Modern German Studies

editor: Peter Heller
associate editor and editor of "The McMasters Colloquium on
German Literature": Hans H. Schulte
editorial board: Georg Iggers, Volker Neuhaus
volume 15

Gustav Mahler
Man on the Margin

by Henry A. Lea

1985

Bouvier Verlag Herbert Grundmann · Bonn

For Charlene

CIP-Kurztitelaufnahme der Deutschen Bibliothek
LEA, HENRY A.:
Gustav Mahler - man on the margin / by Henry A. Lea. — Bonn: Bouvier, 1985.
(Modern german studies; Vol. 15)

ISB N 3-416-01881-8

NE: GT

ISS N 0170-3013

CONTENTS

PREFACE

Gustav Mahler's many-faceted life and work invites a variety of interpretations. He can be seen as a late romantic, the last of the great Austro-German symphonists; as an early modern, paving the way for certain innovations in twentieth-century music; as an existentialist expressing the anxiety of the isolated individual; as a fin-de-siècle composer, preoccupied with artistic expression in an age of political decline; as a Freudian figure uncovering heights and depths of the inner life. I have chosen to treat him as a man without a country. Except for this aspect, my study is not intended to be an exhaustive or encompassing work on Mahler. A brief account of his life has been included for the orientation of the reader.

Many place names have changed since Mahler's time. In such cases, the name used when Mahler was living is given first, followed by the present name. Most of the unpublished translations of German texts are my own.

I owe a debt of gratitude to numerous persons and institutions for their help in preparing this book. My special thanks go to Anna Mahler, the composer's daughter, for her kind permission to make use of her father's and mother's unpublished letters. The following persons generously provided information, material and ideas: Professor Sigrid Bauschinger, Professor E. M. Beekman, Professor Jack Brin, Professor David Bronsen, Professor Frank Brownlow, Professor Ursula Chen, Dr. John Clapham, Professor Dan Collins, Professor Leonard Ehrlich, Professor Milton Gordon, Dr. Stephen Hefling, Professor Allan Janik, Dr. Hans Lamm, Professor Klaus Peter, Professor Edward Reilly, Professor Robert Rothstein, Professor Eva Schiffer, Professor Harry Seelig, Dr. Eric Simon, Professor Miriam Whaples and Professor David Wyman. For the use I've made of the information given to me and its interpretation I am solely responsible.

I am grateful to the Internationale Gustav Mahler Gesellschaft in Vienna for making their archive and library available to me and for patiently answering many questions. I am particularly indebted to Professor Kurt Blaukopf, Dr. Herta Blaukopf and Frau Emmy Hauswirth for their assistance and courtesy during a sabbatical stay in Vienna in 1979. The staffs of the University of Pennsylvania Library, the Wiener Stadtbibliothek, the Beinecke Library at

Yale and the Library of the University of Massachusetts in Amherst gave me access to important documents and helped locate material. I thank the Czechoslovak Society of Arts and Sciences, particularly Professor Wilma Iggers, for inviting me to present a paper on Mahler's Czech background in Washington, D.C., in October 1980. The University of Massachusetts supported the preparation of this book with a generous grant, for which I am most grateful.

The following publishers have kindly given me permission to use material which has previously appeared in different form:

> Lothar Stiehm Verlag, Heidelberg, publisher of *Aspekte des Expressionismus*, ed. Wolfgang Paulsen.
>
> Verlag Delp, Bad Windsheim, publisher of *Views and Reviews of Modern German Literature: Festschrift for Adolf D. Klarmann*, ed. Karl S. Weimar.
>
> Carl Winter Universitätsverlag, Heidelberg, publisher of *Jews and Germans from 1860 to 1933*, ed. David Bronsen.
>
> Bergin and Garvey Publishers, Inc., South Hadley, Massachusetts, publishers of *Passion and Rebellion: The Expressionist Heritage*, ed. Stephen E. Bronner and Douglas Kellner.

A special word of appreciation goes to Mrs. Olga Schiffer for sharing her knowledge of the Mahler country with me and for giving me important source material over the course of many years. I deeply regret that she did not live to see the publication of this book.

Professor Peter Heller and Professor Jules Piccus kindly read the entire manuscript and made many valuable suggestions. Mrs. Mélanie Fletcher-Howell carefully and patiently typed numerous drafts of the manuscript. My deepest gratitude goes to my wife, Charlene, for her abiding interest, incisive criticism and unfailing support.

Amherst, Massachusetts
April 8, 1985

INTRODUCTION

Of the major composers of Western classical music Gustav Mahler is the only one without a national homeland. His birth on the edge of the German-speaking area, in a tri-cultural region (German, Jewish, Slavic) of the Austrian Empire, placed him squarely between East and West and made him literally a man without a country. There have been many exiles who have left their homeland, voluntarily or not, but very few who have no homeland at all. And since the Austrian Empire has been the only supranational state in modern times, the phenomenon of a nationally unanchored art in a nationalistic age is probably unique. This situation was compounded by Mahler's Jewishness, which he experienced as an unwanted burden. Mahler was an assimilated Jew who had no ethnic roots, did not come from the ghetto and was not a Zionist. But unlike Felix Mendelssohn, another prominent converted Jew, who lived earlier and in Northern Germany when there was somewhat greater tolerance, Mahler lived for ten years in a city ruled by an anti-Semitic mayor at a time when anti-Semitism had taken on an ugly racial aspect. Yet Vienna offered an unusually cosmopolitan setting which inspired important Jewish cultural contributions. The combination of Viennese supranationalism and Jewish-Czech marginality, each reinforcing the other, can be heard with great intensity in the homelessness of Mahler's music. It is this aspect of Mahler that I wish to examine in this study.

Among the enormous literature on Mahler there seems to be only one book which focuses on this central fact of the composer's existence. Adorno's book on Mahler, published in 1960 on the occasion of the composer's centenary,[1] is a sociologically oriented study in which the composer is seen musically and socially as an extreme outsider. His music is interpreted as an expression of someone who is unable to affirm the world as it is. Adorno traces Mahler's spiritual torment directly to his social situation. Only Kurt Blaukopf's excellent study, which is more in the nature of a biography, also treats Mahler from the perspective of his complex heritage.[2] Adorno's book is very rich and wide-ranging, but it is also unduly apodictic and written in a socio-philosophical idiom accessible only to those who are familiar with his vocabulary and his thinking; this accounts for the fact that his book has not yet been translated.

The purpose of my study is to explain the social and musical implications of Mahler's background to American readers. I will discuss the music as non-technically as possible, showing how it evolved from the German tradition of the nineteenth century, yet was indelibly marked by Mahler's marginality as well as by his historical position as one of the first modern composers.

My background in German and Austrian literature and culture as well as music may help me to explain to non-musicologists certain aspects of Mahler's music that lie beyond the range of a strictly biographical or musicological approach. Mahler is unusually multi-layered, so much so that each performance of his music reveals inner voices and details that one has not heard before, no matter how familiar one is with his music. It is, moreover, exceptionally allusive and associative music, with a richness of reference rarely found in a composer to this degree. To elucidate some of these references is one of the goals of this study.

Mahler's music continues to communicate with compelling emotional force. While containing German, Austrian, Czech and Jewish elements, it is more than the sum of its parts. It is exceptionally knowing music, which speaks to the listener in a most personal, direct, modern voice. The desire to explain a vital source of this communicative power inspired me to write these pages.

NOTES

[1] Theodor W. Adorno, *Mahler: Eine musikalische Physiognomik* (Frankfurt/Main: Suhrkamp Verlag, 1960).
[2] Kurt Blaukopf, *Gustav Mahler oder Der Zeitgenosse der Zukunft* (Vienna-Munich-Zurich: Verlag Fritz Molden, 1969); English translation by Inge Goodwin (London: Allen Lane, 1973).

BIOGRAPHICAL ESSAY

Gustav Mahler was born on 7 July 1860 in Kalischt (Kaliště), a village in Bohemia near the Moravian border in present-day Czechoslovakia. At that time this area belonged to the Austrian Empire, there being no independent Czechoslovakia. Demographically it was a volatile region, inhabited by Czechs, a large German minority and a small Jewish minority. Mahler was the son of a tavernkeeper and distiller; his petit bourgeois parents, who were assimilated, unreligious, German-speaking Jews, were struggling to emerge from the restrictions imposed on Jews in the Austrian Empire. The lifting of these restrictions at about the time of Mahler's birth enabled the family to move to the larger nearby town of Iglau (Jihlava), where a better life was possible. However, Mahler's childhood was darkened by the death of many of his brothers. He was the second-oldest of fourteen children — eleven boys and three girls — of whom eight boys died in infancy and one, Ernst, at the age of fourteen. The deaths of these children, especially of Ernst, left a deep mark on the young boy, as did the unhappy marriage of his ill-matched parents.

He was educated in the Iglau public schools, with the exception of an unhappy semester in Prague, and graduated from its high school in 1877, but being a day-dreamer preoccupied with music he was a mediocre student. At an early age he began to take piano lessons and first appeared in public at the age of ten. The rich musical atmosphere of the Iglau area, with its Czech and German folksongs and its military trumpet calls, was a vital source of musical inspiration for him. In 1875 his father was persuaded to send him to Vienna to study music. At the Vienna Conservatory, where one of his fellow-students was Hugo Wolf, his interest shifted from piano to composition. He won composition prizes but also aroused hostility for his independence and sharp wit; throughout his life he refused to bend to authority. After completing his musical studies in 1878, he studied briefly at the University of Vienna where he had taken courses in 1877-78. He attended classes in the humanities and Bruckner's lectures on harmony. In 1880, during another brief enrollment at the same university, one of his teachers was Eduard Hanslick, the noted critic, who later supported Mahler's appointment as director of the Vienna Opera.

The years 1878-80 were unsettled years during which Mahler eked out a bare living by giving piano lessons and accompanying recitalists. In one of his few political gestures, he joined a group of young intellectuals of socialist leanings. He also composed his first important work, the cantata *Das klagende Lied (The Song of Lament)*, for which he had written the text. He submitted this work for the Beethoven Prize competition, but the jury found the piece too modernistic. Faced with the need to make a living, Mahler chose to be a conductor. He acquired an agent who obtained a job for him in a small theater in Bad Hall, an Austrian spa not far from Linz. Here, at the age of nineteen, he conducted operettas for a few months under primitive conditions. But this inauspicious debut was the beginning of a distinguished conducting career. Mahler rapidly progressed through a series of increasingly important Central European opera posts to world renown at the most prestigious musical centers. Relentlessly he climbed to the top of his profession, often negotiating for a better position soon after accepting a new appointment.

There followed positions in Laibach (Ljubljana), now in Yugoslavia, and Olmütz (Olomouc), now in Czechoslovakia, where critics recognized his ability and high artistic standards. His performance of *Carmen* in Olmütz attracted the attention of a producer who recommended him to the theater in Kassel, Germany. Between these engagements he lived in Vienna and in 1883 was chorus director there for a season of Italian opera. Often he visited his parents in Iglau and, as the oldest surviving son, helped his brothers and sisters financially and in other ways.

Before going to Kassel, Mahler made the obligatory pilgrimage to Wagner's home in Bayreuth, five months after Wagner's death, and heard *Parsifal*. His two-year engagement in Kassel, 1883-85, was important musically as well as biographically, but his position as second conductor forced him to perform mediocre works and, typically for him, involved him in many quarrels with the principal conductor and the management. After hearing a concert conducted by Hans von Bülow, Mahler wrote an emotional letter to the famous conductor, begging him to take Mahler along as his disciple; not only was the reply negative, but Bülow sent Mahler's letter to his superior in Kassel, which made the young conductor's situation there even worse. Yet his unrequited love for Johanna Richter, one of the singers in Kassel, inspired him to compose the song cycle *Lieder eines fahrenden Gesellen (Songs of a Wayfarer)*, which in turn became the main source of his First Symphony. The Prussian code of behavior at the Kassel theater, which he frequently violated, and his subordinate position prompted him to accept a better post in Prague. He ended his tenure in Kassel with an enthusiastically received performance of Mendelssohn's oratorio *St. Paul* on 29 June 1885, but not without incurring some virulent anti-Semitic attacks in the press from partisans of the principal conductor who had been passed over for this festival concert in favor of Mahler. It was in Kassel that Mahler became fully aware of his abilities as a conductor and where he first expressed his ambition to direct the Vienna Opera. He left Kassel, one day before his 25th birthday, as a supremely self-confident master of his craft.

During the 1885-86 season Mahler served as conductor at the German Opera in Prague, with the same rank as two other resident conductors. He immediately impressed the director, Angelo Neumann, with whom he had better relations than with most managers. Making his debut in Prague on 17 August 1885 in the presence of the Austrian Emperor, Mahler quickly established himself with vivid performances of the operas he loved best and on which his fame as conductor rests — the operas of Mozart, Beethoven and Wagner. A performance, on short notice, of Beethoven's Ninth Symphony and excerpts from Wagner's *Parsifal* won him a letter of appreciation from the academic community of the German University in Prague. But even in Prague, where Mahler felt more at home than in many other places, a serious dispute arose between him and the director over a question of musical interpretation. An agreement was worked out, but such episodes occurred wherever Mahler conducted, owing to his uncompromising musical demands and the stubbornness with which he defended them. While in Prague, he heard operas by Smetana, Dvořák and Glinka and recommended them to the director in Leipzig, Max Staegemann, before leaving Prague.

Mahler spent two highly productive seasons in Leipzig, Germany (1886-88), but his subordinate position to the chief conductor, Arthur Nikisch, irritated him greatly. In fact, only a few months after arriving in Leipzig he submitted his resignation because he might not be permitted to share a performance of Wagner's *Ring* with Nikisch, as the director had promised. But when Nikisch became ill, Mahler conducted three of the four *Ring* dramas with great success. In Leipzig he met Carl Maria von Weber's grandson, Carl von Weber, who asked Mahler to complete the sketches for Weber's unfinished opera *Die drei Pintos*. Mahler did so and the work had its premiere in Leipzig on 20 January 1888 under his direction. The production was highly successful and brought Mahler international attention and some needed funds.

In his last year in Leipzig, 1887-88, Mahler composed hectically, inspired by a hopeless passion for the wife of his patron, Marion von Weber. He completed the First Symphony and the first movement of the Second Symphony, and he became engrossed in the German folksong collection *Des Knaben Wunderhorn (The Youth's Magic Horn)*, many of whose songs he set to music. In Leipzig he met Tchaikovsky and Richard Strauss — the latter his competitor, rival and friend. The friendship with Strauss was not close, because of differences in personality and artistic outlook, but they did appreciate and promote each other's work. Tchaikovsky and Strauss were among a long list of composers and musicians whom Mahler met and who include Brahms, Bruckner, Debussy, Dvořák, Rachmaninoff, Schoenberg and Sibelius.

In Leipzig, as in most places where Mahler conducted, the critical reception of his performances was very mixed. There always seemed to be at least one major critic who strongly opposed him because his conducting was untraditional. His tempos were found to be arbitrary, the dynamics extreme, the conducting style too intense, the interpretations too subjective. Clearly, Mahler alienated conservative critics. When he resigned his position in Leipzig after a bitter quarrel with the stage manager, one of the leading critics reported tersely that Mahler had been replaced by someone else.

In September 1888, at the age of twenty-eight, Mahler was appointed director of the Royal Opera in Budapest. His appointment, with a ten-year contract, caused much surprise in the press because of his youth, the large salary, and because he was Jewish. For these reasons and because he was not Hungarian, the nationalistic Hungarian press did not welcome him. He did what he could to satisfy Hungarian patriotism, engaging native singers, commissioning Hungarian translations of Wagner operas, and even studying Hungarian himself. Laboring prodigiously against considerable resistance, Mahler won over his detractors with his performances of the first two *Ring* operas in January 1889. The orchestral execution received special praise. Though Mahler's first season in Budapest was highly successful, shadows were cast by anti-Semitic remarks in the Hungarian Parliament and by charges that he treated his musicians ruthlessly.

1889 was a particularly difficult year for Mahler. He lost both parents and his sister Leopoldine, and he had to undergo a serious operation. And his First Symphony, the premiere of which he conducted in Budapest on 20 November 1889, was severely criticized. The 1889-90 season ended in bitterness for him because of a persistent press campaign against his directorship.

After the death of his parents Mahler had to look after and, in part, support his surviving brothers and sisters; for a time his sister Justine managed his household for him until he got married.

A new production of Mozart's *Don Giovanni* in the fall of 1890 earned Mahler the enthusiastic approval of Brahms who told him that this was the finest performance of the opera he had ever heard. And Mahler scored another great success with the first performance outside of Italy of Mascagni's *Cavalleria rusticana*. Despite these successes, he had to contend with rebellious singers and an unfriendly press. Two singers even challenged him to a duel, but the director sided with Mahler and would not permit a duel. The final straw was the impending appointment of Count Gezá Zichy as director. Count Zichy planned to take charge of all artistic and administrative affairs of the opera house. Upon being appointed in January 1891, he attempted to change Mahler's contract, whereupon the composer promptly accepted a position at the Hamburg Opera with which he had previously negotiated. At his final Budapest appearance, the audience shouted "Viva Mahler!", but most of the press was glad to see him go. Audiences often responded to Mahler's performances of the classics more favorably than music critics, who with some notable exceptions found his musical conceptions too advanced. Yet he had also found influential friends in Budapest, who later recommended him to the Vienna Opera. The affair illustrates the strong feelings aroused by opera politics in European countries and the high visibility and vulnerability of conductors at important European opera houses.

In the fall of 1890, while in Budapest, Mahler received a visit from the violinist Natalie Bauer-Lechner who had been a fellow-student of his at the Vienna Conservatory. A close friendship developed between them that ended only when Mahler became engaged to his future wife. During their ten-year friendship which never became a romance, Natalie, who loved Mahler, became his confidante and faithfully recorded his ideas and opinions.

Mahler made his debut in Hamburg on 29 March 1891 with Wagner's *Tannhäuser* and at once impressed the critics. In contrast to the Budapest position, the Hamburg post was that of first conductor with responsibility for singers and orchestra, but not as the administrator of the entire opera house. Yet the position was an important one, for Hamburg was Germany's second largest city, a cosmopolitan port city with a well-equipped opera house and sophisticated audiences. The director, Bernhard Pollini, was an able and experienced manager, but he was more concerned with the commercial side of his job than with artistic considerations. The stage direction in particular was neglected during his regime. He promoted the "star system" and exploited the musicians, but he did assemble a distinguished group of singers in Hamburg. Apparently he hired Mahler because he considered him a star conductor who would attract large audiences.

Mahler immediately won the approval of the distinguished pianist-conductor Hans von Bülow, though Bülow did not appreciate Mahler's own music. When Bülow died in 1894, Mahler succeeded him as conductor of the Hamburg subscription concerts. With this assignment Mahler began his career as a symphonic conductor. His first international tour took place in March 1897 when he conducted concerts in Moscow and Budapest.

On 18 May 1891 Mahler for the first time conducted Wagner's *Tristan und Isolde*, an opera for which he had a special affinity and with which he is closely identified. A highlight of the Hamburg years was the German premiere of Tchaikovsky's opera *Eugene Onegin*, on 19 January 1892 under Mahler's direction, in the presence of the composer who had high praise for the performance. In June and July 1892 Mahler conducted a season of German opera in London. The reception was enthusiastic, and even George Bernard Shaw, then a music critic, was impressed.

Despite his heavy conducting schedule, Mahler completed his Second and Third Symphonies and numerous songs. At its premiere in Berlin in 1895, the Second Symphony received a largely negative response from the critics, but the audience was deeply impressed by the work. This performance marked the beginning of Mahler's career as a recognized composer.

Mahler often complained bitterly that his conducting duties left him little time for composition, but the impression is that on some level he enjoyed being a performing musician. He loved the major operas and knew how to stage them effectively, and he enjoyed the acclaim of audiences. His outstanding musical gifts carried him through whatever opposition he aroused. Conducting also enabled him to present his own works, whose instrumentation he revised after rehearsing and hearing them in public, and it may have given him an opportunity for self-expression that was, psychologically speaking, a change from his intense absorption in composition and in his own thoughts.

Beginning with the summer of 1893, Mahler spent the summers on composition, sketching a new work in one summer and orchestrating it in the following summer. Calling himself a "summer composer," he retreated to scenic locations in the Austrian Alps where the Second Symphony was completed and all subsequent symphonies were written. At each of these residences he built a secluded cottage where he could work free from interruptions and noise, to which he was extremely sensitive. When at work he would tolerate no intrusions. In the mountains he could also indulge in his favorite sports — hiking, swimming, cycling and mountain-climbing.

When the Hamburg Opera employed the 18-year-old Bruno Walter as a coach, Mahler gained a life-long friend, disciple and musical interpreter. Two important personal events of the Hamburg years were the suicide of his musically gifted brother Otto and the passionate love affair with the singer Anna von Mildenburg, which he terminated when their relationship proved to be professionally damaging.

As in all other posts he held, Mahler grew restless in Hamburg. He did not get along with the director and he aspired to the highest musical position, the directorship of the Vienna Opera. Because the incumbent director, Wilhelm Jahn, was ailing, the position was known to be available. Mahler used every influence, every intermediary, every strategem he could to obtain this position. He even converted to Catholicism. The negotiations were successful, and Mahler was appointed conductor on 15 April 1897 and director on 8 October 1897. For ten years he presided over the Vienna Opera with great energy, intensity and devotion, bringing new life to the repertory and the staging and raising the performance standards, but also arousing much controversy with his autocratic manner and unconventional ideas. In 1898, when Hans Richter resigned as conductor of the Vienna Philharmonic subscription concerts — mainly because he no longer felt comfortable in Mahler's presence — Mahler was appointed to succeed him. During his brief tenure (1898-1901) he led the orchestra on a tour to the International Exposition in Paris in 1900; when there was not enough money left to pay for the musicians' return trip, Mahler personally went to see Baron Albert Rothschild and obtained the necessary funds. In the following year he resigned as conductor of the orchestra because of illness and dissension with the musicians.

Mahler was an exceptionally intense, volatile man. He was given to sudden shifts of mood, fluctuating between emotional extremes. Endowed with great richness of personality, he was capable of unusual warmth and compassion, but in the opera house or concert hall he was a relentless martinet. In musical matters he would defer to no one, not even to the Austrian Emperor. In pursuit of his artistic ideals he literally wore himself out. What he accomplished as a composer and performer in a relatively short life marked by bouts of ill health is astonishing.

In the fall of 1901 Mahler fell in love with Alma Schindler, the daughter of a well-known Viennese landscape painter, and married her on 9 March 1902. She was a strikingly attractive, high-spirited, self-assured, musically gifted young woman who was nineteen years younger than Mahler. Alma, who was not Jewish, had already composed a number of songs. The marriage turned out to be an uneasy union because each partner demanded more than the other was able or willing to give. Mahler demanded that his wife give up composition, look after the family's needs and manage his affairs. Though he loved her, he was authoritarian and self-centered. They had two daughters, Maria and Anna, whom he adored, but most of his time and energy was taken up with his work. Clearly he was only a part-time husband and father, particularly in the later years when he had increasing health problems. For her part, Alma was an assertive, self-important, willful, demanding woman who was not disposed to play a subordinate role. This constellation led to a marital crisis when Mahler discovered that Alma was being courted by an eager suitor. Deeply shocked, he decided to consult Freud. At their brief meeting, which took place in Leiden,

Holland, in August 1910, Mahler proved to be an adept psychoanalytic patient. The marriage held, probably because in Alma's eyes his rival could not match Mahler's distinction.

In 1907 a heart ailment was diagnosed, at the very same time that the Mahlers' older daughter died at the age of four. He was told to slow down but was constitutionally unable to do so. In the same year he resigned his post in Vienna, partly because he may have felt that he had accomplished as much there as he could, partly because of continuing anti-Semitic attacks in the press, partly because the management was dissatisfied with his absences on concert tours. Earlier that year he had received an offer to conduct at the Metropolitan Opera in New York. This offer attracted him mainly because the high salary would enable him in a few years to retire to the Austrian Alps and devote himself entirely to composition.

He conducted his last performance at the Vienna Opera, Beethoven's *Fidelio,* on 15 October 1907; before departing for the United States in December 1907 he conducted in Russia and Finland. In Finland he met and liked Sibelius but did not care for his music. Mahler made his debut at the Metropolitan Opera with *Tristan und Isolde* on 1 January 1908. In the following season, 1908-09, a new manager at the Metropolitan brought in Toscanini, a man so different temperamentally and musically that there could be no relationship between them. For this reason Mahler accepted an offer to become conductor of the New York Philharmonic, beginning with the 1909-10 season. The summers of the American years were spent in Toblach (Dobbiaco) in the Dolomites, now in Italy, where Mahler composed *Das Lied von der Erde (The Song of the Earth)*, the Ninth Symphony, and the Tenth, which he did not live to complete. In September of 1910 he experienced his greatest public triumph when he conducted the premiere of his Eighth Symphony in Munich before a distinguished audience.

During his fourth American season, 1910-11, Mahler became seriously ill. On 21 February 1911 he conducted his last concert while running a high fever. He was found to have a streptococcus infection for which there was then no cure. In April 1911 he returned to Europe, first to Paris to consult a specialist and then to Vienna where he died on 18 May 1911. As was his wish, he was buried next to his little daughter in the Grinzing cemetery in Vienna.

Chapter I

THE MARGINAL MAN

Mahler was born on 7 July 1860 in the small town of Kalischt (Kaliště) in Bohemia near the Moravian border, approximately half way between Vienna and Prague. At the time of his birth both Bohemia and Moravia were provinces of the Austrian Empire. The fact that his family was Jewish, spoke German and lived in a Czech area gives some idea of the complexity of his background which notably lacks any specifically national or ethnic identification. His triple heritage is a central fact of Mahler's existence and goes far to explain what is striking about his persona and his music.

Culturally and artistically speaking, Mahler belongs to a distinctive group of creative men who were born in the region of present-day Austria and Czechoslovakia in the last half of the nineteenth century and who include, among others, Alban Berg, Hermann Broch, Sigmund Freud, Hugo von Hofmannsthal, Franz Kafka, Gustav Klimt, Oskar Kokoschka, Karl Kraus, Robert Musil, Rainer Maria Rilke, Egon Schiele, Arthur Schnitzler, Arnold Schoenberg, Anton von Webern, Otto Weininger, Franz Werfel, Ludwig Wittgenstein, and Stefan Zweig. Visionaries with a strong sense of cultural despair, they created mythogenic works of great complexity, allusiveness and world-weary sophistication. Their work is to an unusual degree innovative and supranational, the latter quality reflecting the multinational makeup of the Austrian Empire. Of these figures, those who are Jewish and those who were born in what is now Czechoslovakia fit into the sociological category known as "marginal man."

A marginal man is defined as "any individual who is simultaneously a member (by ascription, self-reference, or achievement) of two or more groups whose social definitions and cultural norms are distinct from each other."[1] Two other definitions are also pertinent — the first one more fully articulated and the second one more poignant: an "individual who through migration, education, marriage or some other influence leaves one social group or culture without making a satisfactory adjustment to another [and] finds himself on the margin of each but a member of neither" and "the man who lives in two worlds in both of which he is more or less a stranger."[2]

Of overriding importance in defining cultural marginality is the divided heritage, a more acute problem for the Jew because he is an outsider by birth. In fact, the Jew, especially when he is emancipated, is "historically and typically the marginal man, the first cosmopolite and citizen of the world."[3] Since marginality requires a degree of assimilation in order to create a cleavage between two distinct cultures, the Western or Westernized Jew is more likely to be a marginal personality than an Eastern Jew, who retains a stronger allegiance to the Jewish religion, is less likely to intermarry or become converted, and usually has a stronger sense of Jewish identity. But both Eastern and Western Jews were drawn to the large cities, "which have always been the final refuge of the detribalized, denationalized, and emancipated."[4] In the metropolis they are less conspicuous and better tolerated and the atmosphere is more liberal, but there is also a certain impersonality and rootlessness.

Closely connected with the marginal Jew's affinity for the city is his supranationalism. Because Jews do not have a nationality, being without a country, a government and a common language, they lack a national identity.[5] Their enemies have used this argument to accuse them of lack of patriotism and even treason, but it is much easier to document patriotism in Jews than the lack of it. It is rather that these detractors resent the Central European Jews' lack of "folk feeling," their inability to identify with the folklore, in its widest sense, of the host country. Assimilated Jews of Mahler's time and place may have had less affinity than others for national, religious or regional traditions (parades, dances, dialects, customs, rituals, epics, sagas, etc.). This lack of local color, which is perhaps most striking in Kafka's work, was accentuated by the rise of nationalism in Central Europe in the nineteenth century, which tended to affect Jews adversely. Furthermore, Vienna, as the capital of a multinational empire, had a cosmopolitan character of its own that attracted many Jewish figures. Viennese cosmopolitanism combined with its Jewish counterpart to produce a uniquely rich, wide-ranging, sophisticated and skeptical culture in which the Jews provided an essential creative ferment.

The skeptical temper often found in marginal persons derives from their half-way position vis-à-vis the establishment. Being largely assimilated but not fully accepted gives them a dual perspective, an outsider-insider view of the dominant culture, which is apt to be more critical than that of the native. Since marginal persons are by definition subordinate to the dominant culture, they are likely to be more detached and even ironic in their stance. This is particularly true of Jews, who have for centuries had good reason to be wary of those in authority. For this reason their creative work is sometimes laced with bitter satire that tends to make more enemies for them; Heine, Kraus, Tucholsky, Marx, Mauthner, Schnitzler come immediately to mind. The bitterness stems from a combination of diagnosing the weaknesses of the establishment while at the same time resenting the lack of social acceptance. For an assimilated Jew there is the additional problem of not being fully Jewish — the dilemma of having lost his ties with Judaism but of not being admitted to non-Jewish society. Even if this person consciously gives up his Jewishness, as by conversion, the Gentile world does not forget it and will not let him forget it.[6] Mahler's life is a prime example of this situation. Though he had little affinity for the Jewish religion and actually converted to Catholicism, he continued to be hounded by anti-Semitism. Though his conversion enabled him to become director of the Vienna Opera, it was hardly the "ticket of admission to European culture," as Heine had claimed.[7]

But as Thorstein Veblen has pointed out in a relevant essay,[8] the record of Jewish achievement suggests that it is only by leaving his Jewish roots and entering the Gentile community that a creative Jew often develops his gifts to their fullest capacity. The inquiring, skeptical mentality of the creative or intellectual Jew could find itself too constricted by the traditions of his own people. But even though the talented Jew will inevitably go into fields dominated by Gentiles because "there is nowhere else to go,"[9] this does not mean that he will adopt Gentile traditions or that he will be adopted by Gentiles. On the contrary, the implication is that a non-accepting Gentile environment is a spur to this type of Jewish accomplishment. Thus, the Jew's innate skepticism is a double-edged sword: it puts him "in the vanguard of modern inquiry,"[10] but only "at the cost of losing his secure place in that scheme of conventions into which he has been born, and at the cost, also, of finding no similarly secure place in that scheme of gentile conventions into which he is thrown. . . . He becomes a disturber of the peace, but only at the cost of becoming an intellectual wayfaring man, a wanderer in the intellectual no-man's-land. . . ."[11] With the exception of Schoenberg, another marginal man, no composer comes to mind who disturbed the peace or typified the restless wanderer as much as Mahler did.

In his essay "The Stranger," the philosopher and sociologist Georg Simmel, himself a baptized Jew, mentions several aspects of marginality that pertain directly to Mahler's situation: 1. though the stranger finds himself in a certain area or ambience, his position in it is essentially determined by the fact "that he doesn't belong to it initially, that he brings to it qualities which do not and cannot originate in it";[12] 2. he is a supernumerary in the sense that he has no property rights in the area — physical or spiritual — in which he finds

himself; 3. his specific characteristic is mobility, which means that he en-
counters every component of his environment but is not organically connected
with any of them through local or ethnic or personal rootedness; 4. his relationship with the group is a special blend of remoteness and nearness, indifference
and involvement. While he is not bound "by custom, piety, antecedents,"[13] this
may make him an object of suspicion and distrust; 5. the stranger shares only
certain general traits with the group, not specific ones; the group's awareness of
this brings out those traits in him that are not shared, and tends to set him apart.

Mahler was well aware of his situation as a stranger. Though he had
little affinity for the Jewish religion he made the oft-quoted statement: "I am
three times homeless: as a Bohemian among the Austrians, as an Austrian
among the Germans, and as a Jew in the whole world. Everywhere an intruder,
nowhere welcome."[14] — a statement that could just as well have been made by
Freud or Kafka or Werfel. It was a literary critic who viewed Mahler as the
spiritual father of this apocalyptic group of artists and remarked on their "Slavo-
Jewish Germanness"[15] that placed them at the margins of German culture.
Though German-speaking, educated in German schools and brought up in
the German cultural tradition, they were not German and did not consider
themselves German. But as mediators between different cultures, they offer
insights and perspectives that have only been recognized in recent years. Undoubtedly, such figures as Mahler, Rilke (born in Prague but not Jewish) and
Kafka have added new dimensions to German music and literature. They have
opened a window to the East — an area that has more often than not been re-
garded with suspicion and prejudice in Germany — and they have enriched
German culture with their non-Germanic art. (In music, this means a higher
priority on the sound.) A recent writer notes the loss of these qualities in
present-day Germany, attributing a lack of cosmopolitanism to the loss of
Jewish cultural contributions.[16]

The effort to live in two diverse cultures, particularly when they are
antagonistic, produces chronic tension and stress that led Robert E. Park,
the sociologist who coined the term "marginal man," to establish him as a
personality type. Park finds that such a person lives in a state of permanent
crisis, suffering from "spiritual instability, intensified self-consciousness, restlessness and malaise."[17] Thus the Central European Jew veered back and forth
between submission and defiance, between vying for acceptance and fighting
the establishment, with inevitable consequences for his personality, self-esteem,
mental health and of course his relationships with Gentiles. Because he con-
tinually looked at himself through the eyes of others and was uncommonly
concerned with injustice, he often developed a hypersensitivity and emotional
intensity that Gentiles found difficult to accept. The mixture of pathos and

irony, often found in Jews, is a result of the difficulty of being Jewish, combined with a sense of the absurd that makes it possible to survive in a hostile
world.

A recent writer on Jewish relations with Gentiles, writing from a pro-
Jewish point of view though not Jewish himself, argues persuasively that the
problem turns on Jewish rejection of Gentile concepts of civility.[18] His chief
examples are Marx and Freud. Pointing out that both "experienced civility
as censorship,"[19] the author sees Marxism and Freudianism as two ideologies
that crashed through Gentile decorum by "overthrowing property and out-
raging propriety."[20] In his article on Prussian censorship Marx wrote as follows: "You demand restraint and you proceed from the enormous unrestraint
of making the civil servant a spy of the heart. . . . On the one hand, you force us
to acknowledge unrestraint, on the other, you forbid us unrestraint."[21] As for
Freud, he acknowledged that Jews have bad manners because they were emancipated late and are still learning to adapt to their social environment. But more
than that, "Freudianism was to be indiscreet on principle. . . . The therapeutic
hour . . . puts an end to decorum."[22] In his essay on Freud, Stefan Zweig speculated that Freud would have found recognition more easily if he had expressed
himself more politely, but he rejected such a compromise. The author's thesis
is that both Marx and Freud resisted the temptation of "embourgeoisement,"
of "becoming respectable."[23] Both "exhibited the unconscious desire of Jews,
as social pariahs, to unmask the respectability of the European society which
closed them out."[24] In Mahler's case one can observe an analogous attitude
toward musical tradition, in performance as well as composition. "What you
theater people call your tradition is nothing but your indolence and slovenliness" is Mahler's most famous dictum.[25] By revising the instrumentation of
symphonies by Beethoven and Schumann and conducting the classics in an unconventional style — with a wider dynamic range, greater rhythmic flexibility
and much more intensity — he challenged the musical establishment.

Jewish writers have been called "disturbers of the peace" by a Jewish
author.[26] In his study of German-Jewish writers, Reich-Ranicki defines their
situation as an adversary one that precluded an easy, unselfconscious, objective
relationship with Gentiles. Viewing society and life itself not from the center
but from the periphery, they saw what is familiar and well-known in a new
way. (This is not to say that non-Jews do not have this capacity; it was merely
more pronounced and more pervasive among Central European Jews.) This
observation is particularly relevant to Mahler, who composed music that is
decidedly not mainstream. As I hope to show in these pages, Mahler's music is
extreme, emotionally and formally, tonally and technically. In his life and in
his work he exhibits the tendency to be radical, provocative and uncompro-

mising that Reich-Ranicki detects in Jewish writers. Highly applicable to Mahler, too, is this author's statement that membership in a persecuted minority affects the psychic structure of Jews; in their creative work they express the disappointment of the rejected and the sadness of the homeless. Mahler's letters, beginning with one written when he was not yet nineteen, are filled with longing for a haven.

Having been born to a Jewish family in a cultural borderland, having left this area for Vienna and married a Gentile woman, Mahler fits the definition of "marginal man" in more than one respect. The division between Eastern and Western Jews, so troubling in this part of the world, is clearly shown in Mahler's strong assimilationist tendencies and in his derogatory remarks about Jews he saw in Poland, Russia and New York City.[27] As a resident in increasingly large cities (Kassel - Prague - Leipzig - Budapest - Hamburg - Vienna - New York) and as a composer of notably non-national music, Mahler was a cosmopolitan without a permanent home, except for his affiliation with Austria which was itself supranational.[28] (What I mean by 'non-national' will be explained later in this book; briefly stated, it is the transcendence of the triadic harmonies that are the foundation of national music and the resulting deregionalization of marches, dances and folksongs by pushing them beyond their harmonic, rhythmic and emotional limits.) The most dramatic evidence of Mahler's marginality is his conversion to Catholicism on 23 February 1897,[29] less than two months before his appointment as conductor at the Vienna Opera. Nevertheless, throughout his life, both before and after his conversion, he was the target of anti-Semitic attacks. His life and career exhibit all the hallmarks of cultural marginality which was greatly intensified by his prominence and visibility and especially by his high-ranking appointment which had to be approved by the Emperor himself.

NOTES FOR CHAPTER 1: THE MARGINAL MAN

1 *A Dictionary of the Social Sciences,* ed. Julius Gould and William L. Kolb (New York: Free Press of Glencoe, 1964), p. 406.

2 The first definition appears in Everett V. Stonequist, *The Marginal Man* (New York: Charles Scribner's Sons, 1937), pp. 2-3; the second one is found in Robert E. Park, *Race and Culture* (Glencoe, Illinois: The Free Press, 1950), p. 355. — It is worth noting that it was an American sociologist, Robert E. Park, in his essay "Human Migration and the Marginal Man" which appeared in the *American Journal of Sociology* in May 1928, who first formulated and studied this concept, perhaps as the by-product of a pluralistic society with more understanding of the outsider than could ever be found in Vienna. — I am indebted to my colleague, Professor Milton Gordon of the Sociology Department of the University of Massachusetts, for giving me these and other references on this subject.

3 Robert E. Park, *Race and Culture*, p. 354. — There are, of course, other marginalities; those based on race and sexuality are far more common than the Jewish variety. There is also the rare marginality of genius to which, in Mahler's case, can be added the marginality of the classical musician who lives in a world that is profoundly inaccessible to most people. Of all the arts, music is the most inward and sets its disciples apart.

4 Ibid., p. 135.

5 There is Biblical evidence that the Jews were destined by God to be not a national but a religious people and that the two are incompatible with each other. When Balaam, the prophet sent by the King of Moab to curse the people of Israel, is converted by the Lord to Israel's side, he calls them "a people dwelling alone, and not reckoning itself among the nations" — words directly inspired by the Lord (Numbers 23:9). This line is interpreted to mean that "Israel is not a nation like other nations but a people set apart for a special destiny." (*The Oxford Annotated Bible with the Apocrypha*, Revised Standard Version, ed. Herbert G. May and Bruce M. Metzger [New York: Oxford University Press, 1977], p. 195). In Deuteronomy 26:19, Moses tells the people of Israel that if they will keep God's commandments, "he will set you high above all nations that he has made, in praise and in fame and in honor, and that you shall be a people holy to the Lord your God, as he has spoken." Further references to the distinction between the Jews and the nations occur in I Samuel 8:42, Nehemiah 1:8, Jeremiah 29:14 and 30:11, Ezekiel 12:15, Hosea 9:17, Amos 9:9, Malachi 3:12 and Romans 4:17. In this designation of Israel as God's people rather than as a nation among nations may be found the origin of Jewish destiny and of the special calling of the Jews to spiritual leadership. This supranationalism is evident in much Jewish thought and art, even though the founding of the State of Israel has made this mission inoperative.

6 The German-Jewish statesman Walther Rathenau wrote as follows: "In the youth of every German Jew there comes a moment which he remembers with pain as long as he lives: when he becomes for the first time fully conscious of the fact that he has entered the world as a citizen of the second class, and that no amount of ability or merit can rid him of that status." Quoted in Gordon A. Craig, *The Germans* (New York and Scarborough, Ontario: The New American Library, 1983), p. 141.

7 Heinrich Heine, *Sämtliche Werke*, ed. Ernst Elster (Leipzig-Vienna: Bibliographisches Institut, 1887-1890), VII, 407. Heine had been just as secretive about his conversion (in 1825) as Mahler was about his; see Jeffrey L. Sammons, *Heinrich Heine. A Modern Biography* (Princeton: Princeton University Press, 1979), pp. 107-108.

[8] Thorstein Veblen, "The Intellectual Pre-Eminence of Jews in Modern Europe," in: *The Portable Veblen*, ed. Max Lerner (New York: Viking Press, 1950), pp. 467-479. The essay was written in 1919 and first appeared in the March 1919 issue of the *Political Science Quarterly*.

[9] Veblen, p. 475.

[10] Veblen, p. 473.

[11] Veblen, p. 475.

[12] Georg Simmel, "Exkurs über den Fremden," in: *Soziologie*, 3rd ed. (Munich-Leipzig: Duncker und Humblot, 1923), p. 509.

[13] Ibid., p. 511.

[14] Alma Mahler, *Gustav Mahler: Erinnerungen und Briefe* (Amsterdam: Allert de Lange, 1940), p. 135.

[15] Felix Stössinger, "Hermann Broch," in: *Deutsche Literatur im 20. Jahrhundert*, ed. Hermann Friedmann and Otto Mann, 5th ed. (Bern and Munich: Francke Verlag, 1967), II, 207.

[16] Bernt Engelmann, *Deutschland ohne Juden* (Munich: Franz Schneekluth Verlag, 1970), pp. 423 and 425.

[17] Robert E. Park, *Race and Culture*, p. 356.

[18] John Murray Cuddihy, *The Ordeal of Civility: Freud, Marx, Levi-Strauss and the Jewish Struggle with Modernity* (New York: Basic Books, 1974).

[19] Cuddihy, p. 116.

[20] Cuddihy, p. 116.

[21] Cuddiny, p. 127, footnote 17.

[22] Cuddihy, p. 32, footnote 5.

[23] Cuddihy, p. 82.

[24] Cuddihy, p. 38. The author is quoting Howard M. Sachar in *The Course of Modern Jewish History* (New York: Dell, 1958), p. 100.

[25] *Gustav Mahler: Im eigenen Wort — Im Worte der Freunde*, ed. Willi Reich (Zürich: Verlag der Arche, 1958), p. 49. The German text reads as follows: "Was ihr Theaterleute euere Tradition nennt, das ist nichts anderes als euere Bequemlichkeit und Schlamperei." The more familiar version, "Tradition ist Schlamperei" — "Tradition is slovenliness," is catchier but erroneous; Mahler was referring to a particular group's attitude toward its own tradition, not to tradition in general. He was criticizing them for taking their tradition for granted rather than constantly reexamining it.

[26] Marcel Reich-Ranicki, *Über Ruhestörer: Juden in der deutschen Literatur* (Munich: R. Piper Verlag, 1973).

[27] For example, when he described the Jews he saw in Lvov, Poland, as the dirtiest people imaginable. See Alma Mahler, *Gustav Mahler: Erinnerungen und Briefe*, p. 283.

[28] In his essay "The Non-Jewish Jew," the historian Isaac Deutscher finds that the marginality of Jewish intellectuals excludes them from any national or religious orthodoxies: "All of them [Spinoza, Heine, Marx, Freud, et al.] had this in common, that the very conditions in which they lived and worked did not allow them to reconcile themselves to ideas which were nationally or religiously limited and induced them to strive for a universal *Weltanschauung*." (Isaac Deutscher, *The Non-Jewish Jew and Other Essays*, ed. Tamara Deutscher [London-New York-Toronto: Oxford University Press, 1968], p. 30).

[29] Kurt Blaukopf, ed., *Mahler: A Documentary Study*, tr. Paul Baker, Susanne Flatauer, P. R. J. Ford, Daisy Loman and Geoffrey Watkins (New York-Toronto: Oxford University Press, 1976), p. 209.

Chapter II

BETWEEN PRAGUE AND VIENNA

1. Political and Social Background

To give the reader some sense of the complexity of Mahler's milieu, I will present a few facts about the area in which he grew up and lived, with special attention to the situation of the Jews in Austria-Hungary at the end of the nineteenth century.

The Austrian Empire, in which Mahler was born in 1860, had two distinctive characteristics: it consisted of many different, often antagonistic, peoples, and it was a Catholic empire. As the successor of the Holy Roman Empire — full title: Holy Roman Empire of German Nationality — it inherited the ideal of a united Christian Europe under German leadership. And its geographic and ethnic composition made it a meeting place, and at times a battleground, between East and West. From a Western perspective it was the easternmost outpost of West European and particularly German culture. This heterogeneous, polyglot realm, with its capital in Vienna, was ruled, except for a brief interlude in the eighteenth century, by the Habsburg dynasty from 1438 to its end in 1918. Under the Habsburgs it was the only major power not founded on nationality.

In the latter half of the nineteenth century, this empire was increasingly buffeted from without by powerful neighbors in the East and West, and threatened from within by the national aspirations of its various peoples. The 1848 Revolution had fanned these aspirations and demanded constitutional limitations on the absolutism of the crown. Though German was the official language and dominant culture and the government was run by German-speaking Austrians, they were in the minority. In the 1910 census they made up 35.6% of the population in the Northern and Western provinces (comprising present-day Austria, Bohemia, Moravia, Austrian Silesia and Austrian Poland) and only 23.9% in the entire empire.[1] The German Austrians were more prosperous than the other groups, dominated intellectual and economic life, and held a majority of positions in the civil service. Politically they were split between the Austro-Germans, who were loyal to the Habsburgs, and a small but militant group of Pan-Germans who advocated union with Germany.

Of the empire's non-German peoples, which included Slavs, Hungarians, Rumanians and Italians, the Czechs, inhabiting Bohemia and Moravia, were incorporated into the empire in 1526. Together with the Hungarians they were the first sizable non-German group to become members of this common-wealth. Bohemia and Moravia — today two of the three provinces that make up Czechoslovakia — were predominantly Czech but had a large German minority. According to the 1910 census, Bohemia had a population of 6,770,000 of whom 63.2% were Czechs and 36.8% Germans; of Moravia's population of 2,622,000, 71.8% were Czechs and 27.6% Germans. In the same census the Jewish population was 85,927 (1.27%) in Bohemia, 41,255 (1.57%) in Moravia.[2] It is worth noting that the Jews were not listed separately as a nationality (and may have preferred not to be so listed); this underlines their marginality by setting them apart from all other groups and points up the continuing con-troversy over whether the Jews are a nationality, as the Eastern Jews and Zi-onists tend to believe, or whether they are simply a religious denomination, as the assimilated Jews and the authorities consider them to be. It was in this melting pot which would not melt that Mahler's family originated.

In addition to being the westernmost non-German province of the empire, Bohemia-Moravia was also its most closely divided district, between Germans and non-Germans. This division frustrated the Czech demand for home rule which was granted to the Hungarians in 1867. No formula could be found to reconcile the conflicting interests of Czechs and Germans — an im-passe which may have contributed more than anything else to the disinte-gration of the empire.

The nationality struggle between Czechs and Germans aggravated their own relationship as well as the situation of the Jews. The Czechs had grown culturally, economically and politically more rapidly than any other group in the empire. Their active and sophisticated musical culture inspired Smetana and Dvořák whose music Mahler later conducted and who made other coun-tries take notice of Czech achievement. Between 1882 and 1912 the number of Czech newspapers and magazines rose from 176 to 1209, a nearly sevenfold increase compared with a less than threefold rise in German publications.[3] Bohemia and Moravia became industrialized earlier, more quickly and more extensively than other parts of the empire and became its industrial center; this circumstance accounts for better communications with the capital, such as roads, railroads and telegraph. Prague and Brünn (Brno), the respective capitals of Bohemia and Moravia, had train connections (financed by Salomon von Rothschild) with Vienna before Salzburg and Innsbruck did; with its eleven telegraph offices Bohemia had the most advanced communications in the entire empire.[4] Rising Czech nationalism extracted some concessions on the use of Czech as a national language and led to the establishment of a separate Czech university in Prague in 1882.

As Czech political expression grew, so did the opposition to Czech autonomy, in Vienna and particularly among the Germans in Bohemia and Moravia. Moreover, the Germans developed their own nationalism, in response to Czech pressure and to the unification of Germany in 1871 which greatly intensified Pan-German sentiment. Economic factors also divided the two groups: whereas the Germans lived mainly in the larger towns, the Czechs, who inhabited the countryside, were beginning to compete with them in the urban centers. This struggle between Czechs and Germans placed the Jewish population in a peculiarly vulnerable position.

The Jews in Bohemia and Moravia were largely of German orientation, culturally and linguistically. Although most were, largely for economic reasons, bilingual they tended to speak German. And the more affluent they were, the more likely they were to identify with German culture. The Jews preferred the German language because it was the administrative language of the empire and its lingua franca and because it was a prestige language, a gateway to the West.[5] Furthermore, Jews had received a German education because this was required of them by legislation passed in 1797. Under the so-called *Judensystemalpatent* (an edict on the legal position of Bohemian Jews) of that year, Bohemian Jews could obtain a marriage license only if they had completed a German elementary school. This legislation had been preceded by the *Toleranzpatent* (Tolerance Edict) of 1782 which directed Jews to establish German-language elementary schools for their children and permitted them to attend public high schools and universities. The goal of this effort by Emperor Joseph II was to promote Jewish assimilation. As a result, Jews were well schooled in the German classics, particularly Schiller whom many German teachers idolized and whose moral fervor and vision of human freedom strongly appealed to Jewish readers. It is reported that Schiller was one of the most popular and widely read authors in the lending libraries of ghettos.[6] Mahler himself knew many of Schiller's poems by heart and at the age of twelve he had appeared in Iglau (Jihlava) as a piano soloist at a celebration of Schiller's birthday.[7] For the first song that Mahler composed he chose a poem by Gotthold Ephraim Lessing.[8] He became an avid reader and admirer of Jean Paul and E. T. A. Hoffmann, with both of whom he shares a special irony and grotesquerie, but among the German classics his favorite author was Goethe, whom he read widely and whose verses he set to music in the Eighth Symphony. The important aspect is the attachment of the Jewish community of Bohemia and Moravia to German culture. Freud, who declined most honors, took special pleasure in winning the Goethe Prize that was awarded to him in 1930.[9]

Characteristic for Mahler's background is the high degree of assimilation among Bohemian and Moravian Jews, who had little contact with Eastern Jews before World War I[10] and whose identification with the Jewish religion was minimal. And as they rose economically, they tended to align themselves with the ruling German sector for reasons of class interest, and during the Liberal period (1860-1879) for political reasons. Perhaps Jews had good reason to side with the crown, particularly after it granted them full rights in 1867, not only because they owed whatever status they had acquired to the monarchy, but because they were more likely to prosper as citizens of a multinational federation than as partisans of any of its rising nationalities.[11] But in the eyes of the Czechs, their German orientation made them agents of Germanization and allies of the hated Habsburgs,[12] while the Germans, on their part, did not accept them as Germans. For both Czechs and Germans, Jews were simply too non-national to be trusted. This, in very brief terms, is the marginality of the Jews of Bohemia and Moravia.

A careful student of the problem points out that it was the misfortune of the Jews of this area that their emancipation took place at the very same moment when the Czechs were struggling to assert their own identity.[13] The Jews in this region were mainly engaged in trade, because they were barred from the professions by anti-Jewish legislation. Mahler's father was a self-taught carter, distiller and liquor dealer who through thrift, tenacity and hard work acquired a tavern and bakery, and became a respected citizen in the town of Iglau.[14] Both Mahler's and Kafka's fathers' careers were typical: they worked their way up from itinerant tradesmen in small towns to more established and more successful businessmen in larger towns.[15] As restrictions were gradually being lifted in the 1860s, the Jews rose rapidly, thus competing with the Czechs who were also fighting for their place in the sun. The economic success of the Jews resulted, as it did elsewhere, in a serious rise in anti-Semitism, both on the Czech and German sides.

A few examples of anti-Semitism in this region will give the reader some idea of the climate in which Mahler grew up. Czech anti-Semitism tended to be economic — resentment of Jewish competition — and political — suspicion that Jews did not identify with Czech nationalism. During an economic crisis in 1866 there were serious anti-Jewish riots by poverty-stricken workers provoked by inflammatory rhetoric: "This is a war against the Jews, and the Jews must all be killed . . . it would be my greatest joy if a Jew were hanged at every corner . . . we must bathe in Jewish blood."[16] In 1870 posters in Southern

Bohemia invited the population "to act against the Jews, to strangle, hang, drown and shoot them."[17] In a brochure entitled *Fear of Judaism* (1870), the Czech publicist Jan Neruda described the Jews as the "power of all powers" who had to be excluded by their host countries because they were determined to rule the world.[18] In the end it didn't matter whether the Jews sided with the Czechs or the Germans — they lost either way.

The German brand of anti-Semitism at that time tended to be racial, being based on a belief in the biological superiority of the German people, in accordance with the theories of Gobineau, Wagner and Dühring.[19] The racial basis of German anti-Semitism is made clear in the following excerpt from a German-language publication in Bohemia: ". . . The actual basis of the German student's anti-Semitism who doesn't yet know anything about politics and earning a living is not the fear of the complete Judaization *(Verjudung)* of all professions, but the instinctive national distaste of young Germans for the foreign and completely materialistic spirit of the Jewish race which he finds more or less sharply marked in every single exemplar among Semitic 'colleagues.'"[20] It is reported that in the Bohemian town of Eger (Cheb) café owners put up signs that read "Czechs, Jews, dogs not allowed here."[21]

Between 1867 and 1914 there were twelve ritual murder trials in the Austrian Empire.[22] 'Ritual murder,' sometimes called 'blood libel,' refers to the charge that Jews kill Christians in order to obtain blood for Passover or other holidays. It is noteworthy that this ancient canard was very much alive in Mahler's time. There were 42 blood libels in the nineteenth century.[23] One of the most notorious was the Polna case of 1899 in which Czech and German anti-Semites collaborated. The murder of a young Czech woman near the town of Polna, located near Iglau where Mahler grew up, led to charges of ritual murder against a Jewish vagrant. The defendant, Leopold Hilsner, was tried and convicted on dubious and incomplete evidence and sentenced to death. The trial became the occasion for an anti-Semitic campaign throughout Europe, recalling the Dreyfus case. When Thomas Masaryk, then a professor at the Czech University in Prague, called for a review of the trial, he was suspended from his position. Emperor Franz Joseph commuted Hilsner's sentence to life imprisonment, and Emperor Charles I pardoned him shortly after succeeding to the throne in 1916.[24]

Against this massive evidence of anti-Semitism, a few positive events can be cited, two of them in the year of Mahler's birth. On 18 February 1860, Jews in most Austrian provinces were given the right to own property, though in Galicia and Bukovina this right was restricted to those with some education; the few Jews in Upper Austria, Styria, Carinthia, Tyrol and Vorarlberg were excluded from the law and had to wait for the 1867 constitution. In the same year a libel suit by Father Sebastian Brunner, a Catholic priest and anti-Semitic journalist, against Ignaz Kuranda, a Jewish editor and publisher, was decided in favor of the defendant. Kuranda had forced Brunner to sue him for libel by accusing him of publishing charges against the Jews that were repeated from earlier anti-Semitic writers and of doing so in order to increase his paper's circulation. Kuranda was acquitted and Brunner was severely rebuked by the judge. In the following year (1861) Kuranda was elected to the Diet of Lower Austria in which he served for twenty years. He also served in the Vienna city council as a member of the Liberal Party.

A similar suit was decided in favor of the Jewish defendant in 1883. August Rohling, a German priest and professor at the German University of Prague, had written a book, *Der Talmudjude (The Talmud Jew)* (1871), in which he attacked the Talmud on flimsy or corrupt evidence. He was challenged by Joseph Samuel Bloch, a rabbi, publicist and politician in Austria, who attacked Rohling's scholarship and accused him of lying and perjury. Rohling was forced to sue Bloch for libel, but he withdrew the suit before the trial was to begin because Bloch had accumulated a vast amount of evidence against him. Rohling lost his professorship and withdrew from public life but continued to publish anti-Semitic tracts. *Der Talmudjude* was translated into several European languages and influenced the anti-Semitic doctrines of the Nazis.[25]

Highly encouraging was the reply of Prince Liechtenstein, the Emperor's lord chamberlain, to one of Mahler's supporters who had mentioned the Jewish issue as a possible bar to Mahler's appointment: "Happily, we in Austria have not yet reached the point where the anti-Semites can dictate our decisions to us."[26] It is hard to know how sincere this statement was — it may simply have been provoked by the question to show that the court was above such matters — but the fact that it was made at all is remarkable. Against it may be cited the Emperor's response to a critic of Mahler's appointment: his Majesty simply pointed to Mahler's religion — Catholic — in his personnel file and considered the matter closed; as long as Mahler had converted, the appointment was defensible.[27]

It is perhaps not well known that in Austria Jews fared considerably less well at that time than they did in Germany. First of all, most German Jews were born in Germany and did not migrate there from a non-German area; they were thus one degree less marginal than the many Austrian Jews who were born in the non-German provinces of the empire. Second, those who did come from the East did not all go to Berlin but went to various other cities, such as Königsberg, Stettin and Breslau. Third, the great majority of German Jews had lived longer in Germany and were probably more accepted there than was the case with the Austrian Jews. Finally, the number of Jews was much larger in Austria than in Germany. According to the 1910 census, Jews made up 4.7% of the population in northern and western Austria (1,342,884 out of 28,572,000) and 3.9% in the empire (2,013,210 out of 51,390,000), whereas Germany had a Jewish population of only 0.95% in the same year.[28] The great majority of Jews lived in Galicia and Hungary, whereas Tyrol, Styria and Carinthia did not accept any Jews. In Vienna the Jewish population increased dramatically during the Liberal era. In 1848 Vienna had only 4000 Jews. Eight years later there were 15,600 (3.3% of the population), and in 1880 10% of Vienna's population was Jewish. In 1900 there were 146,926 Jewish residents out of 1,674,957 inhabitants in the city (8.77%).[29] The reasons for this migration to the capital were twofold: the restrictions against the Jews, particularly in freedom of movement, permission to own real property, and choice of vocation, were being lifted, and many Jews, especially young ones, such as Mahler, came to Vienna in search of social, economic and cultural betterment. In view of the widespread and virulent anti-Semitism, the rise, assimilation and cultural achievements of the Jews in Vienna (not in the provinces) are remarkable. The work of Mahler, Freud, Schnitzler, Herzl, Kraus, Schoenberg and many others constitute a true golden age at a time when Jews found themselves socially and politically increasingly imperiled.

The large influx of Jews to Vienna during the last half of the nineteenth century also created problems between the newcomers and the assimilated Jews already living in Vienna. Most of the migrants from the Eastern provinces were poor, looked exotic and retained their customs and speech habits. Since many were small shopkeepers and tradesmen, they were resented by the already established businessmen who saw them as undesirable competitors. And the assimilated Viennese Jews found them not only alien to their lifestyle and a throwback to what they themselves had left behind, but a threat to their position by provoking anti-Semitism. Mahler himself was an assimilated Jew who harbored such prejudice against Eastern Jews. (See below, pp. 45-46). Thus there developed a serious cleavage between the impoverished, orthodox Eastern Jews and the emancipated, sophisticated, urban Jews who increasingly dominated the cultural scene in Vienna and played a prominent part in the professional and financial life of the country. They were especially visible in medicine, law, journalism and the arts. In 1881, 61% of Vienna's doctors were Jews; in 1888, there were 394 Jewish lawyers out of a total of 681;[30] according to one source, approximately one-half of the students at the University of Vienna were Jewish.[31]

The university was rife with anti-Semitism when Mahler was a student there (in 1877-78 and 1880). Arthur Schnitzler, who entered the university in 1879, gives a vivid description of the discrimination against Jewish students.

In his memoirs he cites the growing polarization between liberal and nationalist fraternities, which led to the exclusion of Jews from the latter. Schnitzler himself was removed from a committee that distributed financial aid to needy students, most of whom were Jewish and came from the Eastern lands, so that the nationalist members could discontinue assistance to Jewish students. Members of nationalist fraternities went out of their way to provoke Jewish students, who had become such adept swordsmen, out of sheer self-defense, that the non-Jewish students summarily declared them to be unqualified to fight a duel *(satisfaktionsunfähig)*.[32] In 1883 Theodor Herzl, another Jew devoted to German culture, resigned from a nationalist fraternity at the University of Vienna because its members had taken part in an anti-Semitic demonstration.[33]

The problem for German-oriented Jews was the split in the ranks of the German population in Austria between Liberals and Nationalists. Assimilated Jews, particularly if they were well-to-do, generally identified with the Liberals because they had enacted civil rights legislation, were culturally and politically German and solidly middle-class, and because they led the movement for constitutional government; moreover, they were anti-clerical and centralist rather than federalist in their policy toward the non-Germans. But by about 1880 this policy was arousing strong opposition from the working classes and the clergy who resented the social elitism of the Liberals, their secularism and the Jewish influence in their party. Increasingly, the Liberals were being outvoted by a combination of populists, Pan-German nationalists and Catholic voters, all of whom shared strong anti-Semitic sentiments. The socio-economic anti-Semitism was represented by the Christian Socialist party headed by Karl Lueger who became mayor of Vienna in 1897, while the racial anti-Semites were led by the Pan-German politician Georg von Schönerer.[34]

Ironically, the Christian Socialists and the Pan-Germans, as well as the Social Democrats, all split off from the Liberals. In the Linz Program of 1882, a group of young, progressive members of the Liberal Party proclaimed a policy of strengthening the German orientation in Austria by, among other provisions, closer cultural, economic and political cooperation with Germany and by centralizing Austria under German leadership.[35] Oddly enough, the drafters of the Linz Program included the Pan-German leader Georg von Schönerer, the future Christian Socialist Robert Pattai, two future leaders of the Social Democrats, Victor Adler and Engelbert Pernerstorfer, and the Liberal historian Heinrich Friedjung; of these Adler and Friedjung were Jewish and born in Bohemia-Moravia. In 1885, when Schönerer added to this program the provision that Jewish influence must be eliminated from all fields of public life, a decisive split occurred between the Pan-Germans and those whose German orientation was purely cultural.

The relevance of these matters to Gustav Mahler lies in his brief membership in the Pernerstorfer Circle, a group of young intellectuals strongly attracted to German culture.[36] Originating in 1867 in an organization of university students, the Pernerstorfer Circle represented a curious amalgam of German nationalism, socialism, and an idealism based on Wagner's theory of the redemptive power of art. Its members included Engelbert Pernerstorfer, Victor Adler, Siegfried Lipiner, Heinrich Friedjung and Richard von Kralik, of whom Adler, Lipiner and Friedjung were Jewish and born in the Slavic provinces. Together with Mahler, these marginal men found themselves in the anomalous position of identifying with German culture just when the Pan-Germans were denouncing Jews as pollutors of German culture, but then these men were not free of anti-Semitism themselves. The tension between the German orientation of the Pernerstorfer Circle and its socialism was never quite resolved, nor did the anti-Semitic issue actually diminish its devotion to German culture,[37] but it is to Pernerstorfer's credit that he did not abandon the Jewish members. It seems that this controversy moved the politically active members — Pernerstorfer, Adler and Friedjung — further toward socialism; even in Mahler's case, two rare recorded political actions are his vote for Victor Adler in 1901 and his accompanying a workers' procession on May Day in 1905.[38]

Mahler was introduced to the group by Lipiner in 1878 when he was only eighteen years old,[39] but his membership could not have lasted very long and must have been rather sporadic, for he was neither a joiner nor a political activist and he began to get conducting assignments that took him away from Vienna; as an ambitious young musician anxious to build a career, he was too preoccupied to be an active member of an organization. When he joined the Pernerstorfer Circle, Mahler was earning so precarious a living as a piano teacher that Victor Adler helped him find students.[40] Kralik reports that Mahler "played fiery accompaniments when the members sang";[41] at one meeting — probably in 1880 — they sang "Deutschland, Deutschland über alles" accompanied by Mahler, not to the usual Haydn melody but to the tune of the song "O du Deutschland, ich muss marschieren."[42] This is musically odd because the latter song, which is much more military than "Deutschland, Deutschland über alles," is composed in 3/4 rhythm while "Deutschland über alles" is written in 4/4,[43] but politically it testifies to this group's strong German sympathies. For Mahler at least, this enthusiasm waned later on, as his treatment of military and patriotic music and his choice of texts clearly show. Except for his close friendship with Lipiner, a poet and philosopher with whom he shared a similar background and sense of artistic mission, the impact of this group on Mahler is difficult to assess. Undoubtedly he passed through a Wagnerian phase as a very young man, but there is evidence that his enthusiasm for Wagner and Nietzsche as thinkers was later considerably tempered — most likely by Nietzsche's elitism and Wagner's racism. Mahler's symphonies completely lack the cultural nationalism and the communal aspirations of Wagner and the Pernerstorfer Circle. My own feeling is that the influence of Mahler's membership in this group on his Third Symphony, which was written fourteen to fifteen years later, may have been overestimated. (See below, pp. 86-87).

An association that has evoked hardly any comment is Mahler's friendship with some figures from the Dreyfus Case. This is of some interest because it brought him in contact, though indirectly and belatedly, with a famous Jewish cause. Mahler and his wife were on friendly terms with three prominent Frenchmen who were supporters of Alfred Dreyfus: Colonel Georges Picquart, Paul Clemenceau, and Paul Painlevé, a statesman and mathematician. They respected and admired Mahler greatly. Mahler had met them and Paul Clemenceau's wife Sophie in Paris in 1900 during a concert tour, and he met his future wife at the home of Sophie's sister, Bertha Zuckerkandl, in Vienna in the following year. (The Zuckerkandls were friends of Alma's family.) Mahler and Alma met Picquart in Strassburg in 1905 when Mahler conducted his Fifth Symphony; apparently Picquart made the trip to hear this performance. Picquart was the first to discover that Dreyfus had been convicted on forged evidence, and he insisted that justice be done even at great cost to his own career. When Dreyfus was exonerated in 1906, Picquart was promoted to general and appointed Minister of War in Georges Clemenceau's cabinet. He learned of his appointment in Vienna while attending a performance of *Tristan und Isolde* conducted by Mahler and had to leave in the middle of the opera (19 October 1906).[44] Picquart and Painlevé remained Alma's friends after Mahler's death.

The episode is remarkable for the attraction felt by these people for Mahler's music and personality. Any interest of politicians and even more of military men in classical music is rare — though perhaps less so in Europe — but when the music is by a contemporary composer or when it is Wagnerian opera, such interest is remarkable. They must have been very unusual people to have initiated this friendship. Though nothing is said about a discussion of the Dreyfus Case, not even in Bertha Zuckerkandl's own account of Mahler in her memoirs,[45] it seems reasonable to suppose that the matter came up. Even this rather incidental association with a Jewish issue is a refreshing item in Mahler's biography.

Nothing else in the available record indicates any interest in Jewish matters on Mahler's part, except when it directly and personally affected his life or career. Not even the election of the anti-Semitic Karl Lueger as mayor of Vienna, at just about the time of Mahler's appointment to the Vienna Opera in the early spring of 1897, nor the tumultuous funeral of Theodor Herzl in July 1904,[46] when Mahler was not far away in the Austrian Alps, elicited any comment from him. Yet he lived and worked in a political climate that was becoming increasingly radicalized and to which he could not have been oblivious. The year 1897 saw the decisive defeat of the Liberals, who had actively promoted Jewish emancipation and had attracted the support of many Jewish intellectuals. 1897 was also a milestone in Jewish history, being the date of the first World Zionist Congress which met in Basel under Herzl's leadership to plan for a Jewish state. Politically, the fall of the administration of Count Kasimir Badeni who had tried to work out a solution to the Czech-German conflict, sharpened the tensions between Germans and Slavs. And artistically, 1897 saw the founding of the Secession Movement by the painter Gustav Klimt, whom Mahler knew well, in an effort to break new ground in painting, architecture and the decorative arts, a development that led to an authentically modern art style. Thus 1897 is a watershed year: politically it polarized Austria with respect to the Jewish question and the nationalities conflict — both ominous developments in the life of the empire; artistically it produced vital new impulses, perhaps as a response to political failure, that pointed the way to expressionism in music and art and later in literature. It was in this atmosphere of political reaction and artistic ferment that Mahler's career as a composer and conductor unfolded.

2. The Czech Connection

Of the major composers in German music, Mahler is the only one to have been born outside the German-language area, thereby sharing Kafka's similar position in German literature. Both hold a special place in German culture by reason of their Jewishness and their origin in a Slavic area. Both are, through their lack of ethnic affiliation, truly trans-national figures.

The town of Kalischt (Kaliště) in which Mahler was born is located in southeastern Bohemia, about nine miles northwest of the Moravian border and about eighteen miles northwest of Iglau (Jihlava), a larger town in Moravia where the family moved 4-1/2 months after Mahler was born. His immediate ancestors came from various small towns in southeastern Bohemia. Kalischt was located in a Czech area, and despite his residence in the German-speaking island of Iglau, he paid visits as a young man to relatives in Ledeč, his mother's hometown, and to friends in Vlašim, Želiv, Ronov and Moravany — all Czech towns.[47] Even though Mahler spoke German it can reasonably be assumed that he knew some Czech; most Jews in this region were to some degree bilingual. Mahler told the Czech composer Josef Bohuslav Foerster that he spoke only Czech during his earliest years.[48] Since this statement was made to a Czech in a context of expressing allegiance to his homeland, Mahler may have overstated his knowledge of Czech, but Foerster also reports that Mahler understood the libretto for Smetana's opera *Prodaná nevěsta (The Bartered Bride)* well enough to correct the German translation by Max Kalbeck.[49] He is also said to have learned many Czech folksongs from a Czech maid employed in his parents' home.[50]

Given this mixed background, it is not surprising that national or ethnic loyalties have become entangled in the discussion of this matter. The musicologist Guido Adler, who also grew up in Iglau and became a loyal friend of Mahler, called him a "Deutschböhme" because, one senses, he was trying to play down Mahler's and his own Jewish origin while emphasizing the German in him.[51] After World War I, Theodor Fischer, a boyhood friend of Mahler, writing in 1931, identifies him as a Sudeten German because he had grown up in the predominantly German town of Iglau, but aside from the geographical inaccuracy the publication in which Fischer's article appeared has a markedly nationalistic title, the more so since it was published by and for an irredentist group in the new and consciously Czech nation.[52] In this case one feels that the writer is claiming Mahler for a beleaguered German minority — a tragic irony in view of this minority's actions only a few years later. On the other hand, a distant relative named Arnošt Mahler, who died in Prague in 1975, claims Mahler for the Czechs, for similarly patriotic motives. Writing in 1972 in a German journal, for German and Western consumption, Arnošt Mahler cites Mahler's birth in a Czech town, the Czech origin of some of his relatives, his familiarity with Czech folksongs and his reported knowledge of the Czech language.[53] This account, too, has the tone of a nationally inspired pronouncement, as if the writer were trying to wrest Mahler from the German orbit and incorporate him into Czech culture. The best and most appealing identification is Mahler's own reported statement; when he was asked about his nationality by German journalists in New York, he simply said, "I am a Bohemian." ("Ich bin ein Böhme.")[54] This report suggests that Mahler intended to disconcert the journalists who expected him to say that he was German; but by identifying himself as a Bohemian rather than as a German or Austrian he avoided the question of nationality. A similar statement, typically more hedged, is said to have been made by Kafka. Max Brod relates that Kafka never felt he belonged to a particular country; at best he felt he was a Bohemian.[55]

The composer Ernst Křenek, himself of Czech ancestry, wrote that "Kaliště was a purely Czech settlement," whereas Iglau was "largely inhabited by Germans. . . ."[56] Guido Adler described Iglau as "a German-speaking island in a turbulent sea of nationalism *(eine deutsche, national umbrandete Sprachinsel)*, a town with an old culture . . . where the religious groups lived peacefully side by side and where the ever-growing aspirations of the Czech minority challenged the indigenous Germans who administered the town conscientiously . . . Mahler found rich musical nourishment in the folksongs of the two nationalities among whom he spent his youth."[57] Mahler lived in Iglau from 1860 to 1875, graduated from its German high school in 1877 and spent his summer vacations there until the death of his parents in 1889.

Iglau had a strong German orientation, beginning with its settlement, in the thirteenth century, by Bavarian miners, artisans and farmers under the patronage of the Teutonic Order of Knights.[58] As late as 1921, almost half of the town's 28,000 inhabitants were German. In the nineteenth century, Czech families in southeastern Bohemia often sent their sons to Iglau because of its excellent schools. In 1860 the Czech population was about 6%, in 1890 18%.[59] Its Jews can also be traced back to the thirteenth century. The first extant document explicitly mentioning Jews in Moravia is the Iglau city law of 1249. In 1426 they were expelled for allegedly supporting the Hussites. In the eighteenth century they were admitted to the town for business purposes on payment of a special tax. In 1837, seventeen Jews lived there legally, but more lived there illegally. After 1848 a Jewish community grew rapidly; the Iglau Jewish Community was founded in 1861, a synagogue was opened in 1863 and a cemetery in 1869. In that year 1,179 Jews lived in Iglau, 1,181 in 1921 and 1,025 in 1930 (3.3% of the population).[60] Mahler's father Bernhard was elected to the Jewish community of Iglau in 1878.[61]

Iglau had a rich and active musical life. Its school of singing, established in the sixteenth century, counted among its students the elder Johann Stamitz, Johann Dussek and Bedřich Smetana — all Czech-born composers. As a member of the parochial choir of St. Jacob's Church and the men's glee club, Mahler got to know some of the masterpieces of the choral literature. The Iglau theater performed operas and operettas, which included both German and non-German works. Undoubtedly Mahler saw some of these productions before he left for Vienna in 1875. He appeared as a pianist at several public occasions, such as Schiller's birthday in November 1872 and in honor of a royal wedding on 20 April 1873.[62]

In addition to these formal presentations, Mahler heard a lot of the folk and military music of the region. "Moravian servants, both Germans and Slavs, sing willingly and well. Melancholy songs accompany getting up and going to bed. The bugles ring out from the barracks. The regimental band marches past. And the tiny youngster sings each and every tune after them. At the age of four, someone buys him an accordion, and now he plays them himself, especially the military marches."[63] Thus at a very young age Mahler absorbed the popular, folk and military music of the region, which later found its way into his own music in a highly individual and transformed manner. These childhood impressions were crucial for his creative life, as Mahler himself believed.[64] It is this Bohemian-Moravian background that makes him a significantly different figure from the German symphonic composers with whom he is usually associated.

Beyond the German-language island of Iglau, which was about eighteen miles long and twelve miles wide, Mahler visited nearby Czech villages, some of which were only a few miles from Iglau and could be reached by foot. Friedrich Löhr, a close friend of Mahler, has described how he and Mahler hiked through this area in 1884 and heard Bohemian musicians play folk and dance music.[65] It was music of mingled joy and sadness,[66] with a great deal of rhythmic verve and an emphasis on wind instruments, especially woodwinds. The small itinerant Bohemian bands usually consisted either of a trio (violin, clarinet — mostly in E flat — and double bass) or a quartet (trumpet, viola and double bass, and either a violin or a clarinet); in southern and southwestern Bohemia a trio of bagpipe, violin and E-flat clarinet was customary. Except for the double bass, string instruments tended to be replaced by wind instruments in the latter half of the nineteenth century.[67] After 1860 popular musical groups became brass bands. This had to do with military influences, with the invention of valve instruments and with the development of gymnastic and other patriotic groups in the increasingly nationalistic atmosphere.

All these elements are found in Mahler's music. Bohemian influences are detectable in his uninhibited melodic intensity, the improvisatory element in his music, his unusual rhythm with its frequent shifts in pace, beat and accent, his almost gypsy-like solo fiddle parts (grotesquely tuned in the scherzo of the Fourth Symphony), and his piercing writing for woodwinds, particularly for the high-pitched E flat clarinet which occurs in each of his symphonies except the Fifth.[68] Mahler himself singled out the song "Des Antonius von Padua Fischpredigt" ("Anthony of Padua's Sermon to the Fishes") as sounding Bohemian,[69] but a better example is the parodistic funeral march on the canon "Frère Jacques" in the First Symphony. In his program for this symphony, which he later withdrew, Mahler entitled this piece "The Hunter's

Funeral." He commented that the march is led by "a group of Bohemian musicians, accompanied by singing cats, toads, crows, etc." and "must be imagined played by a cheap band, such as one hears at country funerals"; "in the midst of this, all the coarseness, the mirth and the banality of the world are heard in the sound of a Bohemian village band. . . ."[70] Theodor Fischer noted a resemblance between this sprightly intermezzo and the hatscho, a typical dance of the Iglau area.[71] Here Mahler seems to satirize comic effects often found in Bohemian music, but in such a way that the music hovers between parody and melancholy.

According to Karbusicky, a Czech musicologist, there exists a Czech song that satirizes funeral processions.[72] And he reports that it was customary to use bands at open-air funerals, after which they would march to the nearest inn while playing cheerful marches and polkas. This alternation of solemn and rustic band music can also be heard in the first movement of Mahler's Third symphony and the last movement of his Seventh Symphony. Some of this irony seems to me to be directed at the persistent military music in Central Europe, but the combination of joy and sadness, of folk music and art music, seems to be characteristic of this region — in contrast to German symphonic music, which tends to be more solemn, more structured and stylistically more consistent.

It is in the dance movements or scherzos of Mahler's symphonies and in their slow, retrospective middle parts where the Bohemian influence is particularly noticeable. Being mostly waltzes and ländler (a slower, more rustic waltz) and in one case a polka, they have, in addition to their Austrian tone, equivalents in similar Czech dances, such as the sousedska (a more lyrical ländler) and the hulán. While the basic form and rhythm of the hulán (in 2/4 time) can be clearly heard in the polka-like opening of the scherzo of the Third Symphony[73] — the combination of flutes and clarinets with a ground bass in fact stylizes the manner of Bohemian musicians — Mahler's use of woodwinds and harp, sometimes with brass, is also a characteristically Bohemian instrumentation. One of the forms of the hulán (in 6/8 time), recorded in a village near Iglau, is very similar to a later passage in that same scherzo. The passage occurs in the extended episode for the posthorn and the orchestral response;[74] it is a remarkable example of a multi-cultural music into which has flowed the musical heritage of three civilizations. The music recalls not only a Czech dance and perhaps the posthorn of the mail coach between Iglau and Prague that Mahler probably used between 1871 and 1881,[75] but also a Spanish jota and several German folksongs (see below, pp. 112-114). Other Bohemian echoes have been located in the Second and Fourth Symphonies; there are, specifically, allusions to Smetana's opera *Dalibor* in the first movement of the Second Symphony and to a well-known Bohemian dance, the rejdovák or rejdovačka, in the third movement of that symphony, as well as a reminiscence of a Czech folksong in the slow movement of the Fourth Symphony.[76]

Karbusicky demonstrates in considerable detail what he considers an affinity between the Czech folksong "Pod našima okny teče vodička" ("Under our windows flows a little brook") and a horn episode in the scherzo of the Fifth Symphony. He suggests that the folksong basis of the lamenting horn melody serves to express human sorrow most intensely.[77] Apart from the question of melodic resemblance which I find less convincing in this case because it rests on only one phrase of the folksong, it does seem that Mahler managed to compress into these transmutations of folk music the whole sorrowfulness of human existence. Whenever he alludes to folk music, it sounds estranged and far removed from the folk spirit, like the music of someone who loves folk music but cannot take part in it himself — in contrast to Antonín Dvořák who could have danced one of his own dances.

What then are Mahler's links to nationally inspired composers like Smetana and Dvořák? For one thing, the Czechs are spontaneous musicians who tend to give priority to melody over structure. Mahler, too, can pour forth melodies, even as his strong intellect attempts to integrate them into large forms. Furthermore, the Czech composers' use of folk music in symphonic works, such as the furiant dance in the scherzos of Dvořák's Sixth and Seventh Symphonies or in a work like Smetana's string quartet "From My Life," is analogous to Mahler's use of the waltz and ländler in his symphonies. The difference is that Dvořák's symphonies have a decidedly national coloring, whereas Mahler completely lacks this element because of his complex background. In instrumentation, the Czechs and Mahler share a clarity of texture and vividness of orchestral color, especially in woodwinds and brass, that is not found in German music. Mahler's melos and harmony, moreover, show a decidedly Slavic piquancy. And as to rhythmic novelty, not a strong point of German composers, Mahler has some of the animation and syncopation so characteristic of Slavic composers. Finally, the pervasive melancholy in Mahler's music finds a parallel in much Slavic music.

Mahler gladly identified with his Bohemian origin, perhaps more so as he got older and became aware that he did not truly belong anywhere, perhaps also because of the nationalistic mood in Germany and Austria. Foerster reports Mahler's offer in 1894 to perform his Second Symphony "at a Czech concert" without a fee, because "he came from Kalište near Humpolec, spoke nothing but Czech in his early youth and the melodies of Czech folksongs had a great influence on his music."[78] There is no doubt that Mahler championed Czech music. In a letter written in Prague in 1886 when he was second conductor at the German Theater there, Mahler wrote: "I attended the Bohemian national theater several times and heard some works by Smetana, Glinka and Dvořák, and I must confess that the first one in particular seems very significant to me."[79] During his year in Prague (1885-86), Mahler became acquainted with three operas by Smetana, *The Bartered Bride, Dalibor* and *The Kiss,* and he recommended these works and operas by Glinka and Dvořák to the manager in Leipzig where he was about to become conductor. "Even if Smetana's operas can never enter the repertoire in Germany, it would still be worthwhile to present so thoroughly original and individual a musician to a sophisticated audience like the Leipzigers."[80] On 17 January 1894, as principal conductor of the Hamburg Opera, Mahler gave the Hamburg premiere of *The Bartered Bride* with great success. He later conducted it during his first season in Vienna and performed it five times at the Metropolitan Opera in New York. It was his favorite non-German opera. While in Hamburg he conducted two other Smetana operas, *Dvě vdovy (Two Widows)* and *Hubička (The Kiss)*, during the 1894-95 season, and he gave the Vienna premiere of *Dalibor* on 4 October 1897, the Emperor's birthday. In view of the opera's Czech nationalism, this strikes one as a telling and rather uncharacteristic political comment on Mahler's part. During his tenure as director of the Vienna Opera *Dalibor* was performed twenty times and *The Bartered Bride* forty-two times.[81] And during the 1900-01 season of the Vienna Philharmonic, Mahler conducted the prelude to Smetana's opera *Libussa* and his tone poem *Vltava (The Moldau)*, both of which have strong national overtones.

Wishing to perform Dvořák, Mahler wrote to him in the fall of 1898 and asked him to send a new work. Dvořák sent him two symphonic poems, *Piseň bohatýrská (Heroic Song)* (op. 111) and *Holoubek (The Wild Dove)* (op. 110), both of which Mahler performed — the former work in Vienna on 4 December 1898 in Dvořák's presence, the latter on 3 December 1899. On 24 February 1901 he also conducted Dvořák's Serenade op. 44, a work Mahler liked better than Dvořák's symphonies which he found inflated, probably because he considered nationalism incompatible with the symphonic form.[82] Dvořák and Mahler met in Vienna in connection with a planned production of Dvořák's opera *Rusalka*, but the production did not materialize because they could not agree on the financial terms.[83]

Mahler's links with his Czech homeland include his conducting stints in Olmütz (Olomouc) in 1883 and in Prague in 1885-86, as well as the first performance of his Seventh Symphony which he conducted in Prague on 19 September 1908. He spent a good deal of time in Bohemia and Moravia; as late as the fall of 1909 he was a guest at an estate in Göding (Hodonín) in Moravia. Actually Mahler spent more time in Eastern than in Western Europe and had, in fact, more affinity for the Slavic world than he did for England, France or Italy. There's reason to believe, too, that during his lifetime he was better received and understood in the East than in the West. His plangent sound is much closer to Tchaikovsky than it is to any German or Austrian composer, with the possible exception of Schubert. His emotional intensity, the naked quality of his music link him with the East. Adorno refers to a "pre-bourgeois, not yet fully individuated element,"[84] by which he may mean something unmediated, unrationalized, unassimilated, something primordial that is characteristically Eastern, that is, not yet intellectualized or adequately balanced. Mahler's music expresses crisis situations of human consciousness, extreme soul states, that are also found in Dostoyevsky's novels.[85]

Yet when one compares Mahler with Leoš Janáček who also came from this area, one is struck by the much 'wilder,' more Eastern sound of Janáček's music. Several explanations come to mind. First of all, Janáček did not write symphonies but composed mostly in freer, more rhapsodic forms. Second, Janáček was not beholden to German romanticism, which left an enduring imprint on all composers in the German orbit. Whereas Mahler wrote out of the Austro-German symphonic tradition, Janáček was free of this and perhaps any other tradition; this may explain his greater modernity, even though he was six years older than Mahler. Third, Janáček's music closely follows the speech rhythms of his native Moravian idiom. Fourth, and perhaps most important, Janáček identified with his people, collected their folksongs, and wrote music on regional or national subjects (for example, the Lachian Dances or the opera *Jenufa* on Moravian village life). This would have been alien to Mahler who signally lacked any national or ethnic identity.[86]

Thus, despite the numerous Czech links and echoes in Mahler's life and music, he was not a Czech composer. This was recognized very early by one of his Czech supporters, the composer and critic Otakar Zich, who wrote in 1911: "Mahler's cradle was in Bohemia; through his songs and symphonies runs many a melodic strain that is dear to us Czechs. In the Third Symphony there even occurs a purely Czech Christmas song. . . . Yet his melodies, even the folk melodies, are definitely different from those of Smetana. His music, even when it is melodically very close to our songs, is not Czech. This is evidence for those who think that the mere use of Czech songs is a guarantee that the music is Czech."[87] One is bound to agree with this statement which points up Mahler's distance or alienation from the folk spirit. He so absorbed and sublimated folk music that his music is less national than any other music in Central Europe during this highly national period. Located geographically and psychically in a cultural borderland and drawing on the rich resources of several civilizations,

Mahler's music is, like Kafka's stories, the expression of a national and spiritual diaspora. The folk music it contains, whether it be Czech, Austrian or German, is but a distant echo, an evocation of the folk spirit by a profoundly isolated artist.

NOTES FOR CHAPTER II: BETWEEN PRAGUE AND VIENNA

1. Political and Social Background

[1] Robert A. Kann, *The Habsburg Empire* (New York: Frederick A. Praeger, 1957), p. 43.

[2] The population figures appear in Robert A. Kann, *The Multi-National Empire: Nationalism and National Reform in the Habsburg Monarchy 1848-1918*, (New York: Columbia University Press, 1950; reprinted in 1964 by Octagon Books, New York), II, p. 302, and in the entries for 'Bohemia' and 'Moravia' in the *Encyclopedia Judaica* (Jerusalem: Keter Publishing House, and New York: Macmillan, 1971).

[3] Arthur J. May, *The Habsburg Monarchy 1867-1914* (Cambridge, Mass.: Harvard University Press, 1951), p. 509.

[4] Kurt Blaukopf, *Gustav Mahler oder Der Zeitgenosse der Zukunft* (Vienna-Munich-Zurich: Molden, 1969), p. 19.

[5] Hans Kohn, "Before 1918 in the Historic Lands," in *The Jews of Czechoslovakia. Historical Studies and Surveys* (Philadelphia: The Jewish Publication Society of America, and New York: Society for the History of Czechoslovak Jews, 1968-1971), I, pp. 17-18.

[6] Ruth Kestenberg-Gladstein, "The Jews between Czechs and Germans in the Historic Lands, 1848-1918," in *The Jews of Czechoslovakia* I, p. 55. — "A Jew who speaks only Czech with his clients all year thinks he is superior if he can read Schiller in German. To know German is equivalent to belonging to some kind of nobility." This quotation is given by Christoph Stölzl in his richly documented study of Bohemian Jews, *Kafkas böses Böhmen: Zur Sozialgeschichte eines Prager Juden* (Munich: edition text + kritik, 1975), p. 23.

[7] Henry-Louis de La Grange, *Mahler* I (Garden City, New York: Doubleday, 1973), p. 672 and p. 25.

[8] Ibid., p. 19.

[9] Peter Gay, *Freud, Jews, and other Germans: Masters and Victims in Modernist Culture* (New York: Oxford University Press, 1978), p. 90.

[10] Hans Kohn, in *The Jews of Czechoslovakia* I, p. 19.

[11] "Their civic and economic existence depended not on their participation in a national community, . . . but, on the contrary, on not acquiring such a status. Even if they became assimilated completely to the culture of a given nationality, they could not outgrow the status of converts to that nationality." Carl E. Schorske, *Fin-de-Siècle Vienna* (New York: Vintage Books, 1981), p. 129.

[12] Blaukopf reports that a Czech deputy, speaking in the Austrian Parliament shortly before 1900, attributed anti-Semitic actions in Moravia to the "Germanizing" attitude of the Jews. See Kurt Blaukopf, *Gustav Mahler oder Der Zeitgenosse der Zukunft*, p. 19.

[13] Christoph Stölzl, *Kafkas böses Böhmen*, p. 26.

[14] Henry-Louis de la Grange, *Mahler* I, pp. 6-8.

[15] Kafka's grandfather was born in Humpolec which is located in the same district where Mahler was born. See Christoph Stölzl, *Kafkas böses Böhmen*, p. 21.

[16] Ibid., p. 39.

[17] Ibid., pp. 39-40.

[18] Ibid., pp. 40-41.

[19] Joseph Arthur de Gobineau, author of *Essai sur l'inégalité des races humaines* (1853-1855), argued that race is the decisive and determining factor in human beings and in history. Richard Wagner affirmed Gobineau's theories. Eugen Dühring maintained in his book, *Die Judenfrage als Racen-, Sitten- und Culturfrage* (1881), that the Jews are an inferior race who should not be allowed to live among other peoples. It was the reading of Dühring that first moved Theodor Herzl toward Zionism. See Alex Bein, *Die Judenfrage: Biographie eines Weltproblems*, 2 vols. (Stuttgart: Deutsche Verlags-Anstalt, 1980), a comprehensive and judicious survey of the Jewish question, with excellent documentation. On Gobineau, see vol. I, pp. 218-222, and vol. II, pp. 169-170; on Wagner, II, pp. 173-184; on Dühring, I, pp. 223-226, and II, pp. 185-186.

[20] Quoted by Christoph Stölzl in *Kafkas böses Böhmen*, p. 80.

[21] Elizabeth Wiskemann, *Czechs and Germans. A Study of the Struggle in the Historic Provinces of Bohemia and Moravia*, 2nd ed. (London: Macmillan, and New York: St. Martin's Press, 1967), p. 59.

[22] Hans Kohn, in *The Jews of Czechoslovakia* I, p. 17.

[23] *New Standard Jewish Encyclopedia*, ed. Cecil Roth and Geoffrey Wigoder, revised ed. (London: W. H. Allen, 1975), p. 326.

[24] See entry for 'Hilsner Case' in the *Encyclopedia Judaica*.

[25] See entries for the respective names in the *Encyclopedia Judaica*.

[26] Henry-Louis de La Grange, *Mahler* I, p. 393.

[27] Berndt W. Wessling, *Gustav Mahler: Ein prophetisches Leben* (Hamburg: Hoffmann und Campe, 1974), p. 156. Unfortunately, Wessling does not cite the sources for his quotations. — Twelve years earlier, in 1885, the Austrian government had declined to accept President Cleveland's nominee as U.S. ambassador to Vienna because he had a Jewish wife. Thereupon the President refused to nominate someone else, and for some time the post was left vacant. See *New York Times,* 20 July 1977, p. 20.

[28] The Austrian statistics can be found in Robert A. Kann, *The Multi-National Empire* II, pp. 300, 305, 306; the German figure appears in the *Encyclopedia Judaica*, vol. 7, col. 481.

[29] *Jewish Encyclopedia* (New York and London: Funk and Wagnalls, 1912), vol. XII, p. 437. — Berlin had 130,487 Jews (4.3%) in 1905; see *Encyclopedia Judaica*, vol. 4, col. 650.

[30] C. A. Macartney, *The Habsburg Empire 1790-1918* (New York: Macmillan, 1969), p. 518.

[31] Christoph Stölzl, *Kafkas böses Böhmen*, p. 79.

[32] Arthur Schnitzler, *Jugend in Wien* (Vienna-Munich-Zurich: Molden, 1968), pp. 154-159.

[33] Amos Elon, *Herzl* (New York: Holt, Rinehart and Winston, 1975), pp. 59-62. The demonstration took place at a meeting to observe Wagner's recent death.

[34] See the excellent essay, "Politics in a New Key: An Austrian Trio," by Carl E. Schorske in his book *Fin-de-Siècle Vienna*, pp. 116-180.

[35] Robert A. Kann, *The Multi-National Empire* I, pp. 97-99.

[36] A well-researched study of this group is the book by William J. McGrath, *Dionysian Art and Populist Politics in Austria* (New Haven and London: Yale University Press, 1974).

[37] Kralik reports that Adler and Friedjung found it painful to leave Schönerer's party; see Richard von Kralik, "Gesichter und Gestalten: Victor Adler und Pernerstorfer," a manuscript in the manuscript collection of the Wiener Stadtbibliothek, Ms. I.N. 106.071, fol. 1^r-6^r, p. 3.

[38] The vote for Victor Adler is documented in *Mahler: A Documentary Study*, ed. Kurt Blaukopf, tr. Paul Baker, Susanne Flatauer, P. R. J. Ford, Daisy Loman and Geoffrey Watkins (New York and Toronto: Oxford University Press, 1976), p. 225. Adler, running against the Christian Socialist incumbent in the Vienna district in which Mahler lived, lost the election. — The May Day event is reported by Alma Mahler in her memoirs, *Gustav Mahler: Memories and Letters* third ed., ed. Donald Mitchell, tr. Basil Creighton (Seattle: University of Washington Press, 1975), p. 82.

[39] William J. McGrath, *Dionysian Art and Populist Politics in Austria*, p. 89.

[40] Julius Braunthal, *Victor und Friedrich Adler: Zwei Generationen Arbeiterbewegung* (Wiener Neustadt: Verlag der Wiener Volksbuchhandlung, 1965), pp. 34-35. Adler, an assimilated Jew who once described himself as "the strictest kind of anti-Semite" (Braunthal, p. 29), had a good understanding of music and rarely missed a performance by Mahler, even after they had long lost contact (Braunthal, p. 35).

[41] Richard von Kralik, *Tage und Werke. Lebenserinnerungen* (Vienna: Vogelsang-Verlag, 1922), p. 63.

[42] Richard von Kralik, "Gesichter und Gestalten: Victor Adler und Pernerstorfer," p. 3.

[43] *Allgemeines Deutsches Kommersbuch*, ed. Friedrich Silcher and Friedrich Erk, 25th ed. (Lahr: Moritz Schauenburg, 1883), pp. 80-81 and pp. 19-20. This is a popular and nationalistic collection of patriotic and student songs that had gone through 156 editions by 1966. The song "O du Deutschland, ich muss marschieren" ("O Germany, I must march"), entitled "Zum Ausmarsche 1815" ("On Marching to War in 1815") and intended as a call to action against Napoleon, is necessarily more militant and more militaristic than "Deutschland, Deutschland über alles" ("Germany, Germany above all else"), which is entitled "Das Lied der Deutschen" ("The Song of the Germans") and stresses the need for German unity. The text of "O du Deutschland, ich muss marschieren" was written in 1814 by Ernst Moritz Arndt, the music by Friedrich Silcher; the text of "Deutschland, Deutschland über alles" was written in 1841 by Hoffmann von Fallersleben, the music by Haydn. In the latter song, the music preceded the text.

[44] Alma Mahler, *Gustav Mahler: Memories and Letters*, pp. 104-105.

[45] Bertha Zuckerkandl, *Österreich Intim. Erinnerungen 1892-1942*, ed. Reinhard Federmann (Frankfurt/Main-Berlin-Vienna: Propyläen Verlag, 1970), pp. 38-43 and pp. 67-74.

[46] Franz Loschnigg, *The Cultural Education of Gustav Mahler*, diss. University of Wisconsin/Madison, 1976, p. 132.

2. The Czech Connection

[47] The visit to Ledeč is described in Henry-Louis de La Grange, *Mahler* I, pp. 14-15; the other towns are mentioned in Mahler's letters to Josef Steiner of 17 June 1879, and to Emil Freund of June 1879 and 18 August 1881. See *Selected Letters of Gustav Mahler*, ed. Alma Mahler, revised edition by Knud Martner, tr. Eithne Wilkins, Ernst Kaiser and Bill Hopkins (New York: Farrar, Straus and Giroux, 1979), pp. 55, 57, and 65. The towns are listed on an improvised map of the entire region, which appears on page 29 of Vladimir Karbusicky's study, *Gustav*

Mahler und seine Umwelt (Darmstadt: Wissenschaftliche Buchgesellschaft, 1978). This book is, so far as I know, the most thorough investigation of Mahler's Czech roots.

[48] Foerster is quoted without reference by Arnošt Mahler, "Gustav Mahler und seine Heimat," *Die Musikforschung,* Vol. 25, No. 4 (October-December 1972), p. 437. Mrs. Olga Schiffer of Amherst, Massachusetts, to whom I am indebted for giving me valuable information on this topic, reports that the Jewish population of this area routinely spoke some Czech.

[49] Josef Bohuslav Foerster, *Der Pilger. Erinnerungen eines Musikers*, tr. from the Czech by Pavel Eisner (Prague: Artis, 1955), p. 375.

[50] Arnošt Mahler, "Gustav Mahler und seine Heimat," p. 438.

[51] Guido Adler, *Gustav Mahler* (Vienna-Leipzig: Universal Edition, 1916), p. 38 and pp. 53-55. Much later, in 1935, Adler proudly identified himself as a "Sudeten German," a surprising label for a Jew to choose after Hitler had come to power, but perhaps the term had not yet acquired its later connotation of right-wing agitation. See Guido Adler's autobiography, *Wollen und Wirken* (Vienna-Leipzig: Universal Edition, 1935), p. 2.

[52] Theodor Fischer, "Aus Gustav Mahlers Jugendzeit," *Deutsche Heimat.* Sudetendeutsche Monatsschrift für Literatur, Kunst, Heimat- und Volkskunde, vol. 7, nos. 6-7 (June-July 1931), p. 264.

[53] Arnošt Mahler, "Gustav Mahler und seine Heimat," pp. 437-448.

[54] Mahler's statement is reported by a musician who played under him in New York. It can be heard on Columbia Masterworks Set M3X-31437 which contains Mahler's Fourth and Fifth Symphonies, performed by Leonard Bernstein and the New York Philharmonic, and an interview with musicians who were members of that orchestra when Mahler conducted it from 1909 to 1911.

[55] *Kafka-Handbuch*, ed. Hartmut Binder (Stuttgart: Alfred Kröner Verlag, 1979), vol. I, p. 580.

[56] Quoted in Donald Mitchell, *Gustav Mahler: The Early Years*, ed. Paul Banks and David Matthews (Berkeley-Los Angeles: University of California Press, 1980), p. 3.

[57] The last sentence of this passage is taken from Guido Adler, *Gustav Mahler,* p. 9; the rest of the quotation appears in Guido Adler, "Gustav Mahlers Persönlichkeit," in *Das Mahler-Fest, Amsterdam, Mai 1920*, ed. C. Rudolf Mengelberg (Vienna-Leipzig: Universal Edition, 1920), p. 17, and is quoted in Edward R. Reilly, *Gustav Mahler und Guido Adler,* tr. Herta Blaukopf (Vienna: Universal Edition, 1978), p. 12.

[58] Lillian Schacherl, *Mähren: Land der friedlichen Widersprüche* (Munich: Prestel-Verlag, 1968), p. 127.

[59] Vladimir Karbusicky, *Gustav Mahler und seine Umwelt,* p. 33.

[60] *Encyclopedia Judaica,* entry for 'Jihlava' (Iglau).

[61] Henry-Louis de La Grange, *Mahler I,* p. 841.

[62] Ibid., pp. 18 and 25-26.

[63] Paul Stefan, *Gustav Mahler: A Study of his Personality and Work*, tr. T. E. Clark (New York: G. Schirmer, 1913), p. 12. Quoted in Donald Mitchell, *Gustav Mahler: The Early Years,* p. 19.

[64] Richard Specht, *Gustav Mahler*, 17th and 18th ed. (Stuttgart-Berlin: Deutsche Verlags-Anstalt, 1925), p. 170. Quoted in Vladimir Karbusicky, *Gustav Mahler und seine Umwelt,* p. 22.

[65] *Selected Letters of Gustav Mahler,* ed. Alma Mahler, p. 393.

[66] Vladimir Karbusicky, *Gustav Mahler und seine Umwelt,* p. 26.

[67] Ibid., pp. 26-28.

[68] Mahler is said to have introduced the E flat clarinet into the G minor variation of the last movement of Beethoven's *Eroica* Symphony, according to the interview mentioned in Note 54 above. He told Natalie Bauer-Lechner, his long-time confidante, that even as a boy he was fascinated

by the instrument and had to overcome the opposition of his colleagues who considered its sound vulgar. See Natalie Bauer-Lechner, *Recollections of Gustav Mahler*, tr. Dika Newlin, ed. Peter Franklin (New York: Cambridge University Press, 1980), p. 46.

[69] Natalie Bauer-Lechner, *Recollections of Gustav Mahler*, p. 33. Mahler may have been referring to the clarinet runs marked "with parody" (measures 87-98) and "with humor" (measures 148-156).

[70] Henry-Louis de La Grange, *Mahler* I, p. 749.

[71] Theodor Fischer, "Aus Gustav Mahlers Jugendzeit," p. 266.

[72] Vladimir Karbusicky, *Gustav Mahler und seine Umwelt*, pp. 35-37.

[73] Ibid., p. 47.

[74] Compare the second part of the hulán printed by Karbusicky on page 49 of *Gustav Mahler und seine Umwelt* with measures 285-293 of the third movement of Mahler's Third Symphony in the score edited by the International Gustav Mahler Society (Vienna: Universal Edition, 1974).

[75] Karbusicky (p. 49 of his book) believes that Mahler could not have travelled by another route when he went to study in Prague in 1871.

[76] Vladimir Karbusicky, *Gustav Mahler und seine Umwelt*, pp. 50, 52, 54. As a Czech, Karbusicky whose book is fascinating is understandably eager to establish Mahler's Czech credentials.

[77] Ibid., pp. 57-66.

[78] Quoted in Arnošt Mahler, "Gustav Mahler und seine Heimat," p. 437.

[79] Letter to Max Staegemann, director of the Leipzig Theater, in *Selected Letters of Gustav Mahler*, ed. Alma Mahler, pp. 96-97.

[80] Ibid.

[81] Katalog der Ausstellung "Gustav Mahler und seine Zeit" (Catalogue of the Exhibit "Gustav Mahler and his Times") (Vienna: Direktion der Wiener Festwochen, 1960), pp. 110-112.

[82] Henry-Louis de La Grange, *Mahler* I, p. 613.

[83] Josef Bohuslav Foerster, *Der Pilger*, pp. 715-716.

[84] Theodor W. Adorno, *Mahler: Eine musikalische Physiognomik* (Frankfurt/Main: Suhrkamp Verlag, 1960), p. 105.

[85] Inna Barssowa, "Mahler und Dostojewski," in: *Beiträge '79-81: Gustav Mahler Kolloquium 1979*, ed. Rudolf Klein (Kassel: Bärenreiter-Verlag, 1981), p. 71.

[86] But this did not keep Mahler from wishing to become acquainted with Janáček's opera. When Janáček invited him in 1904 to attend a performance of *Jenufa* in Brünn (Brno), Mahler responded on 9 December 1904: "Dear Sir, . . . I am unable to leave Vienna at the present time, but as I would be very interested to get to know your work, I beg you to be kind enough to send me the vocal score with German words." Since such a score was not available, the matter could not be pursued. See Jaroslav Vogel, *Leoš Janáček*, rev. and ed. Karel Janovický (New York and London: Norton, 1981), p. 228.

[87] Quoted in Karbusicky, *Gustav Mahler und seine Umwelt*, p. 99. And another Czech admirer, the musicologist Zdenek Nejedly, made the following apt judgment in his 1912 monograph on Mahler: "Mahler never attempted to write Bohemian music, just as he didn't care whether his music was sufficiently German." Quoted in Karbusicky, p. 134.

Chapter III

THE ETERNAL JEW

For a Jew, being Jewish is a central fact of life. No matter whether the attitude of the Jew toward being Jewish is positive or negative, Jewishness is a decisive and determining force in a person's existence. To a somewhat lesser degree, a person's Jewishness is also perceived by non-Jews as an essential aspect of personality. "Thus the Jew is in the situation of a Jew because he lives in the midst of a society that takes him for a Jew."[1] An eminent German-Jewish writer, Ludwig Börne, has vividly expressed it: "Some reproach me for being Jewish; others forgive me for it; still others even praise me for it; but they all think of it."[2]

This problem is more acute for assimilated Jews who have, to a large extent, given up their Jewish identity, yet are not fully integrated in the countries in which they live. In Germany the Jews were highly assimilated and enamored of German culture, but lived in a politically volatile country which lacked a democratic tradition and was not united until 1871, eleven years after Mahler was born. Germany was then finding its own identity for the first time and was perhaps not inclined to be particularly tolerant toward a distinctive minority. Moreover, as it evolved under Bismarck's leadership, Germany was a rather authoritarian, nationalistic, bureaucratic state where nonconformists did not thrive. (Unlike England, France and the United States, Germany has not been known as a refuge for exiles.)

While Germany was a quickly rising, ethnocentric Protestant power during Mahler's lifetime, Austria was a declining polyglot Catholic empire that could not control its many nationalities. Its powerful Catholic hierarchy was even less pro-Jewish than the Protestant clergy in Germany, partly because religious anti-Semitism, which holds the Jews responsible for the crucifixion of Christ, was more prevalent in Catholic areas. Another reason for the rise in Austrian anti-Semitism at that time was the large migration of poor Jews to Vienna and the German-speaking parts of the empire from its easternmost provinces.

Like other Jews from Bohemia and Moravia, Mahler was by background
and upbringing an assimilated Western Jew and identified himself as such
in some strongly prejudicial statements about Eastern Jews (see below, pp.
45-46). His family spoke German, not Yiddish, and moved within a culturally German orbit. His father chose to settle in the predominantly German town
of Iglau, but it took him thirteen years to become a citizen (1873); he was so
proud of it that he had the certificate framed and displayed it on his living-
room wall.[3] Though he was elected to the Iglau Jewish Community by a large
majority, he does not seem to have been an observant Jew; indeed, the evidence
points in the opposite direction. By profession a tavernkeeper and a distiller
and seller of alcoholic beverages — which Mahler later did not want to admit,
preferring to call him a businessman[4] — he was an ambitious entrepreneur with
cultural aspirations who sought to improve his and his family's lot and who
tried to educate himself by reading and study — a very typical Jewish career
for that time and place.

Bernhard Mahler was known as a scholarly tradesman because he read
books and had even studied French. Before his marriage he had served as a
children's tutor and he possessed a library of classic and modern works.[5] There
is every indication that he gave his own children a secular and German education. Like Freud, who also came from this area, the young Mahler had little
or no contact with the Jewish religion. There is no evidence that he was ever
confirmed, and he may indeed have been more familiar with Catholic than with
Jewish ritual, as Blaukopf believes.[6] It is true that he had Jewish instruction in
high school and received his only A in this subject, but easy grading was the
rule in this class.[7] Nothing that we know about Mahler suggests any Jewish
identification; on the contrary, he experienced his Jewishness as a burden and
a hindrance to his career.

Mahler himself was more aware of his situation than some of his Jewish
friends who tried to present him as a German composer (Guido Adler, Richard
Specht, Paul Stefan). In one of his earliest letters, written shortly before his
nineteenth birthday, he seems to identify with the Wandering Jew. In a dream-
like scene he envisions the suffering Ahasuerus seeking salvation from an
angel, but the angel withdraws as Ahasuerus "stares after him in immeasurable
grief, then takes his cane and wanders on, without tears, eternal and im-
mortal! . . ."[8] Even after one makes allowances for the emotional effusion of
an intense young man, this letter is a remarkable expression of personal lost-
ness for so young a person.

In fact, the havenless wanderer forms a recurrent theme in Mahler's
life and work. In numerous letters he conveys a sense of homelessness which
he hopes to end by finding a position in Vienna or by getting married or by going

to America, where he hopes to find "a spiritual home," or by being "at home somewhere" as he plans to retire near Vienna.[9] At the age of twenty-six he thinks he is destined to roam the earth without rest.[10] In one letter he describes himself as a "wayfarer" (fahrender Gesell), borrowing a phrase from the title of his first and clearly autobiographical song cycle.[11] His wife speaks of his restlessness, his "Ahasuerism,"[12] reporting that he couldn't stay long anywhere, and his biography reads like a travelogue. For a conductor a lot of travel does not seem unusual, but Mahler's statements go far beyond this. Realizing that he was somehow 'different,' he speaks of his music as being strange even in his own country.[13] As he prepared to leave for America he said he was taking his homeland with him, namely his Alma and his child,[14] yet only six months later, in New York, he complains of being homesick for Vienna and describes himself as "a dyed-in-the-wool Viennese."[15] Toward the end of his unsettled life he did plan to retire in Breitenstein, an Alpine village not very far from Vienna, but he did not live to do so.

Perhaps his most eloquent and intense expression of existential loneliness occurs in the last song from Das Lied von der Erde (The Song of the Earth). Whereas the Lieder eines fahrenden Gesellen (Songs of a Wayfarer) leave the wanderer homeless and bereft because of unrequited love, Das Lied von der Erde ends in such cosmic desolation that it is difficult to think of a parallel. The minor-key ending of Tchaikovsky's Pathétique Symphony, despairing as it is, sounds like a personal elegy by comparison with the open-ended C-E-A chord at the end of Das Lied von der Erde, which conveys a limitless solitude, a sense of earth's beauty and continuity beyond the singer's own death. This song, entitled "The Farewell," is not merely the personal parting from a friend, as in the text, but essentially the withdrawal from life, from earth, from the universe for all eternity. From the text's subjective emotion of not being at home on this earth Mahler distilled an all-encompassing loneness. To what degree this feeling can be attributed to his Jewishness is hard to say. Certainly, non-Jewish poets and composers have sung of loneliness (for example, Schubert's song cycle Die Winterreise [The Winter Journey] or Rilke's poetry) or travelled incessantly (Kleist, Byron, Nietzsche), but Mahler talked of his Jewishness and suffered from it.[16] That his music expresses a deep existential homelessness cannot be denied.

Mahler's references to his Jewish background pertain mainly to career matters and his desire for assimilation. The latter is expressed in quite offensive terms in a few letters he wrote to his wife from Eastern Europe. While guest-conducting in the Galician city of Lemberg (Lvov), he sent the following comment: "Life here has an unusual look. Oddest of all are the Jews who run around here the way dogs do elsewhere. It is extremely entertaining to watch them!

My God, am I supposed to be related to them?! I can't tell you how silly I find
the race theories in view of such evidence!"[17] Describing the Polish city as dirty
— as is customary for many people raised in German-speaking areas when
referring to Poland — Mahler wrote that "no imagination can think up a dirtier
person than a Polish Jew in this place."[18] Alma Mahler reports a similar experience in New York when she and Mahler were walking through "the Jewish
quarter," undoubtedly the Lower East Side. "Are they our brothers?" she
asked him and he shook his head in desperation.[19]

On the other hand, when they were in Warsaw together in 1902, Mahler
was happy when Alma gave money to a poor old Jewish peddler,[20] perhaps
because it expressed sympathy for the Jews by his non-Jewish wife. On another
stopover in Warsaw five years later Mahler looked for this old Jew; "I did not
find him but found quite a few young ones. (I didn't want to bring you one as a
souvenir.) But I did get my money's worth. It is very unusual (etwas sehr Selt-
sames) to see such strange types. One would like to ask each one who he is,
what he does, wants, hopes for."[21]

It is distressing to have to record these unfortunate statements, even
though they were not written for publication. Mahler was even more assimilationist and much less compassionate than Heine, who reacted similarly when
he encountered Polish Jews in Warsaw in 1822.[22] Mahler's remarks are all the
more disturbing because his wife, to whom they were addressed, had anti-
Semitic tendencies of her own.[23] And considering the anti-Semitism he experienced himself, one would have expected a more enlightened point of view.

In the spring of 1885, while he was second conductor in Kassel, he was
chosen over his superior, Wilhelm Treiber, to direct a music festival there. In
the ensuing controversy between Treiber's and Mahler's partisans a local weekly
published, on 2 May 1885, an attack against "the Jew Mahler" who was accused of getting the honors while the Germans were doing the work. In its issue
of 23 May 1885 the same paper published a nasty anti-Semitic poem about the
affair; both papers are in Mahler's Kassel personnel file.[24] The festival committee, to its credit, was not influenced by these attacks which Mahler apparently took with equanimity. Though he wrote to his friend Friedrich Löhr
of these difficulties, he didn't mention anti-Semitism. The crowning irony of
this affair, as de La Grange points out,[25] is that the major work of the festival
was the oratorio *Paulus* by the Jewish composer Mendelssohn.

It was in connection with Mahler's appointment as director of the Vienna
Opera that most of the anti-Semitic events in his life occurred. In no other

position he held did his Jewish origin present an employment problem. In the spring of 1894, when he mentioned the possibility of going to Vienna, Mahler wrote that being Jewish would bar him from any court opera "as matters now stand in the world."[26] Early in 1896, when his negotiations with the Vienna Opera were not progressing, he enlisted the help of Rosa Papier, a singer who had sung under Mahler at the Kassel festival and who was close to a high-ranking opera official in Vienna, Eduard Wlassack. Wlassack at first notified Rosa Papier that Mahler had no chance as a Jew but later used all his influence in his behalf.[27] In late 1896, when it seemed likely that the incumbent director, Wilhelm Jahn, would soon resign for reasons of age and health, Rosa Papier advised Mahler to apply for a conductor's position instead of the directorship, as a maneuver that would make it easier for him to be appointed. He followed this advice, but was informed in January 1897, according to de La Grange, that "under the present circumstances, it is impossible to engage a Jew for Vienna."[28] Unfortunately, de La Grange gives no source for this important statement, but this information appears in two letters Mahler wrote in that same month.[29]

Undoubtedly Mahler was persuaded that "the greatest hindrance of all — my being Jewish *(mein Judentum)*" was blocking his appointment,[30] and he was determined not to let this happen. On 21 December 1896 he wrote to Ödön von Mihalovich, the Hungarian composer whom he had asked to intercede for him: "In Vienna the problem of a conductor-director is acute. At the moment I am high on the list of candidates, but two factors are against me, it seems: my 'madness,' which my enemies mention whenever they want to put difficulties in my path, and the fact that I was born a Jew; as regards this point, I must tell you, in case you don't know it yet, that I was converted to Catholicism very shortly after I left Budapest."[31] And he gave a similar account to the Vienna music critic Ludwig Karpath and to another correspondent.[32] Since Mahler actually converted on 23 February 1897,[33] six years after he had left Budapest, he was falsifying the record. The statement he made to Karpath deserves to be quoted in full:

> You know, what particularly offends and angers me is the circumstance that I had to have myself baptized to get an engagement, that's what I cannot get over. It is of course untrue that I had myself baptized only when the Vienna position beckoned — I had been baptized years before that — but the fact is that the desire to escape from Pollini's Hamburg inferno awakened in me the thought of leaving the Jewish religious community. That is the shameful thing about the matter. I do not deny that it cost me a great deal of effort *(Überwindung)*

to take an action for what one may justifiably call self-preservation and *which one was inwardly not at all disinclined to take*
(emphasis by Karpath).[34]

If one assumes that Karpath is quoting Mahler accurately, this passage
goes to the heart of the matter. The deep ambivalence about being Jewish, the
opportunism and the attempt to hide it, the guilt feelings, the not-quite-con-
vincing protestations are symptomatic of the assimilated Jew of the era who
wanted to get ahead and found that his Judaism stood in his way. One can
readily believe that Mahler objected to baptism as a prerequisite for the position, but he probably got over it without too much trauma. The effort to change
the date was obviously made to forestall the impression of opportunism, which
embarrassed him. But when he gives as his reason for converting the desire to
leave the Hamburg Opera, he is being somewhat disingenuous; the real reason
is his ambition to become director of the Vienna Opera, which was then the
most prestigious musical position in Europe, if not in the whole world. As for
leaving the Jewish religious community, it could be said that Mahler was never
a member of it, in the sense of being a practicing Jew or belonging to a con-
gregation. What he must have meant is that he was leaving a group bound together by an ancient culture, a group, moreover, that has been persecuted for
many centuries. Whether he truly had to overcome a deep-seated reluctance to
do so is open to question; it was a matter of self-preservation only if Mahler's
need to be at the top of his profession can be interpreted as self-preservation —
a strong likelihood in his case. The key clause at the end — 'an action which
one was inwardly not at all disclined to take' — made actually stronger by the
use of litotes and the impersonal pronoun (to avoid using the first person), is
amazingly frank and leaves no doubt that Mahler put career above Judaism.[35]
    It is possible, in the context of the conversation with Karpath which dealt
with Mahler's oscillations between Judaism and Christianity, to interpret that
final clause as his readiness to become a Catholic. It has been argued, notably
by his wife, that Mahler was a Jew who believed in Christ, was attracted to
Catholic mysticism and loved the incense and music of churches[36] — a description that fits Franz Werfel, the poet whom she married later, better than it does
Mahler. According to a more recent writer, Mahler converted "to the faith
whose teachings and ritual had long been familiar to him as the son of a country
stamped by Catholicism, and whose doctrine of redemptive love he had adopted
in his unorthodox way." But he adds correctly that Mahler "was as little a
zealous Catholic as he had earlier been a zealous synagogue goer."[37] His religion
was essentially existential: though he believed in something beyond this world,
this belief was directly bound up with his belief in himself and in his work. He

had a sense of mission as an artist, but beyond that it is highly doubtful that he had any religion in the traditional sense. While no materialist, he was not an orthodox believer; in effect, if not officially, he did not have a confession. He was neither an observant Jew nor an observant Christian, but a modern skeptic. Alfred Roller, Mahler's stage designer, reports that when Mahler was asked why he did not write a mass, he replied that he could not write a credo.[38] Musically he is most convincing when he is least religious.

Mahler's use of (quasi-)Christian texts in the fourth and fifth movements of the Second Symphony, the fifth movement of the Third, the fourth movement of the Fourth and the first movement of the Eighth has led some commentators to attribute Christian convictions to the composer. Though the atmosphere of these texts is certainly Christian, they do not necessarily stamp the composer as a Christian. The two texts in the Second Symphony merely assert a belief in an after-life, without being denominational. In fact, Mahler deleted the specifically Christian elements in Klopstock's ode "Die Auferstehung" ("The Resurrection") — the hallelujah refrains and the reference to Jesus — and substituted his own much more general affirmation that man will vanquish pain and death and rise again.[39] The texts in the Third and Fourth Symphonies, which do mention Jesus and the saints, are a child's personalized vision of heaven, for which Mahler probably couldn't or wouldn't have found substitutes from other religions. The "Veni Creator Spiritus" hymn in the first movement of the Eighth Eymphony is certainly a Catholic prayer, but the monumentality of its treatment clashes with the spirituality of the text, giving it "a secular, humanistic meaning."[40] Furthermore, the movements in which these texts occur fill an important structural function, representing various levels in an ascending view of the symphony from the earthly to the spiritual, in the manner of an expressionist play, without necessarily adhering to a particular religion. I think Mahler used these texts more for artistic than for religious reasons to express his vision of art, just as Goethe introduced a Catholic heaven at the end of *Faust* because the work demanded it, not from religious conviction.[41] Yet in Goethe's drama, as well as in the hymn to human brotherhood which closes Beethoven's Ninth Symphony, one hears if not religious conviction at least a strong affirmation. But in Mahler, and much more in a work like Georg Kaiser's expressionist play *Von morgens bis mitternachts (From Morn to Midnight)*, one senses that the final apotheosis is dictated by formal requirements rather than by faith. That Mahler did not have sufficient faith to make his affirmations sound convincing is another mark of his marginality. One of the most persuasive statements about Mahler's religious situation was made by Bruno Walter when he was asked to differentiate between Bruckner and Mahler: "Mahler was looking for God all his life, Bruckner had found

God."[42] This means that Mahler wanted to believe but found it difficult to do so. If this is correct, he would have found it even more difficult to align himself with a particular confession. He stood above the confessions, as much as he stood above the nations.[43]

It is clear from the evidence that Mahler converted to Catholicism so that he could become director of the Vienna Opera. This act has to be viewed from the perspective of that time, not judged by today's standards which are set by the Holocaust. In 1897 the situation of the Jews, though hardly ideal, was not the same as in 1942 when the poet Franz Werfel refrained from converting to Catholicism, even though he had accepted most of its tenets, because he did not want to leave a martyred minority.[44] And today, unless it is done for compelling religious convictions, conversion would be considered a gratuitous act, since in most areas inhabited by Jews the more serious forms of discrimination have been eliminated. But in Mahler's time conversions occurred more often because of economic, social, cultural and professional barriers against Jews; among the converts were three who touched Mahler's life: Victor Adler, Siegfried Lipiner and Arnold Schoenberg (who later returned to Judaism).[45] But though conversion may have made success possible, as it did for Mahler, it did not stop anti-Semitic attacks against the converts; on the contrary, the attacks intensified, as also happened to Mahler (see below, pp. 51-52). So did the marginality of these Jews who now found themselves in a no-man's-land between a lapsed Judaism and a merely nominal Christianity. The blame for this entire situation rests with the authorities for insisting on conversion as a condition for employment or advancement. De La Grange reports that the word 'Christian' in Mahler's personnel file is underlined, which he interprets as "proof of the importance the Austrian officials attached to this matter"; when the incumbent director, Wilhelm Jahn, resigned in the summer of 1897, opera officials recommended "Kapellmeister Gustav Mahler, a young Christian Austrian of 37. . . ."[46] One can only say that the Vienna Opera got a far better director than it deserved.

Legally Mahler probably could not have been barred, as were Heine and Börne in the early nineteenth century from university and civil service careers, respectively, but *de facto* discrimination was still strong, especially in high-ranking positions. As a greatly gifted and ambitious man, Mahler was not prepared to tolerate obstacles to his career. Throughout his life he was determined to advance to the top, sometimes to a degree that makes the reader uncomfortable. In 1886, after he had signed a three-year contract with the Leipzig Theater but before the season had even begun, he made strenuous efforts to be released from his contract because he did not want to share the podium with another conductor. He went so far as to apply for a position in Wiesbaden before the incumbent director had actually retired, as Mahler heard that he would. Mahler was talked out of this potential breach of contract by Baron von Gilsa who had been his superior in Kassel, and the incumbent director in Wiesbaden, Carl Reiss, not only did not retire but was given a five-year reappointment.[47] Mahler relentlessly searched out and pursued the best possible positions, having an absolutely sure sense of his own ability and worth. As early as January 1885, when he was twenty-four years old, he was determined to become director of the Vienna Opera.[48] Whatever reservations one may have about the way he reached his objective, it can be argued that by advancing his career he benefitted humanity more than if he had retained his tenuous connection with Judaism and not gone to Vienna.

Mahler's appointment in Vienna — as conductor on 15 April 1897, as director on 8 October 1897 — did not, of course, end the anti-Semitic issue. On 10 April, two days after the initial appointment was announced, one of two anti-Semitic, Pan-German newspapers in Vienna, the *Deutsche Zeitung* (the other paper was *Deutsches Volksblatt* — both papers were organs of the anti-Semitic Christian Socialist Party led by Karl Lueger), attacked the "frightening Jewification of art in Vienna" and questioned whether a Jew could perform "our great music . . . our German opera" even if "he had just been baptized three weeks before."[49] Though initially Mahler won over the critic of the *Deutsche Zeitung*, who praised Mahler's debut in *Lohengrin* on 11 May 1897 — "The anti-Semitic papers are either silent or favorable," Mahler wrote[50] — this did not last long. From 12 September 1897 on, so reports de La Grange, they attacked him as a "non-German" who gave German works the lowest priority and yet was considered unfit to conduct *Die Meistersinger* and *Der Ring des Nibelungen* because their "typically German" quality was alien to him; but they gave him credit for doing *Tristan und Isolde* well.[51] The *Deutsche Zeitung* accused him of holding his position only because of the "systematic adulation" of the Jewish press and the hiring of too many Jews.[52] On 18 March 1900, this newspaper published, anonymously, a comprehensive attack against Mahler's performances, repertoire and opera direction.[53]

De La Grange relates in considerable detail the anti-Semitic attacks on Mahler during the first few years of his tenure at the opera and during his 2-1/2 years as conductor of the Vienna Philharmonic (1898-1901). On the day before his first Philharmonic concert Mahler was denounced as the "Jewish musical dictator of Vienna" in a newspaper article;[54] in 1901 he was displaced as the orchestra's conductor by the anti-Semitic Joseph Hellmesberger. Mahler was accused of being overzealous, presumptuous and tyrannical, of abusing his musicians, not choosing the right repertory, tampering with the classics, favoring friends and relatives, getting rid of respected artists, and in one case even of financial irregularities. Though Mahler was, like many eminent conductors, a perfectionist and antagonized some musicians with his fanatic care and some listeners with his unorthodox performances, his devotion to the music and the high artistic standards he maintained are fully attested to. His work at the Vienna Opera literally cost him his health. Most of the accusations against him were malicious and were inspired by anti-Semitic prejudice. It is hard to think of another musician or composer who has been so vilified.

*   *   *   *

Did Mahler write 'Jewish music'? The answer must be no. 'Jewish music' has been defined as "that music which is made by Jews, for Jews, as Jews."[55] Obviously Mahler was not Jewish in any national sense. A comparison with Ernest Bloch, who greatly respected Mahler's music,[56] makes this immediately clear: there are no works on Hebraic themes, such as *Baal Shem* or *Schelomo*, in Mahler's oeuvre. Bloch's statement that he was interested in "the Hebrew spirit . . . which I seek to feel within me and to translate in my music"[57] would have been foreign to Mahler who disliked any national music. It would be difficult even to posit that there is such a thing as 'Jewish music' in the art music of the diaspora, except where traditional chants are used, as in Bloch's *Sacred Service* which is not, strictly speaking, secular music.

What is called 'Jewish music' exists only in the liturgy and in folklore, because there was no national basis on which an authentic Jewish art music could develop.[58] This explains the paucity of classical Jewish composers. Those who did exist naturally composed in the style of their adopted country. The only major exception in Central Europe is Ernest Bloch who was born in an international enclave (Geneva) and identified himself as a Jew in a national sense; all the other prominent Jewish composers were assimilationists. But they may still have absorbed Jewish influences from the liturgy or from folklore, particularly if they came, as Mahler did, from an area heavily populated by Jews. Without characterizing Mahler as a 'Jewish' composer, which he clearly was not, one may perhaps say that his music contains, on three or four occasions, a melody or inflection reminiscent of Jewish folksong; an example is the passage from meas. 39 to 71 in the Frère Jacques movement of the First Symphony.[59] In view of his Jewish background in rural Central Europe and his love of folk music, this is not at all implausible.

Yet identifying Mahler's music as 'Jewish' in any sense raises two troubling questions. First of all, any mention of Jewish characteristics runs up against the problem of stereotyping, both positive and negative, with its prejudicial and reductive aspects. Secondly, any one who attributes Jewish qualities to Mahler's music can be accused of using the same arguments that anti-Semitic critics have used. If I nevertheless venture into this dangerous terrain, I do so because Judaism is a vital part of Mahler's being and belongs to the history of the era. I also wish to expose those critics who argue that one kind of music is superior to another solely on the basis of race, religion or national origin. While recognizing that there are national differences in music or any other art, I am arguing for a multinational or multicultural approach. This is in the spirit of Mahler who not only combined various national or ethnic strains in his own music but who performed an exceptionally wide repertoire of symphonic and operatic music.[60]

Two important writers on Mahler have limited themselves to pointing out a general attitude or stance in Mahler's work that they consider Jewish. Guido Adler cites, with reservations, the composer's "occasionally overintense expressive power, the fanatic exaggeration in imparting his emotions,"[61] but a more pervasive and basic aspect of Mahler's art is identified by Adorno: "What is Jewish in Mahler does not partake directly of what is popular, but expresses itself beyond all that is communicated as something spiritual, unphysical but nevertheless perceivable in the totality of his work."[62] What I think Adorno means is that Mahler tends to delocalize or make abstract whatever folk music he uses so that it loses its folk quality and becomes etherealized; thus transformed, folk music pervades his music without being directly identifiable as such.

In 1916, Max Brod, the novelist, essayist, music critic and editor of Kafka, published the first of his discussions of 'Jewish elements' in Mahler's music.[63] Born in Prague to a German-speaking Jewish family, Brod was himself a marginal man who acted as a cultural mediator between the Jewish, Slavic and German worlds (he translated Janáček's librettos into German and wrote a biography of this composer). But unlike Mahler, Schnitzler, Freud and most of the other creative Jewish figures of that time and place, Brod was a conscious Jew and active Zionist and eventually settled in Israel. Brod identified himself as a "Jewish poet of the German tongue."[64] He was an active and long-time champion of Mahler's music in which he heard the expression of a Jewish soul. Hearing Hasidic songs Brod noticed a striking similarity between their "often sharply marked march rhythm" and Mahler's own marches which seemed to him to symbolize "the firm, resolute, upright gait of a God-filled soul."[65] Denying categorically that Mahler might have been trying to write marches in the German style, as an attempt at musical assimilation, Brod explains Mahler's marches as originating in the wide range of march rhythms in Jewish music.

While it is hard to judge this interpretation without an intimate knowledge of Jewish music, I think that Mahler's marches are multi-cultural (in that they do not evoke one particular national or ethnic group) and that they express a wholly unheroic view of human destiny. Brod finds a parallel between Eastern Jewish folksongs and the loneliness of *Das Lied von der Erde*, but in this lonely music all folk elements have been left far in the distance.

Brod concludes that Mahler, like Heine and Mendelssohn, belongs to German culture with only a part of his being and that his work consequently appears inconsistent and even bizarre from a German perspective, but fully realized if he is seen primarily as a Jewish artist of the emancipation period who was not fully assimilated. Brod rightly points out that this break between German and Jewish components is sharper and more abrupt in Mahler whose German side was less central than it was in Mendelssohn. Brod calls Mahler an "example of a German-Jewish symbiosis,"[66] but the symbiosis was highly tenuous at best and Mahler himself would probably have denied it. Yet it is this arresting mixture that makes Mahler, Heine, Kafka and others of similar background such fascinating figures. The clash between the warring elements of their marginality produced craggy works of art imbued with a deep irony, arising from the special situation of the Central European Jew who is isolated both from his own people and his host people.

To mention features in Mahler's music more likely to have been produced by a Jew — an occasional melody, intense emotionalism, a combination of pathos and irony, spiritualization of popular elements — should not be considered prejudicial, just as one should not denigrate certain Czech influences — prevalence of woodwinds, gypsy-like solo string parts, rhapsodic passages, priority of melody over structure. Yet some chauvinist critics, judging music according to racial criteria, have denounced composers of Jewish origin as aliens who corrupt German music. The first and most prominent writer of this persuasion was Richard Wagner, who in 1850 published a polemical and pseudonymous essay entitled "Das Judentum in der Musik" ("Jewry in Music"). Long before he discusses any music he expatiates on the negative qualities of the Jews. He states without explanation or documentation that the "Jewification of modern art" is obvious and blames Jews for being "a splintered, homeless tribe"[67] who cannot be truly creative because they do not belong to a national community. For this reason, Wagner argues, the Jew has never had his own indigenous art, "merely a peculiar manner of expression"[68] which he superimposes on other people's art. He asserts that Jewish artists lack true originality as well as deep feeling and accuses them of superficiality, triviality and lack of commitment. His two examples are Mendelssohn and Meyerbeer, but he gives not a single musical example in the entire essay.

    Nineteen years later Wagner had this essay reprinted, with "Aufklärungen über das Judentum in der Musik" ("Explanations about 'Jewry in Music'"). This prolix 21-page statement can be reduced to one main point: the Jews have conspired against him because he had written the anti-Semitic essay. As a result, his operas are being rejected by audiences and in the press, and his aesthetic theories cannot gain a hearing. Charging that the press and theater are controlled by Jews, he sees a secret international Jewish organization determined to persecute him. And he blames what he calls the weakness of German music after Beethoven on Jewish influence, forgetting all the while that Mendelssohn was the only Jewish composer among them. Interspersed in this text are various racial slurs: he complains that Leipzig, his hometown, doesn't have enough blond musicians and has become exclusively a "Jewish musical metropolis" *(Judenmusikweltstadt)*; he calls Eduard Hanslick's essay on beauty in music an intrusion of "musical Jew beauty" *(musikalische Judenschönheit)* into a "full-blooded Germanic system of aesthetics" because Hanslick had a Jewish mother; and he wonders whether "the decay of our culture can be stopped by a violent casting out *(Auswerfung)* of the decomposing foreign element."[69] In a later essay he calls the Jews the "demon incarnate of mankind's decay."[70] One of his most offensive statements is recorded in Cosima Wagner's diary for 18 December 1881: irritated by Lessing's play *Nathan der Weise (Nathan the Wise)* whose Jewish protagonist pleads for religious tolerance, Wagner "makes a drastic joke to the effect that all Jews should burn to death at a performance of *Nathan*."[71]

    I have gone into this matter at such length for these reasons: 1. Mahler was an admirer and outstanding interpreter of Wagner's music, though he spoke negatively of Wagner's writings.[72] 2. There is evidence that Cosima Wagner permitted her anti-Semitism to affect her relationship with Mahler. Despite an outwardly friendly correspondence, she never invited him to conduct in Bayreuth and tried to prevent his appointment in Vienna.[73] 3. Anti-Semitic critics attacked Mahler on precisely the same racial grounds that Wagner used against Mendelssohn and Meyerbeer. In contrast to pro-Semitic writers like Brod, Adler and Adorno, these critics adopt a virulent ethnic and racial chauvinism that must not go unchallenged.

    One of the first critics to discuss Mahler's music in Jewish terms was William Ritter, a Swiss painter and critic. Born in Neuchâtel, he wrote in French, studied art at the University of Vienna, traveled widely in Europe, and lived in Munich from 1900 to 1914 and in Switzerland after that. He was a critic of music and art and wrote a biography of Smetana.[74] In Munich he attended a rehearsal for the premiere of Mahler's Fourth Symphony, which took place on 25 November 1901. The music provoked him into writing an extravagantly worded and highly ambivalent review which shows a nationalistically German and anti-Semitic bias that one would not expect of a French-speaking Swiss writer interested in Czech art and music. Writing from an artistically conservative and Christian point of view, Ritter describes Mahler's music as "pagan," "satanic," "monstrous," "caricaturing," "sacrilegious."[75] Attributing his style to "Vienna and his race," Ritter uses some of the stereotypes that later appeared in the writings of German nationalist and Nazi critics: "Asiatic," gypsy, grimacing.[76]

The Fourth Symphony in particular seems to have offended him and other critics as well, apparently because it struck them as frivolous and stylistically wayward. Critics of Ritter's persuasion are invariably disturbed by what the Germans call *Stilbruch* — a sudden shift of style or a combination of styles that do not match. The Fourth Symphony has its full share of stylistic diversity; as a basically pastoral work, it ranges in style and mood far beyond the pastoral. An example occurs in the third movement where the tone shifts drastically four times within fifty-one bars (at meas. 222, 238, 263 and 283). This disparateness is undoubtedly a central element in Mahler's music and differentiates him from his German and Austrian predecessors, with the possible exception of Schubert who did not go nearly as far as Mahler does. Mahler's stylistic shifts can be explained as a deep-seated part of his personality, as an expression of his half-romantic, half-ironic outlook, as a product of his marginality or as an important aspect of his modernism. However it is interpreted, it goes counter to the German tradition which emphasizes stylistic uniformity in symphonic music.[77]

Ritter found the Fourth Symphony dishonest, coarse, sensual, farcical; it destroys "our artistic principles, multiplies Heine's ironies hundredfold . . . [brings] jugglers into the temple [and] a circus into the cathedral."[78] He called it a "musical black mass" and characterized Mahler as "one of the most dangerous adversaries of our national aesthetics"[79] — a judgment that astonishes us today, especially with its final phrase. But when we read that Ritter was converted to Mahler by the funeral march of the Fifth Symphony — he called it "his road to Damascus"[80] — we realize that by national aesthetics he meant unrelieved solemnity. The irony is that this funeral march is anything but Beethovenian; it has Mahler's characteristic mixture of pathos and irony (for example, measures 320-336).[81] What must have persuaded Ritter is the symphony's large-scale conception, its spiritual journey, its aspirations to tragedy and grandeur, its rhetorical gestures. Even so he had his reservations: the first movement conveyed an image of "the devil carried to earth . . . by the apostle of Nietzscheanism"; the instrumentation was "most unexpected, most abnormal"; the scherzo expressed "the new paganism. . . ."[82] But after hearing the Fifth Symphony, Ritter acknowledged Mahler as "a man of bizarre and immense genius who feels keenly that he is a heretic," an artist of "immense inspiration."[83]

For a critic of Ritter's conservatism writing in 1905, he makes some perceptive comments. He points out that Mahler performed the classics in a way that made them seem like avant-garde works by revealing hitherto ignored aspects of them.[84] He finds Mahler's depictions of nature stylized, self-conscious, philosophical — such as a modern urban person might view nature — not concrete, realistic, observed, spontaneous as in Dvořák.[85] He recognizes that the funeral march in the Fifth Symphony does not record the death of an individual but the end of an era.[86] And he hears in the Scherzo of the Fifth "one of the pinnacles of inspiration, technique and miraculous orchestral juggling of Mr. Mahler" — an apt description of this extraordinary piece. "I don't approve of Mahler's oeuvre, but I enjoy it passionately. Must I be ashamed?"[87] Ambivalent to the end, Ritter finally declares that he, "Catholic, traditionalist, anti-Semite, surrenders to the work of the Jewish, Nietzschean sorcerer." Though he surrenders to genius, his prejudices are intact; even in one of his last sentences he mentions the "disintegrating impact of this race on ours."[88]

Other racist critics are not that honest. They argue that European music is basically "Nordic" in content and form (serious, exalted, metaphysical, idealist, highly structured, stylistically uniform, "pure," close to folksong, deep) and therefore superior; that there is no bridge between "Nordic" and other music; and that the Jews are racially "Asiatic" and therefore exert a destructive influence on "Nordic" culture.

A few examples will suffice. Writing in Mahler's lifetime with the knowledge of probably the first six symphonies, the music critic Rudolf Louis finds Mahler's music "terribly repellent"[89] because of its basically 'Jewish' character. What bothers him is not that it is 'Jewish music,' but that it speaks "a musical German, but with the accent, tone and especially gesture of the Eastern, all too Eastern Jews."[90] He considers Mahler's music "inauthentic" because it is not unicultural. Asserting that Mahler is "constitutionally" barred from being a major composer, Louis repeats the racial theory that there is "an unbridgeable gulf" between "the members of Occidental culture and Occidental race" and admirers of Mahler's music.[91] Though he clearly considers German culture superior and Jewish culture inferior, he denies that he is an anti-Semite.

The intrusion of racial criteria into a scholarly book is not an isolated example. The eminent musicologist Hans Joachim Moser, who has a long list of publications to his credit, wrote about Mahler with a strongly nationalist bias and an insidiously denigrating tone that is unworthy of a scholar. About "Revelge" ("Reveille"), one of Mahler's most stirring songs, Moser wrote: "This is some kind of distant Asia or Africa — but hardly Germany."[92] Though he toned down his style in his post-World War II books, he didn't change his point of view. A revised work that appeared in 1958 contains the following statement: "As an Israelite who rejected the Eastern Jews in Lemberg in horror, he seems to have more affinity for an extremely distant style than for the 'inner Germany' which he strove for all his life with touching fervor ever since his early enthusiasm for Brahms and Bruckner. . . ."[93] Apart from the fact that Mahler did not have any enthusiasm for Brahms, it is misleading to say that he "strove for Germany." He had his own style from the very beginning, but since he spoke German, was educated in German schools and grew up in a German cultural environment, he necessarily was strongly influenced by German music, literature and philosophy. The first poem he set to music was by Lessing, the *Rübezahl* libretto shows numerous echoes of the German classics, and the texts he set are for the most part drawn from German literature. Yet he was not a German. Moser's statement makes music a function of a national ideology.

In a publication of 1944 in which the Jews are blamed for causing World War II, the musicologist Karl Blessinger wrote that Mahler initiated "the decisive step toward the dissolution of our tonal order" (p. 152), forgetting that Wagner had taken that step in the prelude to *Tristan und Isolde*. Critics of this persuasion cannot see Mahler's music as an extension of, alternative to or critique of the Austro-German symphony; they can see it only as a disrespectful, irreverent or disintegrating influence: "In the case of Mahler and his jazz followers we are not dealing with self-mockery but with a clear defamation of a great tradition."[94] But just as Wagner did not analyze Mendelssohn's music, these racial critics do not analyze Mahler's music; they simply denounce him as a Jewish decadent. (Analysis is a Jewish concern.)

In a more positive assessment of what is 'Jewish' in Mahler's music, the Prague music critic Richard Batka wrote: "Mahler's relationship to German folk music is a relationship not of calm, natural possession, but of fervent longing."[95] It is true that Mahler did not "possess" or belong to German folk music, but he knew it well because he grew up in a German-speaking area and lived most of his life in Germany and Austria. He simply altered it or it emerged in altered form in his hands because he viewed it from an outsider's perspective. I don't believe this was a conscious process, but a part of his innermost being, inherent in his creative impulse. He had to compose this way. Even his earliest compositions show the hallmarks of his style which is modern in the sense of being critical of tradition; it contains harmonic ambiguity, irony, an extreme emotional and instrumental range, and a special evocative power that derives from deep-seated musical associations (such as the posthorn solo in the Third Symphony). It is psychoanalytic music in that it x-rays both folk music and the symphonic tradition; this is what makes conservative and nationalist critics most uncomfortable.

It is basically a question of cosmopolitanism, of sophistication, perhaps of self-consciousness — qualities often encountered in disaffiliated modern artists, Jewish as well as non-Jewish. Heinrich Heine, with whom Mahler shares the assimilated German-Jewish background, wrote that Jewish artists show a "complete lack of naiveté, but is there, in art, any ingenious originality without naiveté?"[96] This statement is clearly meant to apply to Heine's own writings but could just as well describe an unspontaneous, self-conscious writer like Thomas Mann who lacked the easy identification with nature and the common man, so prized by nationalists, as much as some Jewish artists do. There is no doubt that as a Bohemian of Jewish background Mahler had an uneasy and critical view of "the folk" and popular art, but this must not become the basis for praising or devaluing his music.

It is indicative that during Mahler's lifetime only one of his major works — Das klagende Lied — received its premiere in Vienna. Of his symphonies, only the Ninth was first performed in Vienna, but posthumously. Arthur Schnitzler reports in 1909 that an Austrian musicologist found Mahler's Fifth Symphony "not indigenous and authentic" (nicht bodenständig und wurzelecht).[97] Undoubtedly his music would sound more homogeneous if he had come from a village in Tyrol, but as a marginal man he simply could not write 'native' music.

A certain reserve toward Mahler, as toward Freud, persists in Germany and Austria to this day. Of the two senior conductors in the German-speaking area — both Austrian — Karl Böhm performed him hardly at all, except when accompanying a singer in the songs, and Herbert von Karajan has been performing him only in recent years. Mahler's music is more often performed by exiles or non-Germans (Claudio Abbado, Maurice Abravanel, Leonard Bernstein, Pierre Boulez, Bernard Haitink, Rafael Kubelik, Erich Leinsdorf, James Levine, Zubin Mehta, Wyn Morris, Vaclav Neumann, Simon Rattle, Georg Solti). Among the exceptions are the German conductor Klaus Tennstedt who is currently recording all the symphonies with the London Philharmonic, and the German baritone Dietrich Fischer-Dieskau who frequently performs the songs and has recorded most of them.[98]

The resistance to Mahler in Germany and Austria in the early post-World War II years can be explained, first of all, by the fact that he was simply not known to audiences, having been banned there during the Nazi years. And after a time of national humiliation, his unorthodox and even irreverent treatment of German folk music and the German symphonic tradition may have fallen on unresponsive ears. At that time Mahler was uncomfortable for German and Austrian audiences to hear — just as Heine was uncomfortable for them to read — because he shook up the rather staid nineteenth-century German symphony and uncovered the dark recesses of folk music (just as Freud uncovered the dark underside of the human mind) at the very moment when listeners looked to their music for reassurance and solace. Their discomfort may have been intensified by the fact that Mahler's music originated in the German-speaking area. Furthermore, German concertgoers tend to be very conservative — even more so than in the United States — and orchestral players find Mahler unidiomatic and taxing to play.[99] To some German and Austrian listeners he may sound like an unwelcome guest, a voice from the underground, a subversive. It is therefore heartening that a respected German commentator, opening a Mahler festival in West Germany in 1979, reminded his listeners that the banning of Mahler from concert halls during the thirties and forties was "the result of German barbarism" and that his absence long after 1945 was a collective repression that had to be corrected.[100]

It seems clear that German and Austrian audiences hear Mahler with different ears than do listeners anywhere else. While his music has international appeal as an encompassing statement about the human condition, in Germany and Austria it evokes specific memories and associations — of landscapes, folksongs, dances, marches, of the world of German romanticism — that have been filtered through the critical perspective of an outsider. It is this aspect that makes Mahler such a striking figure. He is the great exile among composers.

NOTES FOR CHAPTER III: THE ETERNAL JEW

[1] Jean-Paul Sartre, *Anti-Semite and Jew*, tr. George J. Becker (New York: Schocken Books, 1965), p. 72.

[2] Ludwig Börne, *Briefe aus Paris*, 74th letter, Paris, 7 February 1832, in *Sämtliche Schriften*, ed. Inge and Peter Rippmann (Düsseldorf: Joseph Melzer Verlag, 1964), III, p. 510.

[3] Henry-Louis de La Grange, *Mahler* I (Garden City, N. Y.: Doubleday, 1973), p. 10. — It was only in 1850, just twenty-three years before, that Mahler's paternal grandparents had finally been permitted to marry legally, but not until their youngest child was born. The number of Jewish marriages had been severely restricted. See de La Grange, p. 6.

[4] Letter to Richard Specht, an Austrian music critic and early biographer of Mahler, in *Selected Letters of Gustav Mahler*, ed. Alma Mahler, revised edition by Knud Martner, tr. Eithne Wilkins, Ernst Kaiser and Bill Hopkins (New York: Farrar, Straus and Giroux, 1979), p. 276.

[5] Kurt Blaukopf, *Gustav Mahler oder Der Zeitgenosse der Zukunft* (Vienna-Munich-Zurich: Molden, 1969), p. 17, and Theodor Fischer, "Aus Gustav Mahlers Jugendzeit," in *Deutsche Heimat. Sudetendeutsche Monatsschrift für Literatur, Kunst, Heimat- und Volkskunde*, vol. 7, nos. 6-7 (June-July 1931), p. 264.

[6] Kurt Blaukopf, *Gustav Mahler oder Der Zeitgenosse der Zukunft*, p. 19. — De La Grange's statement that the family was orthodox is puzzling; see *Mahler* I, p. 412.

[7] Henry-Louis de La Grange, *Mahler* I, p. 22.

[8] *Selected Letters of Gustav Mahler*, ed. Knud Martner, p. 56.

[9] *Selected Letters of Gustav Mahler*, ed. Knud Martner, pp. 221, 319, 350, and Alma Mahler, *Gustav Mahler: Memories and Letters*, third ed., ed. Donald Mitchell, tr. Basil Creighton (Seattle: University of Washington Press, 1975), pp. 210-211.

[10] *Selected Letters of Gustav Mahler*, ed. Knud Martner, p. 104.

[11] Henry-Louis de La Grange, *Mahler* I, p. 119.

[12] Alma Mahler, *Gustav Mahler: Erinnerungen und Briefe* (Amsterdam: Allert de Lange, 1940), p. 86. The passage is deleted in the English edition.

[13] *Selected Letters of Gustav Mahler*, ed. Knud Martner, p. 290.

[14] Alma Mahler, *Gustav Mahler: Memories and Letters*, ed. Donald Mitchell, p. 303.

[15] *Selected Letters of Gustav Mahler*, ed. Knud Martner, p. 319.

[16] "To be born a Jew is like coming into the world with one foot or one arm." This statement by Mahler is reported by the Austrian music critic and biographer Ernst Decsey in his memoirs, *Musik war sein Leben*, ed. Harald R. Hampel (Vienna: Hans Deutsch Verlag, 1962), pp. 9-10.

[17] Alma Mahler, *Gustav Mahler: Memories and Letters*, ed. Donald Mitchell, p. 224. — In view of Mahler's Jewish problem, it is grimly ironic that his niece, Alma Rosé, conducted the orchestra of women inmates in Auschwitz and died there. See Fania Fénelon, *Playing for Time*, tr. Judith Landry (New York: Atheneum, 1977).

[18] Ibid., p. 226.

[19] Ibid., p. 162.

[20] Ibid., p. XXXIV.

[21] Ibid., p. 295.

[22] See Heine's essay "Über Polen" ("On Poland"), first published in 1823, which contains the following statements: "The appearance of the Polish Jew is awful. I shudder when I remember first seeing a Polish village . . . mostly inhabited by Jews . . . ; even the high-minded talk of a high-schooler fired up for gymnastics and fatherland couldn't have tortured my ears as sharply

as the Polish Jewish dialect. Yet this disgust was soon displaced by compassion, after I observed the condition of these people more closely and saw the pigsty-like holes in which they live, talk Yiddish, pray, haggle and — are miserable. . . . The Polish Jew with his dirty fur, his thick beard and garlic smell and Yiddish talk is still preferable to me than many a Jew decked out in all his bureaucratic finery." See Heinrich Heine, *Sämtliche Werke*, ed. Ernst Elster, vol. 7 (Leipzig-Vienna: Bibliographisches Institut, 1893), pp. 194-195.

[23] See her description of Siegfried Lipiner in Alma Mahler, *Gustav Mahler: Memories and Letters,* ed. Donald Mitchell, p. 26, and the passages dealing with her attitude toward Jews in Karen Monson, *Alma Mahler: Muse to Genius* (Boston: Houghton Mifflin, 1983), especially pp. 164-166 and p. 247.

[24] The name of the paper is *Reichsgeldmonopol, Volksblatt für wirtschaftlich-soziale Neugestaltung.* The matter is fully discussed by Hans Joachim Schaefer in his study *Gustav Mahler in Kassel* which appeared between June 1975 and February 1982 in thirty-two installments in *Informationen aus Kassel,* a monthly bulletin on the arts published by the City of Kassel. The anti-Semitic agitation against Mahler is the subject of the tenth installment (April and May 1977). The series has since been published in book form: Hans Joachim Schaefer, *Gustav Mahler in Kassel* (Kassel: Bärenreiter Verlag, 1982). — In the following year, 1886, the *Deutsche Antisemitische Vereinigung,* founded in Kassel, discussed a proposal to get rid of the Jews; see Hannah Arendt, *Antisemitism* (New York: Harcourt, Brace and World, 1968), p. 39.

[25] Henry-Louis de La Grange, *Mahler I,* p. 123.

[26] *Selected Letters of Gustav Mahler,* ed. Knud Martner, p. 152.

[27] Henry-Louis de La Grange, *Mahler I,* pp. 361 and 379.

[28] Ibid., p. 390.

[29] *Selected Letters of Gustav Mahler,* ed. Knud Martner, pp. 207 and 208.

[30] Ibid., p. 207.

[31] Henry-Louis de La Grange, *Mahler I,* pp. 389-390; no source given.

[32] See Ludwig Karpath, *Begegnung mit dem Genius,* second ed. (Vienna-Leipzig: Fiba-Verlag, 1934), p. 102, and Kurt Blaukopf, *Gustav Mahler oder Der Zeitgenosse der Zukunft,* p. 152.

[33] Henry-Louis de La Grange, *Mahler I,* p. 411.

[34] Ludwig Karpath, *Begegnung mit dem Genius,* p. 102.

[35] It was recently revealed that Mahler advised Bruno Walter to convert to Christianity for career reasons. See the new edition of Mahler's letters, *Gustav Mahler Briefe,* expanded and revised by Herta Blaukopf (Vienna-Hamburg: Paul Szolnay Verlag, 1982), p. 223. The relevant sentence, "But above all: *convert* and *do your military service!*" (Aber vor allem: *übertreten* und *abdienen!*) (Mahler's emphasis), had been deleted in the original edition of the letters.

[36] Alma Mahler, *Gustav Mahler: Memories and Letters,* ed. Donald Mitchell, p. 101; see also Alma Mahler-Werfel, *Mein Leben* (Frankfurt/Main and Hamburg: Fischer Bücherei, 1963), p. 24. But she contradicted this view after hearing the chorale-like ending of Mahler's Fifth Symphony, which she found "hymnic and boring." When Mahler cited Bruckner in his defense, she replied astutely: "*He* may [compose like this], but not you." Alma Mahler, *Gustav Mahler: Memories and Letters,* ed. Donald Mitchell, p. 47.

[37] Karl Schumann, *Das kleine Gustav Mahler-Buch* (Reinbek bei Hamburg: Rowohlt Taschenbuch Verlag, 1982), p. 59.

[38] Constantin Floros, *Gustav Mahler* (Wiesbaden: Breitkopf und Härtel, 1977), I, pp. 123-124.

[39] Compare the original poem in Friedrich Gottlieb Klopstock, *Sämtliche Werke,* vol. 7 (Leipzig: Georg Joachim Göschen, 1823), pp. 118-119, with Mahler's text, which may be found in Deryck Cooke, *Gustav Mahler: An Introduction to his Music* (Cambridge and New York: Cambridge University Press, 1980), pp. 59-60. Cooke correctly identifies the author as "Klopstock/Mahler."

[40] Deryck Cooke, *Gustav Mahler: An Introduction to his Music*, p. 93. But elsewhere Cooke states that Mahler's "deep spiritual need impelled him to turn to the Christian faith"; see his essay "The Word and the Deed: Mahler and his Eighth Symphony," in Deryck Cooke, *Vindications. Essays on Romantic Music* (Cambridge and New York: Cambridge University Press, 1982), p. 111. — Religion is not mentioned in Mahler's description of the Eighth Symphony in a letter to the conductor Willem Mengelberg, just after he had completed the work: "Try to imagine the whole universe beginning to ring and resound. These are no longer human voices, but planets and suns revolving." *Selected Letters of Gustav Mahler*, ed. Knud Martner, p. 294.

[41] Johann Wolfgang Goethe, *Conversations with Eckermann*, 6 June 1831.

[42] Interview with Bruno Walter, included in Columbia Set M2L 276 which contains a recording of Mahler's Ninth Symphony by Bruno Walter and the Columbia Symphony Orchestra.

[43] Cf. Karl Schumann, *Das kleine Gustav Mahler-Buch*, p. 59.

[44] See Werfel's letter to the Archbishop of New Orleans, 27 October 1942, in Frederick C. Ellert, "Franz Werfel's Great Dilemma," *The Bridge: A Yearbook of Judaeo-Christian Studies*, vol. 4, ed. John M. Oesterreicher (New York: Pantheon Books, 1962), pp. 215-216.

[45] See the article on 'apostasy' in the *Encyclopedia Judaica*; Julius Braunthal, *Victor und Friedrich Adler* (Wiener Neustadt: Verlag der Wiener Volksbuchhandlung, 1965), pp. 19-20; Constantin Floros, *Gustav Mahler* I, p. 96; Dika Newlin, *Bruckner - Mahler - Schoenberg* (London: Marion Boyars, 1979), p. 258.

[46] Henry-Louis de La Grange, *Mahler* I, p. 445 and p. 905. — Since that time, two Jewish conductors have been appointed by the Vienna Opera: Bruno Walter served as musical adviser from 1936 to 1938, and Lorin Maazel served as director from 1982 to 1984.

[47] Hans Joachim Schaefer, *Gustav Mahler in Kassel*, Installment 29 (February 1981).

[48] *Selected Letters of Gustav Mahler*, ed. Knud Martner, p. 83.

[49] Henry-Louis de La Grange, *Mahler* I, p. 409.

[50] Ibid., p. 430.

[51] Ibid., pp. 449, 531 and 551.

[52] Ibid., pp. 535 and 548.

[53] Ibid., pp. 549-550.

[54] Natalie Bauer-Lechner, *Recollections of Gustav Mahler*, tr. Dika Newlin, ed. Peter Franklin (Cambridge and New York: Cambridge University Press, 1980), p. 121.

[55] *Encyclopedia Judaica* (Jerusalem: Keter Publishing House, and New York: Macmillan, 1971), article on 'music,' vol. 12, col. 555.

[56] His unpublished letter to Alma Mahler, dated 2 January 1948, is in the Mahler-Werfel Collection at the University of Pennsylvania.

[57] *Encyclopedia Judaica*, article on 'Ernest Bloch.'

[58] Peter Gradenwitz, "Mahler and Schoenberg," in *Leo Baeck Institute Year Book* V (1960), p. 263.

[59] Other examples are the main theme of the first movement of the Fifth Symphony — meas. 34-53, 88-113, 322-336 — and its variation in the second movement — meas. 78-86, especially the cello passage at 82-86, repeated by the horns at 108-116 and by the violins at 355-362 and punctuated each time by repeated chords; and the strange melody in the second movement of the Seventh Symphony — meas. 190-207 — written for two cellos against an accompaniment of muted trumpets, military horns and rapid figures in the clarinets, that is extraordinary even for Mahler. Adorno mentions another example, meas. 4ff. of the scherzo of the Fourth Symphony — see his *Mahler: Eine musikalische Physiognomik* (Frankfurt/Main: Suhrkamp Verlag, 1960), p. 192.

[60] At the Mahler Festival in Amsterdam in May 1920, the guests from abroad expressed their thanks for the first opportunity since World War I "to shake the hands of our brethren in art,

irrespective of nationality and race." *Das Mahler-Fest Amsterdam Mai 1920,* ed. C. Rudolf Mengelberg (Vienna-Leipzig: Universal Edition, 1920), p. 71.

[61] See Adler's obituary essay on Mahler, in *Biographisches Jahrbuch und Deutscher Nekrolog,* ed. Anton Bettelheim, vol. 16 (1911), p. 21.

[62] Theodor W. Adorno, *Mahler: Eine musikalische Physiognomik,* p. 192. The German text reads as follows: "Was jüdisch ist an Mahler, partizipiert nicht unmittelbar an Volkstümlichem, sondern spricht durch alle Vermittlungen hindurch als ein Geistiges, Unsinnliches, gleichwohl an der Totalität Fühlbares sich aus."

[63] Max Brod, "Jüdische Volksmelodien," in *Der Jude,* vol. 1 (1916-1917), pp. 344-345.

[64] Max Brod, *Der Prager Kreis* (Stuttgart: Kohlhammer Verlag, 1966), p. 57.

[65] Max Brod, "Jüdische Volksmelodien," p. 345.

[66] Max Brod, *Gustav Mahler: Beispiel einer deutsch-jüdischen Symbiose* (Frankfurt/Main: Ner-Tamid-Verlag, 1961).

[67] Richard Wagner, "Das Judentum in der Musik," in Richard Wagner, *Sämtliche Schriften und Dichtungen,* fifth edition (Leipzig: Breitkopf und Härtel/C. F. W. Siegel [R. Linnemann], V, p. 68 and p. 71. An English translation of this essay is available in *Richard Wagner: Stories and Essays,* ed. Charles Osborne (London: Peter Owen, 1973), pp. 23-39.

[68] Ibid., p. 76.

[69] Richard Wagner, "Aufklärungen über das Judentum in der Musik," in Richard Wagner, *Sämtliche Schriften und Dichtungen,* VIII, pp. 240, 251 and 259.

[70] Richard Wagner, "Erkenne dich selbst," in Richard Wagner, *Sämtliche Schriften und Dichtungen,* X, p. 272.

[71] *Cosima Wagner's Diaries,* vol. II (1878-1883), ed. Martin Gregor-Dellin and Dietrich Mack, tr. Geoffrey Skelton (New York and London: Harcourt, Brace and Jovanovich, 1978), pp. 772-773.

[72] Alma Mahler, *Gustav Mahler: Memories and Letters,* ed. Donald Mitchell, p. 92.

[73] Ibid., p. 12 and p. 101, and Berndt W. Wessling, *Gustav Mahler: Ein prophetisches Leben* (Hamburg: Hoffmann und Campe, 1974), pp. 156-159. The editor of Mahler's recently published letters to Cosima Wagner, Eduard Reeser, believes that it was her desire to see the conductor Felix Mottl become director in Vienna rather than anti-Semitism that caused her to oppose Mahler's appointment. But Reeser does say that Cosima always kept Mahler's Jewish background in mind; it also affected Mahler's professional relationship with Siegfried Wagner, her son. See *Gustav Mahler: Unbekannte Briefe,* ed. Herta Blaukopf (Vienna-Hamburg: Paul Zsolnay Verlag, 1983), pp. 211-240, especially pp. 218-224.

[74] Henry-Louis de La Grange, *Mahler I,* p. 944.

[75] William Ritter, "Un symphoniste viennois: M. Gustave Mahler," in William Ritter, *Etudes d'art étranger* (Paris: Société du Mercure de France, 1906), pp. 244, 248 and 273.

[76] Ibid., pp. 249, 252, 257 and 273. It seems to me to be nonsense to refer to European Jews as "Asiatic" when they have lived in Europe for the last 1500 years.

[77] In German literature, Heinrich Heine has aroused the opposition of conservative critics for the same phenomenon; an example is his poem "Das Fräulein stand am Meere" in his collection *Neue Gedichte.*

[78] William Ritter, "Un symphoniste viennois," pp. 272-273.

[79] Ibid.

[80] Ibid., p. 282.

[81] In a letter to Alma Mahler of 17 January 1925, Ida Dehmel, widow of the poet Richard Dehmel, wrote that the Fifth Symphony expressed to her the essence of the Jewish spirit. The unpublished letter is in the Mahler-Werfel Collection at the University of Pennsylvania.

[82] William Ritter, "Un symphoniste viennois," pp. 283, 281 and 284.

[83] Ibid., pp. 286 and 287.

[84] Ibid., p. 247.

[85] Ibid., pp. 269-270.

[86] Ibid., p. 282.

[87] Ibid., p. 275.

[88] Ibid., p. 288. — Recently published letters from Mahler to Ritter show that Ritter got in touch with the composer after the premiere of the Fourth Symphony and asked him for a copy of the score. Mahler responded affirmatively, as he usually did when a critic showed an interest in his work, and invited him to attend the rehearsals of the Sixth Symphony in Munich in November 1906. Subsequently Ritter wrote more and more positively about Mahler's music. No reference to Ritter's anti-Semitism appears in Mahler's letters to him. See *Gustav Mahler: Unbekannte Briefe*, ed. Herta Blaukopf, pp. 143-154.

[89] Rudolf Louis, *Die deutsche Musik der Gegenwart* (Munich-Leipzig: Georg Müller, 1909), p. 182.

[90] Ibid.

[91] Ibid., pp. 181-182.

[92] Hans Joachim Moser, *Geschichte der deutschen Musik,* vol. 2, pt. 2 (Stuttgart-Berlin, 1924), p. 404.

[93] Hans Joachim Moser, *Musikgeschichte in 100 Lebensbildern*, third ed. (Stuttgart: Reclam, 1958), p. 824.

[94] Karl Blessinger, *Judentum und Musik: Ein Beitrag zur Kultur- und Rassenpolitik* (Berlin: Bernhard Hahnefeld Verlag, 1944), p. 141.

[95] Richard Batka, "Das Jüdische bei Gustav Mahler," in *Der Kunstwart*, ed. Ferdinand Avenarius, vol. 23, July 1910, no. 2, p. 98.

[96] *Encyclopedia Judaica*, article on 'music,' vol. 12, col. 655.

[97] Arthur Schnitzler, *Tagebuch 1909-1912*, edited by the Kommission für literarische Gebrauchsformen der Österreichischen Akademie der Wissenschaften (Vienna: Verlag der Österreichischen Akademie der Wissenschaften, 1981), p. 54.

[98] My conclusion about Mahler performers is based on recordings, radio programs and publications of music festivals. I have not made a statistical study of Mahler performances, but a recent writer hints at the same conclusion, though for somewhat different reasons. See Karl Schumann, *Das kleine Gustav Mahler-Buch*, pp. 105-106.

[99] During the rehearsals for the world premiere of the Seventh Symphony in Prague in September 1908, a trumpet player complained about the muted high notes he was being asked to play. Almost seventy years later, similar criticism was voiced during rehearsals of the Third Symphony in Germany in 1975. See Alma Mahler, *Gustav Mahler: Memories and Letters*, ed. Donald Mitchell, p. 304, and Hans Zender, "Aufzeichnungen während einer Probenwoche zur Dritten" (Notes during a week of rehearsing the Third), in *Mahler: Eine Herausforderung*, ed. Peter Ruzicka (Wiesbaden: Breitkopf und Härtel, 1977), pp. 171-172.

[100] Peter Wapnewski, in *Die Zeit*, 26 October 1979, p. 19.

Chapter IV

A MUSICAL IRONIST

Mahler's symphonies differ from the nineteenth-century symphony as derived from Beethoven in two essential respects: they abandon the idea of a single basic key for an entire symphony and they make abundant use of irony. I am using irony here in the meaning of incongruousness, paradox, contradiction, incompatibility and also as an unmasking or disillusioning device; basically, irony has the purpose and effect of calling into question whatever it is directed against.[1]

According to Friedrich Schlegel, the poet is at once the creator and observer,[2] and it is my intention to show that Mahler's music contains an implicit comment on both the form and the substance of his work. This comment is ironic in that it shows an awareness of incongruities in life and in music. The best-known example of Mahler's irony is the mock funeral march in the First Symphony. Based on the popular canon "Frère Jacques" ("Bruder Martin" in German) which Mahler had often heard sung,[3] this piece transforms the familiar children's song into a grotesque processional. The irony of this transformation lies in the fact that the music expresses the opposite of what is expected. A quick, cheerful children's song becomes a dirge in the minor key, opened portentously by two bars of timpani, followed by the melody of the canon which is played by a solo bass in a high range. (This may be the only borrowed theme that Mahler quotes literally and in its entirety.) Other instruments gradually join in, and at measure 19 a skipping countermelody in the oboe is counterpointed against the main theme so as to undercut it — in the literal sense of 'parody' as 'countersong.' The march is followed by a Bohemian section which is speeded up twice, each time with percussion added, which gives the music a distinctly jazzed-up effect. This section, beginning at measure 45, is marked "with parody," an odd intrusion into a funeral march.[4] And while funeral marches usually have a lyrical middle section which is meant to give consolation, Mahler writes an interlude so sad and lonely that the returning dirge is more sprightly than the consoling interlude, all the more so since the returning

march, played half a tone higher than its initial key, is suddenly and wildly accelerated, at a much faster pace even than before (meas. 139-145).

This funeral march was inspired by a well-known engraving entitled
"The Huntsman's Funeral" by the romantic artist Moritz von Schwind who
specialized in illustrating German legends and fairy tales.[5] The picture shows
a group of forest animals, led by Bohemian musicians, escorting the hunter's
coffin to the grave. Mahler described the mood as "sometimes ironic and merry,
sometimes gloomy and uncanny," adding that the "funeral march must be
imagined played by a cheap band such as one hears at country funerals . . . in
the midst of this, all the coarseness, the mirth and the banality of the world are
heard in the sound of a Bohemian village band, together with the hero's terrible
cries of pain. In its bitter irony and contrasting polyphony it is the most moving
moment!"[6] The hero of the symphony, represented by a leitmotif in the first
and last movements, comes upon death in this grotesque form, as a black-humor
phenomenon that combines tragedy (a person's death) with irony (he is buried
by the animals he tried to kill) and that is celebrated by grotesque music —
meaning that it is distorted and shows an "unresolved clash of incompatibles."[7]

This funeral march is enveloped in multiple ironies: 1. The melody of a
children's song is being used in a manner opposed to its usual function; 2. The
music combines mock-sadness with quasi-dance music, thereby bringing together two disparate styles, each of which is of itself ironic; 3. The march is a
parody of a funeral march, in that it imitates the form but changes the content
and style of serious funeral music; 4. The movement as a whole may be self-
irony, for by quoting one of his *Wayfarer* songs ("Die zwei blauen Augen"
["The Two Blue Eyes"]) in the lyrical interlude, the composer may be marking
his own burial before being reborn in the final movement which was originally
entitled "Dall' Inferno al Paradiso."[8] Death followed by rebirth is the meaning
of the funeral march in Beethoven's *Eroica* Symphony; 5. By including a mock
funeral march in his symphony, Mahler is making an ironic comment on the
form and substance of the traditional symphony. One such comment might be
that the romanticism of the nineteenth-century symphony needs to be leavened
by a satiric counter-music. (It is not surprising that one of his favorite books
was *Don Quixote*, a work that satirizes excessive romanticism.)

In the history of the symphony this funeral march is an original, for
nothing like it had ever, so far as I know, appeared in a symphony before. For
those whose symphonic standard was Beethoven and the Beethoven succession, Mahler's stretching of the stylistic and expressive range of the symphony
must have seemed heretical. Even Berlioz and Tchaikovsky, to whom Mahler
is much closer than he is to the Schumann-Mendelssohn-Brahms group, had not
gone as far in the March to the Scaffold in the *Symphonie Fantastique* or in the

second movement march in Tchaikovsky's Second Symphony. The only previous piece known to me that resembles it is the Funeral March of a Parrot, for mixed chorus, oboe or bassoon, and organ, by Charles Henri Alkan who shares with Mahler his Jewish ancestry, a predilection for marches and a macabre imagination.[9]

Mitchell traces Mahler's march to the miniature funeral march in Mendelssohn's *Midsummer Night's Dream* (op. 61, No. 10a).[10] This very brief piece of only twenty-eight bars, written in C minor and scored for clarinet, bassoon and a pair of kettledrums, is the funeral march for Pyramus and Thisbe in the entertainment within the play. There are indeed striking parallels in rhythm and melody as well as in mood and atmosphere. Notable in both pieces is the concentration on woodwinds and percussion, especially the high notes in the clarinet and the solo use of the bassoon. But whereas Mendelssohn wrote a descriptive piece of theater music, Mahler put his mock funeral march into the middle of a symphony, a form held in some awe since Beethoven endowed it with nobility and moral grandeur. In doing so, Mahler opened the symphony to irony and heterogeneity — two qualities that introduced a specifically modern note into symphonic music. Like a reflective modern writer who is both narrator and commentator (cf. Thomas Mann), Mahler commented on his music, thereby adding a critical dimension to his work.

Hovering between irony, parody, grotesque and melancholy, the Frère Jacques movement combines Bohemian folklore (its orchestration and its mixture of gaiety and sadness) and German romanticism (its lyric intermezzo) with a gallows humor that often characterizes a Jewish outlook. In view of Mahler's youth — he was only twenty-eight when he completed this symphony — this multi-layered, multi-cultural music is a remarkably sophisticated work that still astonishes the listener with its unique sound and conception. Needless to say, it brought him much hostility and even notoriety. At the first performance of the First Symphony (Budapest, 20 November 1889), a critic who was one of Mahler's closest friends described this movement as a "complete disaster."[11] At the first Vienna performance (19 November 1900), "the Funeral March dumbfounded the audience and provoked derisive laughter, and only the absence of a pause between the last two movements prevented the majority from leaving."[12] One critic called the symphony "a stylistic absurdity" and "a total failure," while the eminent critic Eduard Hanslick began his review with the statement "One of us must be crazy, and it isn't I!"[13]

What Mahler intended to express in this music is as difficult to say as it is in all of his transformations of folk music. One critic argues that the music could be considered ironic only if the composer distanced himself from it, but she denies this because she finds the music too expressive of pain.[14] It seems to

me, however, that there is a shift in perspective from the march (meas. 1-38) to
the Bohemian music (meas. 38-70) to the lyric intermezzo (meas. 83-113): the
latter is subjective, romantic music without any distance, while the other two
sound to some degree stylized and therefore less direct than the intermezzo.
If this is so, a comment could be inferred from the first two parts, even if this
comment might extend only to the form. This comment might be that heroic
funeral marches are no longer credible.

The most remarkable aspect of this piece is the minor-key transposition
of Frère Jacques. A minor-key version of the canon is actually attested to,[15]
which Mahler may have known, but this does not end the matter. He had often
heard children sing this song — almost certainly in the major-key version —
but he considered it deeply tragic.[16] Perhaps it reminded him of a missed childhood or it could mean that to an outsider all folksongs have an alienating and
ultimately saddening effect because they are the expression of a community
from which he is, or considers himself to be, forever excluded. However much
folk music may appeal to him as music, it reminds him always of his separate-
ness. This is what makes all of Mahler's folk music allusions so poignantly
meaningful and at the same time critical. He loved folk music without being
able to identify with it, and it is this inherent discrepancy that gives it a touch
of irony, even if this irony may not have been intended.

The self-reference in the intermezzo of this march suggests a measure
of self-irony, which is sometimes found in Jewish humor.[17] He might be attending his own funeral. It is not the only example in Mahler. In the second
movement of the Fifth Symphony, he varies the main theme of the first movement funeral march in such a way that it comes out sounding ironic, even parodistic (beginning at meas. 78): the theme is preceded and accompanied by
chattering woodwinds with off-beat accents and a leaping three-note figure,
also in the woodwinds, that undercut the main theme in the cellos. The effect is
reminiscent of the Frère Jacques march, especially in the swooping glissando
in measure 83. A more obvious example of self-irony occurs in the last movement of this symphony. Three times in this movement Mahler speeds up the
meltingly romantic theme of the preceding adagietto à la Berlioz (meas. 190ff.,
373ff., 630ff.), giving it a decidedly parodistic cast.[18] In each case the theme is
set off by a counter-melody which gets more parodistic itself with each repetition. The effect is to cut down his own romanticism, very much in the manner
of Heine. Distrust of his romanticism is also heard in the trio of the scherzo
of the Seventh Symphony: a poignantly plaintive little melody is rudely cut off
by a sudden and quick satiric passage, after which the plaintive tune resumes,
only to be followed by another putdown (meas. 179-210); a later recurrence of
the satiric passage is marked "screaming" (*kreischend*; see meas. 398). Apart

from the personal and musical self-irony, two time systems clash here: the reminiscence of the past and the sardonic here-and-now (or perhaps the German-romantic and Jewish-ironic realms). In the Ninth Symphony Mahler reverses the sequence: the Rondo-Burleske has a fast and at times distorted version of the sustained, intensely lyrical theme of the last movement (at meas. 320, 444, 454). This example, too, shows Berlioz' influence and perhaps Liszt's, but it is remarkable that the parody precedes the straight version, as if the lyrical version carried within its very conception the seed of its own parody. Mahler first has to dispose of the theme's parodistic capabilities before settling down to a serious statement of it.

Against the weight of critical opinion I believe that the opening horn theme of the Third Symphony and its deployment also expresses irony. The first four bars of this theme recall a well-known German patriotic song ("Ich hab mich ergeben mit Herz und mit Hand") as well as the main theme of the last movement of Brahms's First Symphony. The melody of the song, a Thuringian folk tune, is also used for the student song "Wir hatten gebauet ein stattliches Haus" which is quoted literally near the beginning of Brahms's Academic Festival Overture. Mahler treats this theme as he usually treats folk tunes: he denationalizes it by opening it up harmonically. Whereas the song and the Brahms melody do not leave their basic key and are solidly hymnic, the Mahler theme, hovering between D minor and F major without settling on either, universalizes the melody by unhinging it from its simple harmonic moorings and monumentalizes it by letting eight horns proclaim it fortissimo as the motto theme of a gigantic symphony. Like a typical Kafka story which suspends time and space, the music fans out into infinity. The opening up of the harmony — at the very beginning of the symphony — is followed by the ascent of the theme several notes above the melody's original compass, only to collapse into primal darkness marked by the stroke of a large drum followed by a gong. Unlike the upbeat ending of the song, this theme ends in a downbeat mood. At the recapitulation the ascent is even higher and the descent even darker, with the final chord in the minor key. In the course of the gigantic first movement — one of the longest movements in the symphonic literature — the theme reappears at various points in various guises; two examples occur at measure 273 where it recalls another well-known patriotic song, "Ich hatt einen Kameraden," and at measure 583, where it becomes the leading motif in an increasingly wild march that ends at the recapitulation. It brings the first movement to a climactic close and reappears, in an incipient and transfigured state, in the opening melody of the last movement and close to the end of the work (at measures 251, 267, 303 and 309).

The published correspondence gives no clue why Mahler used this particular theme, but then he does not shed much light on his creative process in his letters. Yet the reference is too obvious to have been unconscious. The song in its patriotic version is extremely well known in Germany — familiar to the point of being trite — and was still regularly sung in German schools in the 1920s and 1930s to instill devotion to country. Since Mahler was a student at the University of Vienna, he probably knew the song in both its patriotic and student versions. In either case I detect irony in his use of it for purposes that are far removed and even antithetical to its normal functions. The irony which may be subconscious arises primarily from the disparity between a popular nationalistic song and a symphony of cosmic proportions. The text of "Ich hab mich ergeben" was written in 1820 by Hans Ferdinand Massmann, the text of "Wir hatten gebauet ein stattliches Haus" in 1819 by August von Binzer; both songs originated in the gathering German unification movement led by Prussia and reflect an atmosphere of patriotic fervor. The student song, "Wir hatten gebauet ein stattliches Haus," was sung in Jena on 26 November 1819 when the fraternity founded there in 1815 to promote German unity was dissolved under political pressure;[19] though unification seemed unattainable, the song affirms its abiding spirit and ends on a Lutheran note. Both songs, in fact, couch their patriotic message in strongly religious terms. The third song, "Ich hatt einen Kameraden," written in 1809 by the poet Ludwig Uhland and set to music by the folksong composer Friedrich Silcher in 1825, was inspired by the same political atmosphere and celebrates comradeship in war. This tragic song is also extremely familiar and served, too, as a patriotic rallying and marching song. It is reasonable to assume that Mahler knew the tune and at least the first stanza. The texts of the three songs follow:[20]

I've given myself with heart and with hand
to you, land full of love and life,
my German fatherland!

My heart, loyally devoted to you, has caught fire,
oh land of the free and devout,
oh glorious Hermann's land!

I will abide and believe in God, devout and free;
I will, oh fatherland, stay
forever steadfast and loyal to you.

Oh God, lift up my young heart's blood
to fresh and joyous life,
to free and fervent mood!

Let me gather strength in heart and in hand,
to live and to die
for the holy fatherland!

*　　*　　*　　*

We had built a stately house
and in it put our trust in God,
in spite of weather, storm and dread.

We lived so serenely, closely, freely,
evil men were shocked,
we lived with too much faith!

The search was on for deceit and betrayal,
denounced and cursed
was the green young seed!

What God gave us, the world has rejected,
unity provoked suspicion
even in good men!

It was called a crime, but wrongly so;
the form can be broken,
but never love.

The form has been broken from without,
but what was suspected within,
was but illusion and sham.

The bond has been cut, it was black, red and gold,
and God permitted it,
who knows what he intended!

The house may collapse — what need is there for us?
The spirit lives in us all,
and our fortress is God!

*　　*　　*　　*

Once I had a comrade,
a better one you won't find.
The drumbeat called us to war,
he walked by my side
in the same step and pace.

A bullet came toward us,
is it meant for me or for you?
It tore him away,
he lies at my feet,
as though he were a part of me.

He wants to take my hand,
as I was reloading.
Can't give you my hand,
rest in eternal life,
my good comrade.

The structure of this symphony clearly shows an ascending development from the earthly to the sublime. Of the various titles Mahler used for the
first movement, none seems to fit the music;[21] his recurring idea of a resurgence
of the life force after a long winter and the victory of summer is hardly adequate
to this stirring and prodigiously imaginative music. But whether the opening
horn call summons nature to wake from its sleep, as Mahler had in mind, or
whether it introduces a vast martial phantasmagoria, its allusions to patriotic
songs and a Brahms theme seem to me highly ironic, but only in the sense of
' incongruous.' By contrast with these musical associations, the gigantic march
which they introduce and which comprises the major part of the movement
sounds like an expressionistically heightened procession of Alpine spirits. Unlike the folksongs, this march transcends all regional and national emotions
to suggest both a mythical Alpine scene and an ironic comment on the spirit of
band-music romanticism. In view of Mahler's background he would have found
it difficult to take patriotic songs or military bands seriously, yet he obviously
loved marches. I am convinced that an ambivalent attitude toward martial
music — a love of such music combined with a disassociation from its extra-
musical connotations — lies behind many of Mahler's marches. In the march
of the Third Symphony there are indications that he is commenting wryly on
military music: the horn trills in measures 343 and 345, the syncopated horn
notes marked "raw!" (meas. 545-552), the parodistic-sounding piccolos (meas.

583-587 and 595-603), the pounding percussion in measures 613-614. By transforming the patriotic songs and using them to introduce this unmartial march, Mahler has stripped them of their original meaning, not by parodying them but by elevating them to a symphonic statement. It is an extraordinary metamorphosis.[22]

A comparable case is the music of Charles Ives who quotes patriotic songs and marches, hymns, folksongs and student songs in his symphonies and other works. Quotations from "Columbia Gem of the Ocean," "Turkey in the Straw," "America the Beautiful," as well as from Beethoven's Fifth and Brahms's First Symphonies occur in Ives's Second Symphony (1897-1901) which has some beautiful writing but does not integrate the tunes into the symphonic structure as deeply as Mahler does. Moreover, Ives quotes the folksongs literally whereas Mahler alters them significantly, either monumentalizing them (as in the Third Symphony) or parodying them (as he may have done with the *Merry Widow* Waltz in the Seventh Symphony) or both at the same time (as in the Frère Jacques march).[23] Ives's irony is more overt, for it is clear from hearing his Second Symphony that he is having fun with American songs; the cacophonous final chord of this harmonically conservative work is openly ironic. Ives's symphony is less complex than Mahler's because Ives's attitude toward American songs was bound to be less complex than Mahler's attitude toward German or Czech songs. Ives was not a marginal man; being a Connecticut Yankee he could afford to make fun of his heritage because it was his own. But when Mahler used German or any other folksongs, he was dealing with material about which he felt ambivalent. Though he loved folksongs he was not German, and as a Jew he was more likely to view such music skeptically, especially if it was nationalistic. Furthermore, American songs and marches do not have the same significance for Americans that German songs and marches have for Germans. Germany was united in 1871 for the first time in its history. Up to that time and particularly during the nineteenth century it had been a quasi-irredentist area with a growing national awareness; after 1871 it became a muscle-flexing empire run by ambitious Prussian rulers, a country in which folksongs and marches took on a strongly political cast. And German folksongs and marches have been around longer and are probably more deeply embedded in the collective psyche than American ones, and because of the many wars in Europe and the resulting national overtones in fraternities and hiking clubs, they carried connotations of national solidarity to an extent not known in the United States. In the one case in which the national integrity of the United States was threatened — the Civil War — similar emotions did attach themselves to songs, for example "Dixie," "Johnny Comes Marching Home" (symphonically treated by Roy Harris and Morton Gould,

among others) and "Battle Hymn of the Republic." Finally, American pluralism simply keeps folksongs from acquiring a nation-wide constituency. It
would be difficult to imagine a group of Americans waxing sentimental over
"My country 'tis of thee" or being whipped into a patriotic frenzy by "Stars and
Stripes Forever," but many Germans did take their songs that seriously, at
least until World War II, and experienced "Die Wacht am Rhein" or "Ich hab
mich ergeben" as calls to national action. This exactly explains the difference
in the treatment of folk music by Ives and Mahler. But both composers loved
folk music with the affection of the born ironist who parodies what he loves
and loves what he parodies. Mahler must have felt this, for when he saw the
score of Ives's Third Symphony in New York, he asked to see it and took it to
Europe with him, apparently intending to perform it.[24]

The use of musical irony by Mahler and Ives anticipates the alienation
effect *(Verfremdungseffekt)* later used by Bertolt Brecht to create distance between the spectator and the play. Brecht defined the alienation effect as a technique "that deprives an event or character of its self-evident, well-known,
comprehensible quality and produces astonishment and curiosity about it."[25]
"Every-day events and persons in our immediate surroundings have something
natural for us, because we are accustomed to them. Their defamiliarization
serves to make them conspicuous to us."[26] The purpose of this distancing technique is, according to Brecht, "to induce in the spectator a probing, critical
stance toward the matter presented."[27] It was Brecht's intention to keep the
spectator from identifying with the action or characters and from experiencing
catharsis, as happens in the traditional Aristotelian theater, so as to train him to
view the play objectively, with his mind rather than his heart, as an alert, detached, skeptical observer who will reflect on it and act to change the conditions
that produced the situation shown on stage.

Defamiliarization is designed to make familiar material seem striking
and unexpected by placing it into an unaccustomed context in order to show
it in a new, usually negative or ironic light and force the spectator to reconsider it. For example, in Act I, Scene 1 of *Die Dreigroschenoper (The Three-
Penny Opera)* the Biblical saying "To give is more blessed than to receive"
appears as the motto of Peachum, who exploits beggars while pretending to help
them. In Scene 12 of *Der aufhaltsame Aufstieg des Arturo Ui (The Resistible Rise
of Arturo Ui)*, a satire on Hitler, a famous quotation from Goethe's *Faust* —
Gretchen asking Faust whether he believes in God — is directed to Arturo Ui,
the Hitler figure, by a woman whose husband Arturo is plotting to kill. In both
cases overly familiar, long revered sayings — clichés — are presented so as to
show that they are no longer meaningful, can no longer be taken seriously,

have nothing more to offer the modern spectator. (With regard to the German classics, it must be remembered that they were widely taught and memorized in German schools and thus became the automatic and unreflected property of every educated German. This also applies to the folksongs alluded to by Mahler.) Being farther removed in time from the classic-romantic German heritage than Mahler, Brecht was less sentimental about it; songs such as "Moon over Alabama" and "Moon over Soho" destroy the nocturnal poetry of the romantics while at the same time offering sharp social comment. Brecht treats this material historically by showing that it is characteristic of a particular era and must be superseded. For Brecht defamiliarization becomes a means to the ideological end of social and artistic reform.

What I am suggesting is that a kind of defamiliarization of overly familiar material takes place in the music of Mahler and Ives. It isn't the Brechtian kind, but an earlier, less ideological, less didactic form that places a folksong or hymn, a march or dance into a symphonic or other large-scale musical context, resulting in an unexpectedly ironic illumination of folk music. Whereas Brecht is less nostalgic and more cynical about the tried-and-true and satirizes it as part of a tradition that has lost its meaning and needs to be replaced, Mahler and Ives express affection for the folk music they defamiliarize and do not attempt to discredit it as part of a moribund tradition.[28] What is remarkable about Mahler's music is that it evokes deeply embedded memories and associations in a way that is half ironic and half valedictory.

The closest previous examples of this treatment of folk music occur in Tchaikovsky's symphonies. In the last movement of the Fourth Symphony (1878) he quotes the Russian peasant song "In the field there stood a birch tree," but this song is not the main theme of its movement and does not carry the kinds of associations that the patriotic songs in Mahler's Third do, nor is it treated ironically, unless the trumpeting of a folksong by a battery of brass instruments be of itself considered ironic. Yet the folksong in Tchaikovsky's Fourth becomes the occasion for the kind of orchestral frenzy that we find in Mahler's Third, as if the two composers are torn between wishing to affirm folk music and being too sophisticated or alienated to feel at home in it. Both Tchaikovsky and Mahler were for different reasons outsiders with a necessarily ambivalent relation to folk music, the difference being that for Tchaikovsky the distance from folk music emerges as his personal destiny with implications of tragedy, whereas for Mahler this distance expresses itself in an expressionistic spiritualization of folk music which strips it of its folk element. Mahler treats folk music with the sophistication of someone who cannot take this music straight, thereby implying an ironic comment on it.

A literary parallel may help to illustrate the point. In the first chapter of Thomas Mann's novel *Bekenntnisse des Hochstaplers Felix Krull (Confessions of Felix Krull, Confidence Man)*, the door chime in Krull's parents' home plays the thrice-familiar song "Freut euch des Lebens" (English version: "Gather ye rosebuds while ye may"), which turns up as a distant echo in the posthorn episode in Mahler's Third Symphony. Thomas Mann's reference falls short of Brechtian defamiliarization because the song is not out of context, but the narrator's perspective is clearly ironic in suggesting that a life style based on such assumptions is suspect. It might be akin to playing "Home on the Range" in an American home. This irony is closer to Ives than it is to Mahler, but this may be merely because verbal irony, like Ives's more explicit quotations, is not as resonant or suggestive as Mahler's more subliminal allusions. As against the plain irony of Mann's simple statement, the reminiscence of the song in Mahler's Third is rich in nostalgia, as if he is memorializing a folk music heritage that cannot be his and is in any case too simple for modern ears. This was not as obvious in 1896 as it is in our own day.

The cited examples of musical irony in Mahler are so deeply integrated in his work that ironic intent is difficult to prove. He was probably not aware of it himself. That is, it is unlikely that he consciously intended to write a march that sounds like an ironic comment on Central European band music. Yet this march has a distinctly ironic flavor, both intrinsically and by being combined with several stylistically different musics in the manner of a collage. Mahler heard marches with the ears and mind of an outsider. Important, too, is the listener's response and association vis-à-vis these songs. Eggebrecht cannot think of a plausible reason why Mahler would have "parodistically distorted" the songs in the opening theme of the Third Symphony.[29] My own explanation is that he altered them in the direction of musical irony because as a marginal man he could not take their patriotic sentiments seriously.

A more traditional example of parody in the sense of a comic or satiric imitation occurs in the final movement of Mahler's Seventh Symphony (meas. 53-78) where the waltz from Lehár's *Die lustige Witwe (The Merry Widow)* may have been parodied.[30] A comparison of this passage with Bartók's famous parody in the fourth movement of his Concerto for Orchestra (1943) is illuminating. Bartók parodies both the "Maxim" aria from *The Merry Widow* and the march theme from the first movement of Shostakovich's Seventh *(Leningrad)* Symphony (1941). Parody is here applied simultaneously to two very different pieces of music and with different intentions. The Shostakovich theme is quite simply burlesqued — unfairly so, I think, in view of the life-and-death struggle depicted in the *Leningrad* Symphony — evidently because it sounds obvious and perhaps banal and is repeated many times, but the Lehár theme is parodied because it represents a bygone era about which one may wax nostalgic but which cannot be revived. Leaving aside the Shostakovich parody which seems to be inspired by plain dislike and lacks any personal identification, the Lehár parody brings us closer to Mahler because Lehár was, like Bartók, Hungarian, *The Merry Widow* treats a Hungarian story, and Bartók, though keeping his distance from Lehár's world, is consequently commenting on something close to home. The operetta was first performed in 1905 when Bartók was 24 years old, and it can be assumed that he was familiar with it. His attitude toward Lehár's music must necessarily be more subjective and more complex than toward Shostakovich with whom he has little in common, either biographically or musically. In the Lehár case Bartók slips into irony, which has been defined as an "attitude of detachment and sophistication and a tendency to perceive life in terms of the incongruities that occur between appearance and reality."[31] Bartók's irony in this case is based on the incongruity between Lehár's world and Bartók's in 1943; being a quotation that is not intrinsic to the music, the irony is overt, explicit and easily identifiable.

Mahler's putative parody of the Lehár waltz is much more insinuating because it is not set off as a quotation, being simply the second theme of the movement. It would probably not strike the listener as a parody at all, and again I cannot prove that it is. Mahler was phenomenally receptive, and he heard and conducted a great deal of music, some of which resonates in his own music — often, I think, unwittingly. If this passage is indeed a parody, it has Mahler's characteristic multi-faceted quality, being a parody within a parody. While its first occurrence sounds more nostalgic than parodistic, the composer varies it later to parody his own statement of this theme (see meas. 327-330, 341-344). Thus we possibly get Mahler parodying Lehár and then proceeding to parody his own parody of Lehár. And this does not exhaust the parodistic content of this movement which also makes fun of the Viennese waltz and then parodies his own comments on the waltz (cf. meas. 100-106 with meas. 430-437 and 486-492).

Two important aspects of parody apply to Mahler: his affection for the music he parodies and his modernist view that "art is a legitimate subject of art."[32] The first is a psychological component, based on the assumption that if someone takes the trouble to write a parody, that person must identify at least to some degree with the object of the parody. Since Mahler never seeks merely to ridicule the models but more often raises them above themselves, this affection is even more evident. He presents us with the novel question whether a parody which is larger and richer than the original is still a parody.

Actually, the term 'parody' in Mahler applies more accurately to certain compositional types and genres, especially marches and dances, than to individual melodies.[33] And this marks him as a modernist who could only treat such traditional forms in the spirit of parody or quasi-parody. It is as the inquiring, skeptical type of artist that he invites comparison with the ironic novelist Thomas Mann who once wrote, "the love for a form of art, in the historical possibility of which one can no longer believe, will inevitably beget parody."[34] As a modern writer he renewed established forms, themes and myths by psychoanalyzing them (as for example in *Tristan* and *Doktor Faustus*), whereas Brecht re-interpreted them along Marxist lines (as in *The Three-Penny Opera* and *Saint Joan of the Stockyards*). Mahler, too, comments on older music, both folk and art music, by shining a penetrating light on it; his illuminations of folk music invariably tend to denationalize it by stripping away the local or regional elements of such music. The irony of this treatment lies in the fact that folk music so treated ceases to be folk music, just as Thomas Mann's *Tristan* — a Tristan sans Isolde — ceases to be a love story. Neither Mahler nor Mann could believe in the traditional function of these genres.

Here it may be appropriate to comment briefly on the *Death in Venice* controversy. In 1971 the Italian director Luchino Visconti made a film version of Thomas Mann's story *Der Tod in Venedig (Death in Venice)*. In the film the protagonist of Mann's story, the writer Gustav Aschenbach, becomes a composer who is chiefly modeled on Mahler. Much of the music used in the film is by Mahler, and flashbacks to Aschenbach's past life are drawn from Mahler's biography. The motivation for this stems from the following circumstances. In the late spring of 1911 Mann was on a brief holiday on the Adriatic, first on Brioni Island where he heard the news of Mahler's death (18 May 1911), and then in Venice. Mann's story was conceived on this trip and was in part inspired by his reflections on Mahler's persona. As Mann revealed nearly ten years later (in a letter of 18 March 1921 to the artist Wolfgang Born), he was so deeply affected by Mahler's passing that he gave his protagonist the composer's first name and physical features. Mann had met Mahler twice in Munich, once before and once after the premiere of the Eighth Symphony on 12 September 1910 which Mann attended, and he was deeply impressed by the composer's personality. In the caves of his mind Mann seems to have associated Mahler's psyche with that of his protagonist. But the only significant biographical resemblance between Mahler and Aschenbach is the fact that the latter's grandfather was a Bohemian conductor. In all other respects they are markedly different. Mahler's humble Jewish ancestors from the Bohemian countryside bear no relationship to Aschenbach's solidly bourgeois, Protestant forebears who served the King of Prussia in various official capacities. Aschenbach won early fame and became an established writer at a young age, whereas Mahler had to struggle long and hard for recognition as a composer. And the cause and manner of Aschenbach's death, precipitated by a fateful attraction for a young boy, has no parallel in Mahler's life or death. Though both were fin-de-siècle artists whose work is strongly autobiographical, they lived and worked very differently. Aschenbach's hard-won discipline and representative stature as a writer, his austere personality, his artistic path from a Dionysian to an Apollonian vein, his highly controlled and self-conscious writing style are antithetical to Mahler's mercurial temperament, his emotional music, his more intuitive and untrammeled way of composing, and the wide-ranging, heterogeneous substance of his work. Crucial is the difference between writing and composing which Visconti ignored. Writing is probably a more intellectual, more conceptual, less emotional activity than composing. To create a literary work requires a different kind of creative process, with different kinds and levels of psychic energy, than composing a piece of music. Because music is more emotive than writing, it is hard to imagine a composer being as reined in as Aschenbach who lived, as Mann put it, with clenched fists. And it is even harder to associate Aschenbach's painstaking way of writing, his preoccupation with form, his manner of weaving together, tapestry-like, a large work out of many small details, with Mahler's much more spontaneous, more dramatic compositional style. While it is true that Mahler kept revising the orchestration of his compositions, he did not resemble the Flaubert-like stylist that Aschenbach represents. And so one may conclude that biographically and artistically, any resemblance between Mahler and Aschenbach existed only in Mann's imagination. Perhaps he thought of them as marginal men, but whereas Mahler's marginality is cultural, deriving from his divided heritage, Aschenbach's is psychic, arising from a repressed erotic life. The figure of Aschenbach is, as so often happens in Mann's fiction, a stylized self-portrait, with an admixture of traits of other figures — including Mahler as Mann saw him — whom Mann respected and/or wished to parody and whom he sometimes envied for qualities that he did not himself possess.

More relevant are certain parallels between Mahler and Adrian Leverkühn, the protagonist of Mann's late novel *Doktor Faustus*. Here, much more than in *Der Tod in Venedig*, the central character is a composite of numerous figures, the chief inspiration being Nietzsche, but the main point is that Adrian Leverkühn is not a writer but a composer. Among Leverkühn's works is a song cycle on poems by Clemens Brentano, one of the editors of *Des Knaben Wunderhorn (The Youth's Magic Horn)*, the titles and description of which strongly recall Mahler's songs; Leverkühn has written a cantata with a final adagio for orchestra, which is described as a "revocation" of Beethoven's Ninth Symphony — an apt description of Mahler's own Ninth Symphony; Leverkühn is able to evoke "the intimate, fearful, gruesome landscape of the German folk-song"; and he is aware that "all the methods and conventions of art today *are good for parody only*" (Mann's emphasis). Once Mahler is even mentioned as a musical influence on Leverkühn. Finally, Mahler comes particularly to mind in the following comment by a Jewish figure in *Doktor Faustus*: "To be German means above all to be national — and who would find nationalism believable in a Jew? . . . In us Jews nationalism would be impudent enough to provoke a pogrom." In *Doktor Faustus* Mann was writing about a late-born composer who, not unlike Mahler, was deeply indebted to the romantic tradition but could not compose in it without subjecting it to irony and parody. It was Mahler's ironic treatment of traditional forms that seems particularly to have fascinated Mann and that constitutes the most significant point of contact between them.[35]

Mahler's irony, which is more evident in the symphonies than in the songs, whose musical treatment is determined by the texts, differentiates him from Bruckner, with whom he is often linked, and in fact from all previous symphonists except possibly Berlioz. Irony appears whenever two or more types or levels of music are juxtaposed, as for example in all of Mahler's scherzos. By relativizing the romantic element — pitting it against the sardonic or the parodistic — Mahler creates an ironic effect by calling into question the ro-mantic style and his own nostalgia. It is difficult to say to what degree this was intentional, for he "moved in the uncertain realm between irony and senti-mentality,"[36] but it is clear that this musical ambiguity gives his music its unique fascination. (When it lacks this quality, as in the Adagietto from the Fifth Symphony, it is invariably less original and less interesting.) The ambiguity is also another mark of his marginality. By introducing irony, ambiguity and parody into an august musical form, Mahler injected a critical note into sym-phonic music that gives his music its modern sound and transnational per-spective.

NOTES FOR CHAPTER IV: A MUSICAL IRONIST

[1] See the respective definitions in Webster's *New Collegiate Dictionary* (Springfield, Mass.: G. and C. Merriam Company, 1973); D. C. Muecke, *The Compass of Irony* (London: Methuen, 1969), p. 159; *Oxford Universal Dictionary*, ed. C. T. Onions (abridged edition) (Oxford: The Clarendon Press, 1955); D. C. Muecke, *The Compass of Irony*, p. 159; D. C. Muecke, *Irony and the Ironic* (London and New York: Methuen, 1982), p. 46; *Brockhaus Enzyklopädie*, 17th ed., vol. 9 (Wiesbaden: F. A. Brockhaus, 1970), p. 244.

[2] D. C. Muecke, *Irony and the Ironic*, pp. 24-25.

[3] Henry-Louis de La Grange, *Mahler* I (Garden City, N. Y.: Doubleday, 1973), p. 142 and p. 755.

[4] Mahler once described this movement as "ironic in the sense of Aristotle's 'eironeia'" — see *Selected Letters of Gustav Mahler*, ed. Knud Martner (New York: Farrar, Straus and Giroux, 1979), p. 178 — but it is difficult to associate Mahler with Aristotle's use of the word 'eironeia' which meant 'dissimulation,' 'mock modesty,' 'understatement' and 'self-depreciation,' except perhaps in the last sense, for Mahler does seem to make a critical comment on his own manner, in this and in other works. In the last movement of the Fifth Symphony he speeds up the sentimental adagietto; see measures 372-385. All references are to the Critical Edition of Mahler's works, edited by the International Gustav Mahler Society in Vienna.

[5] *Selected Letters of Gustav Mahler,* ed. Knud Martner, p. 177.

[6] Henry-Louis de La Grange, *Mahler* I, pp. 748 and 749.

[7] Philip Thomson, *The Grotesque* (London: Methuen, 1972), p. 27.

[8] Henry-Louis de La Grange, *Mahler* I, p. 747 and p. 784.

[9] The Marche Nocturne in Berlioz' *L'Enfance du Christ* (op. 25; 1854), though not directly reminiscent of Mahler's piece, is a remarkable combination of mystery, beauty and foreboding and is superbly orchestrated. In rhythm and tone it shares the off-beat quality of some of Mahler's marches. As a piece of music and certainly as a march, it stands out as a particularly original and characteristic work. In simultaneously suggesting the promise of Christ and his betrayal, this piece manages to compress a wide emotional range into its brief span. — An unexpectedly Mahlerian march is Sibelius' strange-sounding funeral march *In Memoriam* (op. 59; 1909).

[10] Donald Mitchell, *Gustav Mahler: The Wunderhorn Years* (Boulder: Westview Press, 1976), pp. 294-296.

[11] Henry-Louis de La Grange, *Mahler* I, p. 205.

[12] Ibid., p. 600. — But the music critic Max Kalbeck entitled his review of the symphony in the *Neue Wiener Tagblatt* of 20 November 1900 "Gustav Mahler's Sinfonia ironica"; see *Gustav Mahler Briefe*, ed. Herta Blaukopf (Vienna-Hamburg: Paul Zsolnay Verlag, 1982), p. 255.

[13] Henry-Louis de La Grange, *Mahler* I, p. 601 and p. 600.

[14] Monika Tibbe, *Über die Verwendung von Liedern und Liedelementen in instrumentalen Symphoniesätzen Gustav Mahlers* (Munich: Musikverlag Emil Katzbichler, 1971), p. 79.

[15] Ibid., p. 75. — My colleague, Professor Leonard Ehrlich, recalls singing the minor-key version in a Jewish school in Vienna in 1934.

[16] Natalie Bauer-Lechner, *Recollections of Gustav Mahler*, tr. Dika Newlin, ed. Peter Franklin (Cambridge-New York: Cambridge University Press, 1980), p. 158.

[17] Two examples: Two Jews are sitting on a park bench discussing anti-Semitism. A bird flies overhead and misbehaves on them. "See what I told you," one Jew says to the other, "for the Gentiles they sing." — A Jew whose application for membership in a country club is rejected replies: "I wouldn't join a club that accepts me as a member."

[18] The difference between Berlioz' distortion of themes in the *Symphonie Fantastique* and Mahler's distortions is that Berlioz' themes, being more extroverted, believably portray the artist's life he is recounting, while Mahler's themes sound intrinsically autobiographical.

[19] Ludwig Erk, *Deutscher Liederhort*, ed. Franz M. Böhme (Hildesheim: Georg Olms, and Wiesbaden: Breitkopf und Härtel, 1963; reprint of Leipzig edition of 1893-1894), vol. III, p. 501.

[20] The texts appear in the popular anthology *Allgemeines Deutsches Kommersbuch*, ed. Hermann and Moritz Schauenburg, musical editors Friedrich Silcher and Friedrich Erk, 156th ed. (Lahr/Schwarzwald: Moritz Schauenburg Verlag, 1966), pp. 9, 212, and 171, respectively. The original texts follow:

> Ich hab mich ergeben mit Herz und mit Hand
> dir, Land voll Lieb und Leben,
> mein deutsches Vaterland!
>
> Mein Herz ist entglommen, dir treu zugewandt,
> du Land der Frei'n und Frommen,
> du herrlich Hermannsland!
>
> Will halten und glauben an Gott fromm und frei;
> will, Vaterland, dir bleiben
> auf ewig fest und treu!
>
> Ach Gott, tu erheben mein jung Herzensblut
> zu frischem, freudgem Leben,
> zu freiem frommem Mut!
>
> Lass Kraft mich erwerben in Herz und in Hand,
> zu leben und zu sterben
> fürs heilge Vaterland!

*   *   *   *

> Wir hatten gebauet ein stattliches Haus
> und drin auf Gott vertrauet,
> trotz Wetter, Sturm und Graus.
>
> Wir lebten so traulich, so innig, so frei,
> den Schlechten ward es graulich,
> wir lebten gar zu treu!
>
> Man lugte, man suchte nach Trug und Verrat,
> verleumdete, verfluchte
> die junge grüne Saat!
>
> Was Gott in uns legte, die Welt hat's veracht't,
> die Einigkeit erregte
> bei Guten selbst Verdacht!

Man schalt sie Verbrechen, man täuschte sich sehr;
die Form kann man zerbrechen,
die Liebe nimmermehr.

Das Band ist zerschnitten, war Schwarz, Rot und Gold,
und Gott hat es gelitten,
wer weiss, was er gewollt!

Die Form ist zerbrochen, von aussen herein,
doch, was man drin gerochen,
war eitel Trug und Schein.

Das Haus mag zerfallen — was hat's dann für Not?
Der Geist lebt in uns allen,
und unsre Burg ist Gott!

*   *   *   *

Ich hatt einen Kameraden,
einen bessern findst du nit.
Die Trommel schlug zum Streite,
er ging an meiner Seite
in gleichem Schritt und Tritt.

Eine Kugel kam geflogen,
gilt's mir oder gilt es dir?
Ihn hat es weggerissen,
er liegt mir vor den Füssen,
als wär's ein Stück von mir.

Will mir die Hand noch reichen,
derweil ich eben lad.
Kann dir die Hand nicht geben,
bleib du im ewgen Leben,
mein guter Kamerad.

*   *   *   *

Oddly enough, the song "Ich hab mich ergeben" appears in an American song book, to the same melody but with a text adapted to American needs:

A Pledge

I pledge myself faithful,
With heart and with hand,
To thee, my own fair country,
To thee, my native land.

Thy flag I will honor,
The flag of the free,
I'll keep thy laws unbroken,
Wherever I may be.

Though danger may face me,
Though trouble may fret,
This pledge so freely given,
I never shall forget.

See Osbourne McConathy, W. Otto Miessner, Edward Bailey Birge and Mable E. Bray, *The Music Hour,* Fourth Book (New York-Boston-Chicago-San Francisco: Silver Burdett Co., 1937), p. 67. My colleague, Professor David Wyman, reports that this book was used in the fourth grade in the Newton, Massachusetts, public school system in 1937-1938.

[21] Mahler considered numerous descriptive titles for this symphony and its individual movements; they are listed in Henry-Louis de La Grange, *Mahler* I, pp. 798-799.

[22] In his essay "Mahler and Freud: The Dream of the Stately House" (in *Beiträge '79-81: Gustav Mahler Kolloquium,* ed. Rudolf Klein; vol. 7 of the Beiträge of the Österreichische Gesellschaft für Musik [Kassel: Bärenreiter-Verlag, 1981], pp. 40-51), William McGrath finds a link between Mahler and Freud in this very same song. In 1898, during a political crisis in the Austrian Parliament over the conflict between Germans and Czechs, Freud who was then working on *The Interpretation of Dreams* had a dream "in which a house built out of stone collapsed ('We had built a stately house') and which thus, because of this allusion, could not be used" (Freud's words, p. 42). McGrath interprets Freud's censorship of this dream as the suppression of his pro-German sympathies in light of the anti-Semitic agitation by pro-German elements in Vienna at that time. These sympathies hark back to Freud's membership in the Reading Association of German Students of Vienna *(Leseverein der deutschen Studenten Wiens),* an organization tinged with German nationalism, whose members were well acquainted with this song. Through his membership in the Pernerstorfer Circle, Mahler also traveled in these circles when he was very young and shared similar sympathies. McGrath also cites the following statement by Mahler, which strongly suggests that the composer had this song in mind when he wrote the beginning of the Third Symphony: "I simply had to proceed like a builder who put the forms of his building in the correct relationship to each other." (p. 46) Where I differ with him is that he interprets Mahler's use of this song, in contrast to Freud's, as "a proud reaffirmation of his youthful beliefs" (p. 47), whereas I think that Mahler used this song ironically. As McGrath points out (p. 47), by 1896 Mahler could no longer hold to the pro-German position that he espoused in 1878-1881. By 1896 he had lived in Germany intermittently, had experienced anti-Semitism and had become much more skeptical about what McGrath calls "the goal of psychic wholeness which pointed the way to community with others" (p. 48). As a matter of fact, Mahler seems an extremely lonely and highly individual voice, not at all the composer of "communitarian music," as McGrath calls him elsewhere, with reference to the first movement of the Third Symphony. (See McGrath's book *Dionysian Art and Populist Politics in Austria* [New Haven-London: Yale University Press, 1974], p. 244). Musically, the theme of the student song is so estranged by Mahler, made so irregular, that even the opening statement of it is not "triumphantly announced," as McGrath describes it (p. 50), but is full of harmonic ambiguity and ends not at all on an affirmative note. Even the affirmative end of this fascinating movement does not conjure up

Binzer's text which I was the first Mahler scholar to publish (in *Views and Reviews of Modern German Literature: Festschrift for Adolf D. Klarmann,* ed. Karl S. Weimar [Munich: Delp, 1974], p. 95), but opens up sounds that to my ears are far removed from any patriotic or national feelings. But in the final analysis, the meaning of music eludes precise definition. Mahler in particular, because of his many musical allusions and the problem of intent associated with them, can be heard with different ears by different listeners, each of whom brings a different perception to his music. I agree with Mr. McGrath that Mahler is a Freudian composer, not so much for any programmatic statements he made about dreams or Greek mythology (p. 41) — theorizing was not Mahler's forte — but for the highly associative quality of his music and because he dug deep into the musical subsoil to uncover unsuspected depths (as in the demonic scherzos of the Sixth and Seventh Symphonies) and heights (as in the sublime final measures of the adagio of the Fourth Symphony). In the opening horn call of the Third Symphony, far from being proud of it he sublimated all the patriotism of Binzer's song to produce a heightened, denationalized proclamation and then unleashed the spectors of "rustic brutality" (Adorno's phrase) in the wild march that follows. In Mahler's statement of Binzer's song and his subsequent treatment of it — a song that was drummed into my head in a German school when I was a young boy — I can only hear an ironic comment on the nationalism that was and is so endemic in that part of the world. By cleansing the melody of its patriotic qualities, Mahler rejected this nationalism as much as Freud did.

[23] See the excellent article by Robert P. Morgan, "Ives and Mahler: Mutual Responses at the End of an Era," *19th Century Music,* vol. II, no. 1 (July 1978), pp. 72-81, especially pp. 74-75. — Mahler quotes only himself literally; the only exception seems to be the quotation of the last eight bars of Schumann's song "Das ist ein Flöten und Geigen," the ninth song in the cycle *Dichterliebe (Poet's Love),* at the end of the scherzo of the Second Symphony. See Monika Tibbe, *Über die Verwendung von Liedern und Liedelementen in instrumentalen Symphoniesätzen Gustav Mahlers,* pp. 58-59.

[24] Ives himself reports that his Third Symphony was copied in 1911, that Mahler saw it in the copyist's office, expressed interest in it and asked for a copy. (Charles E. Ives, *Memos,* ed. John Kirkpatrick [New York: W. W. Norton, 1972], p. 55 and p. 121). The editor of Ives's *Memos* concludes that Mahler took the score with him on his last return trip to Europe in 1911. But another Ives scholar, David Wooldridge, states that the score was copied in 1910 and that Mahler played it in Munich in the summer of 1910. As evidence he cites an unsigned note in Mahler's hand to the music librarian of the Deutsche Museum in Munich, which had a concert series, asking for the parts of the symphony so that he could rehearse the work. Wooldridge also tells of meeting a retired timpanist in Munich in 1954, who recalled having played the Ives symphony under Mahler in the summer of 1910. This evidence sounds convincing. See David Wooldridge, *From the Steeples and Mountains: A Study of Charles Ives* (New York: Knopf, 1974) pp. 121, 150-151, 206.

[25] Bertolt Brecht, *Gesammelte Werke,* edited by the Suhrkamp Verlag in collaboration with Elisabeth Hauptmann (Frankfurt/Main: Suhrkamp Verlag, 1967), vol. 15, p. 301.

[26] Ibid., p. 347.

[27] Ibid., p. 341. — This technique was first formulated, without Brecht's socio-political program, by the Russian critic Victor Shklovsky in the essay "Art as Technique" (1917). To keep perception from becoming habitual and automatic, art must "make objects 'unfamiliar' . . . make forms difficult, to increase the difficulty and length of perception" (p. 12). The writer "makes the familiar seem strange" in order to call attention to it and deepen the reader's perception of

it. The English translators use the term 'defamiliarization' to render the Russian word 'ostra-
neniye,' which literally means 'making strange' (p. 4, note 3). See *Russian Formalist Criticism:
Four Essays*, tr. Lee T. Lemon and Marion J. Reis (Lincoln: University of Nebraska Press, 1965).
The reference is cited in Robert P. Morgan, "Ives and Mahler," p. 74.

[28] Robert P. Morgan expresses it aptly in his paper, "Ives and Mahler": "One of the most characteristic features of their music is the way it transforms the familiar, distancing it so as to re-
kindle its affective force" (p. 74). And my colleague, Professor Miriam Whaples, writes about
Mahler that he is "the first composer to realize the affective possibilities of parody" (in her essay,
"Mahler and Schubert's A minor Sonata D. 784," p. 263; see Note 32 below).

[29] Hans Heinrich Eggebrecht, *Die Musik Gustav Mahlers* (Munich-Zurich: R. Piper, 1982), p. 49.

[30] We know from Alma that she and Mahler saw *The Merry Widow* in Vienna. (Alma Mahler,
Gustav Mahler: Memories and Letters, ed. Donald Mitchell [Seattle: University of Washington
Press, 1975], p. 120). Though the reference occurs in a chapter on the year 1907, two years after
the completion of the Seventh Symphony, the passage is a more general one and need not refer
to 1907. Since the operetta had its premiere in Vienna on 30 December 1905, it is likely that the
Mahlers saw it earlier than in 1907. Alma also reports that Mahler was still working on the
symphony in the winter of 1905-1906 (ibid., p. 96) and even in 1907 (ibid., p. 119). However, his
revisions were usually confined to changes in instrumentation rather than thematic substance.
Admittedly the matter is conjectural, but at least two other writers mention allusions to *The
Merry Widow*; one of them also in the last movement of the Seventh Symphony, the other in the
First and Ninth. (See Peter Ruzicka, "Befragung des Materials: Gustav Mahler aus der Sicht
aktueller Kompositionsästhetik," in *Mahler — eine Herausforderung: ein Symposion*, ed. Peter
Ruzicka [Wiesbaden: Breitkopf und Härtel, 1977], p. 111, and Theodor W. Adorno, *Mahler:
Eine musikalische Physiognomik* [Frankfurt/Main: Suhrkamp Verlag, 1960], pp. 53 and 211).
Adorno's reference to the "Maxim" song in the First Symphony, which must pertain to measures
110-115 in the first movement, is startling because this symphony was completed seventeen
years before the premiere of Lehár's work, but it is true that Mahler sometimes anticipated
melodies that became popular much later.

[31] *Dictionary of World Literary Terms*, ed. Joseph T. Shipley, revised and enlarged ed. (Boston:
The Writer, Inc., 1970), p. 165.

[32] Miriam K. Whaples, "Mahler and Schubert's A minor Sonata D. 784," *Music and Letters*, 65
(1984), p. 263.

[33] See Robert P. Morgan, "Ives and Mahler," p. 75. It is possible that Jews, being outsiders, have
a special affinity for the parodistic. Parody is often directed against what is traditional, familiar,
rhetorical, but marginal people are apt to view such material more critically, for in the eyes of
the stranger the familiar takes on an aspect that the native would not see. Four Jewish writers
come to mind whose unerring sense for what is provincial, parochial and chauvinistic often
expressed itself in parody: Fritz Mauthner, Karl Kraus, Robert Neumann and Friedrich Torberg.
Their connection with Mahler is that they invariably took aim against nationalism. Needless to
say, Jews of the diaspora are not the only critics of nationalism, but they are by definition more
vulnerable to it and therefore more critical of it.

[34] In *Almanach der Rupprechtpresse auf die Jahre 1921-22* (Munich, 1922), p. 33; quoted in Erich
Heller, *Thomas Mann: The Ironic German* (Cleveland and New York: Meridian Books, 1961),
p. 253. The identical text, in German, appears also in Thomas Mann, *Briefe 1889-1936*, ed. Erika
Mann (Frankfurt/Main: S. Fischer, 1962), p. 187: ". . . dass Liebe zu einem Kunstgeist, an
dessen Möglichkeit man nicht mehr glaubt, die Parodie zeitigt."

³⁵ References to the *Death in Venice* problem are:

> Thomas Mann, *"Death in Venice" and Seven Other Stories,* tr. H. T. Lowe-Porter (New York: Vintage Books, 1954), esp. pp. 8-15.

> Thomas Mann, *Briefe 1889-1936,* ed. Erika Mann (Frankfurt/Main: S. Fischer, 1962), pp. X and 195.

> Ernest Wolf, "A Case of Slightly Mistaken Identity: Gustav Mahler and Gustav Aschenbach," *Twentieth Century Literature*, 19 (1973), 40-52.
> Hans Rudolf Vaget, "Film and Literature. The Case of *Death in Venice:* Luchino Visconti and Thomas Mann," *German Quarterly*, 53 (1980), 159-175.

References to *Doctor Faustus* are as follows:

> Thomas Mann, *Doctor Faustus*, tr. H. T. Lowe-Porter (New York: Knopf, 1970), pp. 182-184 (Brentano songs); pp. 489-490 ("revocation" of Beethoven's Ninth Symphony); p. 183 (comment on German folksong); p. 134 (on parody); p. 162 (mention of Mahler); pp. 406-407 (on Jews). I have, in part, used my own translations.

The corresponding page references in the German text are:

> Thomas Mann, *Doktor Faustus* (Frankfurt/Main: S. Fischer, 1974; vol. 6 of Gesammelte Werke in 13 Bänden), pp. 243-245 (Brentano songs); p. 649 ("revocation" of Beethoven's Ninth Symphony); p. 244 (comment on German folksong); p. 180 (on parody); p. 215 (mention of Mahler); pp. 539-541 (on Jews).

³⁶ Pierre Boulez, "Gustav Mahler up-to-date?," in *Gustav Mahler in Vienna*, ed Sigrid Wiesmann, tr. Anne Shelley (New York: Rizzoli International Publications, 1976), p. 25.

Chapter V

TRANSNATIONAL MUSIC

Stefan Zweig identified two related aspects of Viennese culture: the combination of heterogeneous elements and a supranationalism of the spirit *(geistige Übernationalität)*,[1] to which he might have added a characteristically unheroic tone. An example is the music of Mozart, which fuses Italian and German features of form and expression. Even more characteristic is Schubert, who combines folk and art elements in such a way that marches, dances, and folksongs are absorbed into large musical forms. The middle section (trio) of the scherzo of the C major symphony (no. 9) is a processional that sounds like band music; by way of relaxing the symphonic mood it introduces a popular note without disturbing the form or musical substance of the symphony. In Viennese literature, the plays of Franz Grillparzer contain an occasional Viennese inflection or colloquialism in the elevated verse dialogues between historical or mythological figures, thereby establishing a link between what is specifically Viennese and universally human.[2] A different facet of the absorption of popular material into high art is found in Hofmannsthal's play *Der Rosenkavalier* in which all social classes, each speaking in its own language, are represented in the manner of world theater — the presentation of life as a great stage in which everyone plays his assigned role. This conjunction of popular and high art, so evident in Mahler's music, is closely related to the cosmopolitan quality of Viennese culture, which in contrast to that of the Austrian provinces has benefitted not only from Vienna's traditional democracy in the arts but from the creative impulses of the many peoples that inhabited the empire. Even in this fiercely nationalistic age, Viennese art of this period was, at its best, truly supranational. In this important respect Vienna and assimilated Jewry found a common meeting ground.

Art produced by Jews in the diaspora, i.e., outside of Israel, noticeably lacks a national accent. In the case of Heine, for example, his marginality reveals itself in the critical, satiric stance that undermines the poet's as well as the reader's belief in a romantic view of life; the diction, mixing traditionally

poetic with sophisticated modern words, breaks up the romantic mood which
is practically a prerequisite for a German poem in the nineteenth century.[3]
It is this stylistic disparity within an individual work that keeps it from acquiring
a national tone. While some of Heine's early poems, such as "Die Lorelei,"
retain the character of folksongs by not breaking the mood, most of his later
poems introduce a sharply satiric note which puts them beyond any national
category. Being too sophisticated, they lack the directness and consistency of
style that are usually inherent in national art.

Nationalism in music, which is limited here to the nineteenth century,
usually evokes a regional landscape or a popular gathering.[4] (This is different
from the modern kind of nationalism in Janáček, Bartók and Kodály, which is
less political and more musicological.) It expresses itself most obviously in the
use or adaptation of folksongs and folk dances, as, say, in *Hänsel und Gretel*
or *The Bartered Bride*. But beyond that one can detect in nineteenth century
music a national flavor which emanates from the melodic contours, harmonic
inflections, rhythm and instrumentation and which gives even nonprogram-
matic music a definite ethnic or regional stamp. Particularly is this true in
Northern, Central and Eastern Europe, in irredentist areas and those with an
awakening self-awareness. Thus it is easy to identify a Tchaikovsky symphony
as Russian, a Dvořák symphony as Czech, a Schumann symphony as German,
a Sibelius symphony as Finnish and an Ives symphony as American. It is this
national element which is missing in Mahler's symphonies.[5]

Most nineteenth-century symphonies are symphonies of place, symphonies that suggest a setting. When one hears a symphony by Schumann
or Brahms, one senses that this music is unmistakably German. (This is not
to say, of course, that Schumann and Brahms do not transcend their national
imprint; it is simply a matter of identifying their national roots.) In Schumann
it is the fanfares and hunting-horn effects, the repetition of basic rhythmic
patterns and the chordal writing; in Brahms it is the earnest solidity of the
music, the lumbering rhythm and the hymnic passages. Since romanticism
and nationalism were for political reasons closely interlinked in Germany,
the entire body of German romantic music is permeated with a distinctly national flavor that first appeared in the music of Carl Maria von Weber. In certain
parts of *Der Freischütz* — the horn quartet in the overture and the hunting
chorus, for example — the hymnic character of this music, built as it is on
solid, triadic, chorale-like chords, its folkloristic flavor, the simple direct
melodies, the hearty mood and regular rhythm seem to evoke a characteristically
rustic German atmosphere, in keeping with the setting of this opera. In more
sophisticated form this mood is found in Wagner's *Tannhäuser* and *Die Meistersinger* and in the last movement of Brahms's First Symphony. The essential

ingredients are the martial tread of the music, the four-square rhythm and a certain unrelieved solemnity — all probably derived from Protestant hymns.

Because of the link between romanticism and nationalism in Europe, most nineteenth-century composers actually wrote pieces of national significance, such as Chopin's Polonaises, Liszt's Hungarian Rhapsodies, Tchaikovsky's *Marche Slave*, Dvořák's Slavonic Dances, Grieg's Norwegian Dances, Smetana's *Má vlast (My Fatherland)*, Elgar's Pomp and Circumstance Marches and Sibelius' *Finlandia*.[6] Characteristically, Mahler did not write this kind of piece. He concentrated on the symphony, a large-scale, highly structured and abstract form of music. He disliked national music and once refused to answer a questionnaire on the national question, partly because he would be asked what a Jew has to do with this matter.[7]

In form and style nineteenth-century instrumental music is predominantly German. The nineteenth-century symphony naturally took its cue from Beethoven, the only heroic composer, who gave the symphony its aspiring character, with the hero prevailing over adversity. Whether these works are nationally colored — as are the symphonies of Tchaikovsky, Dvořák and Sibelius, written in areas where national identity was an issue — or whether they lack national color — as do the symphonies of Berlioz, Franck and Saint-Saëns, written in Western Europe where nationalism was no longer a problem — they share a large-scale design, seriousness of utterance, dramatic intensity, cyclical structure and a wide expressive range that give the listener an encompassing emotional experience. Liszt's *Faust* Symphony and the symphonies of Bruckner, originating in the Austrian Empire, lack a decidedly national color, except perhaps in Liszt's Gretchen movement and in Bruckner's highly characteristic Austrian scherzos;[8] in these works the coming breakdown of tonality is evident in the chromaticism of Liszt's outer movements and in the last two movements of Bruckner's Ninth Symphony, particularly in the harmonically unresolved opening of its scherzo and in the climactic dissonant chord of the last movement.

Mahler's symphonies differ from these works in two essential respects: they abandon the idea of a single basic key for an entire symphony and they make use of irony. Both factors effectively counteract any national quality in the music. National music is firmly embedded in a basic tonality from which it may depart but to which it always returns. This does not mean that all nineteenth-century music written in a basic key is necessarily national, but it does mean that all music of a national flavor is organized around a single tonality. This gives it the solid and sure harmonic and psychological underpinning that is implicit in the concept 'national.'

Until 1888, when Mahler completed his First Symphony, the only change in key was from minor to major to suggest the Byronic theme of the artist's struggle and triumph; among many examples are Beethoven's Fifth and Ninth Symphonies, Brahms's First, Schumann's Fourth, Mendelssohn's Third, Berlioz' *Fantastique*, Dvořák's Eighth, Tchaikovsky's Fifth and Bruckner's Eighth. I know of no symphony before 1888 by a well-known composer that does not return to its initial key at the end.

Of Mahler's symphonies, the First, Third, Sixth, Eighth and Tenth retain a basic key, whereas the Second, Fourth, Fifth, Seventh, Ninth and *Das Lied von der Erde* begin in one key and end in another. "Waldmärchen" ("Forest Legend"), the first part of Mahler's earliest published work, *Das klagende Lied (The Song of Lament)*, begins in three keys: measures 1-3 are in A minor, measure 4 is in D major, measures 5-6 are in F sharp minor which concludes "Waldmärchen," and at measure 7, French horns introduce a theme in D major while the F sharp minor context continues — a very strange and modern effect for this quintessentially romantic work. At measure 11 the F sharp minor context shifts to F minor while the horns shift to D flat. It isn't till measure 26 that the music arrives at C minor, which seems to be its basic key, only to change to C major thirteen bars later. I've counted eighteen key changes in the 126-bar orchestral introduction alone.[9] The frequent key shifts tend to modernize this balladesque work which comes right out of the world of German fairy tales. Its text, adapted by Mahler from a story by Ludwig Bechstein which is also found in Grimm, deals with the murder of a knight by his brother for the love of a queen and the avenging of the murder, and seems as such not well suited to Mahler's sophisticated musical treatment. In *Das klagende Lied* Mahler came as close as he ever did to writing a nationally tinged work; the text has all the trappings of the German fairy tale: deep dark woods, magic, a ruined castle, violent death, and the obligatory macabre touch. The work also has more echoes of Wagner than any other Mahler work. Yet there are no passages which are harmonically straightforward for more than a few bars; the score changes tonality so frequently that nothing resembling a national tone can ever establish itself. Moreover, there are highly modernistic touches, such as the woodwind passage in remote keys in measures 116-128 of "Der Spielmann" ("The Minstrel"), the second part of the original edition and the first part of Mahler's final edition of this work; in the section beginning at measure 336 of "Der Spielmann," each of seven successive bars has a different number of beats, and most extraordinary of all, the vulgar off-stage band music at measures 79-92 of the final part, "Hochzeitsstück" ("Wedding Piece"), repeated twice more, pits the wedding music against the tragic reality represented by the main orchestra in a manner that anticipates the technically and emotionally similar section in Act 2 of Alban Berg's opera *Wozzeck*.[10]

The opening of the First Symphony is also unanchored in tonality. When the main theme of the symphony is introduced in the seventh bar, it lacks a readily identifiable key, is left unresolved and shows an interval of a fourth between the notes in place of the usual third — all of which makes this theme sound remote and mystical rather than regional or national. The music does not settle into the symphony's basic key of D until it reaches measure 62. In the scherzo, usually the most regional-national movement because of its use of dance music, one hears brass fanfares, like outcries, that reach far beyond the movement's A-major compass (meas. 76-77, 79-80, 87-88 and 95-96); alternating with repeated passages for muted trumpets, they introduce a grotesque element which is completely new to the symphony and incompatible with a traditional ländler movement. In the opening and in measure 51 of the last movement of the Seventh Symphony, two different tonalities can be heard simultaneously, like two conflicting musical impulses; the open chord at the end of *Das Lied von der Erde*, to the word 'ewig,' suggests musical, emotional and spatial infinities, anticipating the very similar ending of Berg's Violin Concerto. Even when there is a unifying key, as in the Third Symphony, Mahler's harmonic peregrinations are so wide-ranging and the dimensions so vast that a basic key becomes irrelevant.

The lack of nationality in Mahler's music can be traced to three factors: his divided heritage, his modernity, and the Austrian tradition. It seems clear that a composer with as complex a background as Mahler's is unlikely to produce national music. It is difficult to think of another composer who was similarly situated or another area that could have produced this supranational culture. Deryck Cooke remarks that "the normal composer is a national composer . . . [who] expresses the spirit of his people" and who can "appeal to groups in other countries as a recognizable representative of his own race."[11] While Germany and Austria have treated Mahler as a prophet without honor, his appeal to audiences in other countries may be that of the knowing outsider, for whom present-day listeners may have more understanding than they did in the composer's own day. Though his music may have certain characteristics of German symphonic music — amplitude, intellectual penetration, structural care, unworldliness, idealism — his is the voice of a nationally unaffiliated composer. His marches, dances and folksongs in particular are the expression of a homeless artist communicating the nakedness of human existence.

Marches — Dances — Folksongs

A characteristic feature of Mahler's musical style is his use and treatment of popular forms of music, specifically marches, dances and folksongs. Traditionally these forms are musical expressions of a communal kind: their purpose and effect is to draw people together, to promote joint effort or activity, and to develop solidarity. In using these popular forms Mahler changes their traditional function in a fundamental way: he stylizes them by changing their rhythm, pace, harmony and tone, and thereby enlarges them into universal statements. The effect of this treatment is threefold: it denationalizes what are essentially national forms of music, it transforms them from communal expressions to lone voices and statements about the human condition, and it integrates them so deeply into symphonic structure that they preempt entire symphonies — the march in the Sixth and Seventh Symphonies, the ländler in the Fifth, a patriotic song in the Third.

Marches, dances and folksongs have, of course, appeared in symphonies before Mahler. There are marches in many nineteenth-century symphonies, such as Beethoven's *Eroica* and Tchaikovsky's *Pathétique*. Most classical symphonies have dance movements, and folksongs occur in Tchaikovsky's Fourth and Dvořák's *New World* Symphonies. But Mahler uses these forms more frequently, more centrally as well as more subjectively, in an elevating or ironic vein — sometimes both simultaneously — that suggests a deep-seated personal and cultural ambivalence toward them. The effect of Mahler's treatment is invariably to remove these popular forms of music from their folk roots.

1. Marches

The first piece that Mahler composed was a polka with an introductory funeral march, written when he was about six years old.[12] Astonishingly, at this early age, this title is prophetic: the fascination with popular forms of music which are promptly depopularized, the mixture of pathos and humor, and the use of the march mainly for dark tidings remained characteristic of his music to the end of his life.

Even a cursory examination of Mahler's music shows that it is permeated with marches. The authorized edition of his earliest published work, *Das klagende Lied*, begins with a march. The opening movements of his Second, Third, Fifth, Sixth and Seventh Symphonies are marches, as are the third movement of the First, the last movements of the Second, Sixth and Seventh, the second movement of the Seventh, and the awesome cortege in the first movement of the Ninth. Not a single one of his symphonies is without a martial or processional section. Many of his songs are marching songs, and even *Lieder eines fahrenden Gesellen* and *Das Lied von der Erde*, where one might not expect to find them, contain marches. No such preoccupation with the march comes to mind in any other composer, with the possible exception of Tchaikovsky.

The march, originally "das Signal zum Aufbruch"[13] (the signal to move on, break camp, depart), is an incidental piece, reserved for ceremonial occasions, such as processions, weddings, funerals, and for entertainments, such as parades, band concerts, operettas. It is, of course, the main form of military music and is usually written in the major key, the main exception being the funeral march. Its occurrence in symphonies had been largely limited to program works, such as Haydn's *Military* Symphony (second movement), Beethoven's *Eroica* (second movement) and *Choral* (alla marcia section in last movement) Symphonies, Berlioz' *Symphonie Fantastique* (fourth movement), Dvořák's *New World* Symphony (last movement), Tchaikovsky's *Pathétique* Symphony (third movement). Neither in these works nor in most of the non-programmatic examples (second movement of Beethoven's Seventh, last movement of Brahms's First) does a march occur in the first movement, except in Mendelssohn's *Reformation* Symphony and Goldmark's *Rustic Wedding* Symphony. Of the major works, only the Schubert Ninth and Tchaikovsky's Fifth have a march in the first movement, perhaps because the first movement as the tone-setting movement had to be kept free from programmatic suggestions or because only slow marches were judged fit for a classical symphony. In introducing five of his symphonies, and concluding six of them, with marches, Mahler has given the march a pace-setting role in the structure and meaning of the symphony that drastically alters its traditional ceremonial function in classical music and opens up entirely new dimensions of martial music. Mahler's marches transcend any military or ceremonial functions to symbolize human struggle, aspiration and destiny.

The marches in Mahler's symphonies may be grouped according to the following four types: (a) affirmative (first movement of the Third, last movement of the Seventh); (b) tragic (first movement of the Second, first movement of the Fifth, first and last movements of the Sixth, first movement of the Seventh); (c) slow (processional-recessional) (first movements of the Ninth and Tenth); (d) ironic (third movement of the First, second movement of the Seventh). But since Mahler mixed his genres in true romantic fashion and nowhere wrote a straightforward march, these categories are not strictly observed and are offered for study purposes only.

(a) Affirmative marches

The affirmative march is easily the least important category. The only successful example is the first movement of the Third Symphony, a gigantic march whose musical origin was explained in the preceding chapter (see pp. 71-75), but even here the affirmation is tempered by much dark music. Based on a folk tune that serves as the basis for two patriotic German songs, this piece might well be called "the apotheosis of the march." The instrumentation includes a large battery of percussion consisting of six timpani, two glockenspiels, tambourine, gong, three cymbals, five small drums, one large drum and rod. After a slow introductory section intended as the awakening of nature, martial music begins at measure 225 and increases steadily in volume and urgency until it explodes in a climactic passage ending the exposition (meas. 368).[14] As the music gains in intensity, the martial opening theme is heard recurrently and in different keys, notably in the French horn (meas. 272) where it recalls another patriotic German song, and in the trombones (meas. 330) where it shifts to a heightened level in D major. At such junctures the composer indicates with a double line between bars that the march is entering a new phase. (Some conductors, like Leonard Bernstein in Columbia Set M2L 275, increase the tempo slightly at these points. The device is highly effective.)

After a reprise of the slow introductory music the march gradually returns, gathering momentum but still heard "as if from a great distance" (meas. 467). It returns in full force at measure 530, introduced by a vigorous nine-bar passage for cellos and basses whose nervous energy and offbeat accentuation give a small glimpse into Mahler's personal way with marches. What follows is probably the most tumultuous march Mahler ever wrote. Marked "march" and continuing for 100 bars, this section tosses about the movement's major themes in a whirlwind march that keeps increasing in pace and intensity until it literally disintegrates. Moving through many tonal regions, it pits very low instruments against high ones and uses muted brass conspicuously; rhythmically it is regular, except for the acceleration, the frequent trills and grace notes before the main beat, and the off-beat accents marked "raw" (meas. 545). The use of high woodwinds to counterpoint the movement's basic theme (meas. 564-566, 582-589, 594-602) gives the music a parodistic flavor, but the dimensions are so large and the music is so spine-tingling that it reaches beyond parody to create a super-march, exultant and infernal all at the same time. The end of this march leads without transition to a restatement of the movement's opening theme which begins the recapitulation. Mahler simply directs several small drums "placed at a distance" (meas. 631) to resume the original march tempo without regard to the faster tempo of the subsiding previous march, but the wildness of the fading march makes the return of the original theme sound artificial because the musical content is too free-wheeling to fit the demands of symphonic form. Noteworthy is the alternation between the march and symphonic tone: spatially and temporally the march moves in and out of the symphonic framework, more often than not simply taking it over.

After the recapitulation of the opening theme and the slow introductory music, the march resumes as if it had never stopped[15] and leads to the almost too exulting conclusion of the movement, so that the march has to bear a greater expressive weight than it can sustain. Mahler has transformed a rather solemn martial song both upward and downward: by making it the basis for the opening theme and major statement of a vast symphony and by freeing it harmonically, he has released it from its naively national bonds and raised it to mythic levels; by enveloping it in wild band music and interposing piercingly high counterthemes, he reveals at least a skeptical view of martial music. In his hands this march becomes a vast musical extravaganza filled with tonal symbolism. It is at once a psychoanalysis, a sublimation and an expressionistic magnification of folk music.

It must be remembered that Mahler lived in a part of the world where band music was ever present as a backdrop to daily life. Both Austria and Germany have a rich legacy of band music which was widely performed in those imperial days. Parades were popular, marching bands could be heard on the street, and pupils were marched to certain school functions. In the 1880s and 1890s when Mahler lived in Germany intermittently, the country had become a resurgent world power and its band music undoubtedly reflected this mood. As an outsider he heard its stirring as well as its threatening tone. Though he himself speculated on the influence of Prussian and Austrian military bands on the march in the Third Symphony and thought that his reading of Carlyle's *History of Frederick the Great* was reflected in this march, he was simply incapable of writing a wholly affirmative march.[16] The wild, percussion-ridden march in the middle of this movement does not sound like positive or joyful music. Mahler literally marched to a different drummer.

His only other affirmative march, in the last movement of the Seventh Symphony, deviates even more from a traditional march. The martial introduction starts with a typical Mahler irregularity: the six introductory bars move from E minor in the timpani to B minor in horns and bassoons to G major in flutes and oboes. The second unorthodoxy is the rapidly cascading, countermelodic passage for woodwinds (meas. 15-22) which is appended to the main theme in the brass and counteracts its festive effect. This opening proclamation in C major is brought to a sudden halt at measure 51 where in the middle of the bar the music switches abruptly but in the same tempo to a sprightly A flat major tune — the *Merry Widow* parody mentioned in the preceding chapter. A similar shift between two contrasted sections, a quietly profound change from C major to A minor, is for me the most moving moment in this movement (meas. 242). Soon thereafter the music lapses into a tedious alternation between the martial opening theme, on the one hand, and the sprightly tune and a waltzy theme in triple meter, on the other; the effect is that they negate each other. Conflicting musical impulses keep the initial march from ever establishing itself, perhaps intentionally so. Even just before the closing C major chord, rapid woodwind runs and a dissonant chord interfere with the festive ending of the symphony. He could not end a symphony with a C major peroration even if he tried. I agree with Adorno that his strenuous effort to do so makes this piece his weakest composition.[17]

The irregularity of Mahler's marches is shown in the opening bars of the Eighth Symphony. The work opens with a hymn to the Latin text "Veni Creator Spiritus." Hymns are by definition processional and this one is written in 4/4 meter, but after only two bars in this meter Mahler writes a bar in 3/4, followed by one in 2/4, one in 4/4 and one in 3/4 before returning to the original 4/4 meter. One possible explanation is that he tried to fit the rhythm to that of the opening line of the text, but the recurring rhythmic divergence introduces an agogic element into this venerable old hymn which prevents a processional beat from firmly taking hold. The first movement also contains an orchestral interlude (meas. 169-211) which has twenty-four changes in meter in less than five pages — perhaps an infernal scene through which the souls must pass before ascending to heaven. The concluding choruses of the Second and Eighth Symphonies, however, are rhythmically regular, perhaps signifying the attainment of spiritual clarity, but such passages are invariably less convincing than the irregular parts.[18]

Choruses and marches, whether they occur in a stage work or in a symphony, in a liturgical or secular work, have the capacity to inspire a sense of community among the listeners. This community may be religious or national or social or simply human in a generalized sense; such a communal spirit can be felt when listening to the choruses in Bach or Handel or Haydn or Mozart or Beethoven or Brahms or Bruckner or even in Liszt's *Faust* Symphony, and it can also be heard in the martial music of Beethoven, Mendelssohn, Schumann, Wagner and Brahms. But in Mahler's choruses and marches one hears a highly individualized voice, because harmony and rhythm shift frequently, the orchestration is extremely sophisticated, and the highly emotional quality of the music belies the pieties of the chosen texts or the directness of the march form. The irony of Mahler's marches is that he used an affirmative, collective form of music to express the exact opposite.

(b) Tragic marches

The most frequently encountered march in Mahler's oeuvre is the tragic march. This includes not only funeral marches but any dark, ominous, foreboding march. Four symphonies — the Second, Fifth, Sixth and Seventh — contain tragic marches; of these, the Second, Sixth and Seventh Symphonies are dominated by it. The Second or *Resurrection* Symphony is bracketed by dark marches in its outer movements, except for the affirmative ending of the work. Notable in the funeral march of the first movement is the profusion of triplets, which give the music a restless quality out of character for a funeral march, and the muted brass at measures 18 and 25, which introduces a near-hissing sound that destroys the traditional effect of brass music. Whether it suggests a protest that life has come to an end or a disbelief in ceremony or skepticism about salvation, it adds a negative element to the march.

A remarkable martial passage occurs in the last movement from measure 343 to 380. The march of the souls has ended, and only a few instruments are playing a yearning melody, as if pleading for salvation. In the distance one hears a band consisting of several trumpets, triangle, cymbals and a large drum which intermittently plays martial music, in sharp contrast to the longing strains of the main orchestra. This off-stage band is usually interpreted as the approaching trumpet calls of the Last Judgment. At its entrance Mahler directs this band to play "so softly that it in no way touches the songful character of cellos and bassoons," and he wants it to sound like "isolated windblown sounds of a barely audible music" which very gradually grows in intensity.[19] The most conspicuous feature of this music is its constantly shifting meter from 2/4 to 4/4 to 3/4 to 4/4. One hopes this means that the trumpets of the Last Judgment do not follow a military rhythm. The stereophonic effect of this passage, already found in a similar passage in *Das klagende Lied*, suggests large dimensions of time and space that leave the traditional earthy march far behind.

The Fifth Symphony also opens with a funeral march. It is perhaps the first symphony to open with a slow movement. It is marked "At a measured pace. In strict rhythm, like a cortege." In contrast to these directions and to previous funeral marches (Beethoven's Piano Sonata op. 26a and *Eroica* Symphony, Chopin's Piano Sonata in B flat minor, Wagner's *Götterdämmerung*), this march is irregular in pace and harmony and frequently shifts the main accent away from the first beat of the bar. In the A minor episode (meas. 322-369) the tread of the march is constantly interrupted by syncopated rhythms in the second violins and violas, by a swooping figure in the violas and by the lavish use of triplets. Contrary to common practice, the middle section —

usually a consoling interlude — is much faster and more agitated than the
original march. Harmonically, the piece moves in a twilight zone, touching on
its basic key of C sharp minor only at the beginning, in the middle (meas. 262
and 281) and at the end. The march is further undercut by parodistic variations
on some of its themes in the symphony's second movement (meas. 74-141, 213-
230, 266-288).

Mahler named the Sixth his "Tragic" Symphony.[20] His wife reports that
this symphony was his most personal work and moved him deeply.[21] She describes it as a biographically prophetic work in which he foretold certain fateful
events (the death of their eldest daughter, his serious heart ailment), but it
goes much further to suggest the crisis of Mahler's time and the approaching
war. It is Mahler's fate symphony and the only one of his symphonies to end in
the minor key. Hearing it gives the impression that the world is enveloped in
martiality. The symphony is scored for a very large orchestra that includes
more percussion than any other work by Mahler. Its martial character is announced in the first bar by four heavy regular beats in the cellos and basses
and in the second bar by a military drum; at measure 57 two timpani and two
small military drums beat out the basic, two-bar military theme of the symphony. This motif punctuates the first and last movements and closes the symphony
with its ominous gait. Embedded in it and in the symphony as a whole is a major-
to-minor motto in the horns and oboes — the horns going from fortissimo to
pianissimo while the oboes move in the opposite direction (meas. 59-60) — but
the symphony begins and ends in A minor.[22]

Noteworthy in this dark work, even more than in the other martial symphonies, is the wide contrast between the doom-laden marches and the lyrical
sections; the pastoral interlude (at meas. 198) with its unearthly cowbells sounds
like distant, muted Easter music. This chorale-like passage retains the movement's march rhythm, though at a somewhat slower pace, with the notable exception of measures 239-241 where the second violins play pizzicato chords in
syncopation to the other instruments — a striking example of Mahler's unconventional writing. When clearly played and heard, this passage introduces
an unmistakably contrary note into a hushed, quasi-religious chorale, as if he
were momentarily cancelling out its usual effect — a frequent device of Mahler
that undercuts the main voice by a prominent and disparate subsidiary part.

The lyrical passages, suggesting a better past and future, emphasize
the tragic present, the here-and-now of the march, which is made to sound more
threatening by off-beat accents (meas. 2-6) and by the liberal use of muted brass
(the first time at meas. 19). However, the first movement ends in A major.

The last movement is another gigantic march. It consists basically of three different sets of march rhythms: the main march, equivalent to the exposition (beginning at meas. 114), a very slow march that leads into the exposition (beginning at meas. 16) and concludes the symphony, and an *alla breve* march that introduces the movement and recurs frequently at a more rapid pace (for example at meas. 191). Apart from the frequent tempo shifts, the marches in this movement, as in the first movement, are more regular by comparison with other marches by Mahler. Noticeable in this movement is the oscillation between major and minor, as if the composer was reluctant to let the work end in the minor key, but this ending is far more convincing than the major-key endings of the Second and Seventh Symphonies. Apart from Mendelssohn's *Italian* Symphony, Brahms's Fourth and Tchaikovsky's *Pathétique*, it is hard to think of a symphony before Mahler that ends in the minor. The weight of tradition is also apparent in the conflict between the demands of sonata form and the volatile substance of Mahler's music — a conflict that works against the music in this overly long, repetitious movement. The high significance attributed to this movement by Adorno and Ratz may have more to do with its place in the overall structure and meaning of this symphony — it dooms the symphonic protagonist — than with its intrinsic musical value.[23]

Special mention must be made of the unusually fierce passage at measures 385-403 with its catastrophe at measure 394. This bar has a breath-stopping rest on the first beat where one would expect the climactic chord, and sharply struck fortissimo chords on the three remaining beats. The following two bars proclaim the symphony's major-minor motif which is repeated five bars later, each time followed by loud strokes on the rod, as if the protagonist were being beaten after being struck down. This passage sounds more like the crisis of the movement and of the symphony's protagonist than the famous two hammer blows (at meas. 336 and 479), which sound rather mechanical by comparison. If there is a fatal encounter with destiny it is decided in this passage. The march in this symphony is a battleground between the protagonist and superior forces, and beyond this represents the struggle of man against an insuperable fate.

Of the Seventh Symphony's five movements, three are marches. The first movement begins, like the finale of the Sixth, with several slower marches that introduce the thematic material of the movement. Though this martial music abounds in unorthodoxies — caesuras (meas. 26 and 31),[24] extra measures (meas. 26 and 35), frequent tempo changes, the doubtful tonality (the symphony begins in B minor, the exposition is in E minor and the work ends in C major), the frequent lack of a first beat in the main theme, the general trend to offbeat accentuation and the shift to triple meter at measure 495 — it has strongly processional figures in the introduction, uses a large drum and tambourine and frequent brass flourishes, and has the character of a large-scale accelerated cortege. Occasionally the march relaxes for a glimpse of a better world, only to resume inexorably and even more darkly. Again the lyrical section, more opulent than usual in Mahler (meas. 118-134), seems at a far remove and sets off the somber tone of the main music as the present reality. The conclusion in E major does not sound convincing.

It was Mahler who established the tragic march as a separate genre. His dark processions have forever altered our perception of military music. They command our attention for their prophetic character and their outsider's view of the march. Not only are these marches a needed correction of musical convention, but they lay bare the soul of the stranger as it had not been revealed before.

(c) Slow Marches

Another innovation by Mahler is the placement of a slow movement at the beginning of a symphony. Tchaikovsky ended the *Pathétique* Symphony with a slow movement but did not begin a symphony with one. Bruckner's majestic opening movements move in this direction, but they are not actually slow movements. Mahler introduced his Fifth, Ninth and Tenth Symphonies with a slow movement and closed the latter two works similarly, thereby bracketing rapid movements with reflective or recessional ones and shifting the emphasis from worldly activity to otherworldly concerns.

The opening movement of the Ninth Symphony is a slow processional. Typically it begins with several unorthodoxies: the dotted rhythm and offbeat accentuation in the first two bars and the syncopation in one of the main themes played by a stopped horn (meas. 4-5). In the third bar the harp announces another principal melodic-rhythmic motif, a strongly accented quasi-martial four-note theme but with a rest after the first two notes. This somewhat offbeat motif becomes the main tread of the funeral procession that takes possession of the music twice (at meas. 111ff. and meas. 317ff.), the second time so powerfully that the music soon collapses, dying away in a retrospective coda in which only fragments of the movement's themes remain. This brief cortege is perhaps the most searing march Mahler ever wrote. This too, then, is a *symphonie funèbre* in which death takes precedence over the life that is the substance of the remaining movements.

Similar conclusions could be drawn from the first movement of the Tenth Symphony. It, too, has a measured processional pulse and erupts in its latter pages in an existential outcry (meas. 194) that culminates in two dissonant chords, each followed by a sustained, piercingly high trumpet call (meas. 206-213) before being resolved into the serene F sharp major key of the main theme. This outcry is heard again in the final movement where it is followed by a long, heartfelt lyrical coda that closes the work peacefully. In this symphony death intrudes with a heavy, muffled but powerful stroke on a very large military drum at the end of the fourth movement and the beginning of the fifth movement. We know from Alma Mahler that these drum strokes are Mahler's memorialization of a fireman's cortege which the Mahlers watched from their New York hotel room and which moved the composer deeply.[25] It is a typically magnified treatment of martial music, transforming a fireman's funeral into a cosmic tragedy. In all these examples the march constitutes a transcendent statement about life and death.[26]

(d) Ironic Marches

Mahler's most original marches, in my view, are the ironic ones. Though there is irony in almost every march he wrote, two marches are permeated with it: the Frère Jacques march in the First Symphony, already discussed in the preceding chapter (see pp. 67-70), and the second movement of the Seventh Symphony. This movement, entitled "Nachtmusik" ("Night Music"), is one of Mahler's most sophisticated pieces, written with great delicacy and mastery of musical characterization. (It could be called 'marche caractéristique,' in succession to Schubert.) The opening horn call at once establishes the martial character of the music, which is undercut by the ambiguous tonality of the piece — it hovers throughout between C major and C minor —, by the typical addition of an extra beat just before the main theme (meas. 29), and by the canonic treatment of this theme which introduces a second voice before the first voice has finished its statement. Further distractions from the march are the frequent accents on the fourth rather than the first beat[27] and a profusion of counter-voices in the woodwinds resembling birdcalls, which dominate the coda almost completely and dissolve the march. The movement ends quietly on one note, the dominant, in the cellos and harp. It is in all respects an anti-march.

The rather macabre mood is briefly relieved by an A flat major interlude (beginning at measure 83) which sounds like a rustic counter-procession. But whereas the interlude in Frère Jacques, also in the major key, is straightforwardly nostalgic, this interlude continues the ironic vein by introducing quick, irregularly spaced oompah chords without a downbeat in the horns (meas. 83-86, 88, 90) and giving prominent and countermelodic parts to high woodwinds (meas. 102-105, 109-114). In the repetition of this interlude (beginning at measure 262), the oompah chords are played pizzicato by the violas and reinforced by more military-sounding oompahs in the horns, and the countermelodies in the woodwinds are more prominent, which makes the ironic effect even stronger. For a march the piece is too multi-voiced, not only with its different musical lines but also with respect to tone. The mood keeps shifting between the pastoral, military, grotesque, folkish, nocturnal, sinister and macabre. There is even a Jewish-sounding melody (beginning at measure 190), followed by a hurdy-gurdy effect that adds another ironic layer to this multi-textured music. The last part combines the processional and pastoral moods, as in a recessional that gradually fades away into the distance. It is as if a procession of ghosts or skeletons has come and gone, disturbing a pastoral scene with its apparition — a sinister interlude in the human comedy.

So great was Mahler's preoccupation with the march that of all the symphony movements written in duple meter, only the fourth movement of the Third Symphony, a setting of Nietzsche's poem "O Mensch! Gib acht!" ("Oh man, take heed!"), and perhaps the third movement of this symphony, a polka, lack a martial or processional element. That marches frequently appear in his songs is less surprising, for songs generally favor simple, regular meter and are based on texts that often deal with soldiers. But even Mahler's songs show a striking affinity for marches. Of his thirty-three published individual songs, fifteen are written in march rhythm and four more are in a related duple meter. Of his twenty-four settings of poems from *Des Knaben Wunderhorn (The Youth's Magic Horn)*, a collection of German folk poetry he loved, twelve are military songs; of these twelve, seven are tragic songs about soldiers and are among his greatest songs.[28] Like the symphonic marches, the military songs show Mahler's dark view of the march. Their rhythmic, harmonic and instrumental subtleties, their ironic touches, their expressionistic heightening of the texts and their apocalyptic tone make these marches both unheroic and larger-than-life.[29]

Mahler's highly characteristic marches combine deep affection for march music with a sharply personal point of view. A comparison of his marches with those of other composers with an original view of the march — as in Nielsen's Fifth Symphony, Janáček's Sinfonietta and Bartók's Sixth String Quartet, all written after World War I — shows that their music is not influ-

enced by German romanticism; in Mahler's marches this influence is strong
but defamiliarized by his outsider's perspective. And since he composed no
occasional or incidental music, his marches are all full-fledged, large-scale
creative efforts. Composed shortly before World War I, they are metaphors,
perhaps for a dying era and beyond that for man's journey through life, death
and eternity.[30]

2. Dances

Similar comments apply to Mahler's treatment of dances. With the
exception of the polka in the scherzo of the Third Symphony, they are the
ländler and the waltz. Both are traditional Austrian dances in 3/4 time, the
ländler being slower and more robust than the waltz. Mahler reverses this
situation, making the ländler in most cases a brisk dance expressive of the
active life and the waltz a slow, nostalgic, reminiscent dance evoking the long-
ago. The ländler turns up in many minuet movements of Haydn (as in the
Symphonies No. 88 and No. 96) and Mozart (as in the Symphonies No. 36 and
No. 39) and in piano compositions of Schubert (as in the Piano Sonata in G
major, D. 894). The scherzos in Bruckner's symphonies, though too rapid for a
ländler, retain the heavy, rustic, outdoor quality of this dance. Mahler's
ländlers differ from the previous examples, first of all, in being longer and
musically more complex. They move through remote tonal regions uncharted
in earlier ländler movements, which are musically conservative in keeping with
the character and connotations of this dance; they leave far behind even
Bruckner's Ninth Symphony scherzo, harmonically the most advanced music
of this kind before Mahler. Already in the scherzo of Mahler's First Symphony,
a typical ländler, there are brass flourishes that crash through the tonal barrier
and open up the harmony, thereby unhinging the music from its A major anchor
and thus from its rustic roots.

With the exception of the Second and Third Symphonies where retrospective ländlers occur in intermezzo movements between massive martial
first movements and large-scale scherzos, the ländler movement is the scherzo
in Mahler's symphonies. In the overall design of his symphonies it is the dance
of life, expressing the tumult and confusion of earthly existence — a function
transcending by far the traditional view of the ländler. Though each scherzo
by Mahler has its own noteworthy features — the bitter-sweet Schubertian
trio in the First Symphony, the specially tuned first violin solo in the Fourth,
the agogic trio of "olden times" ("altväterisch") in the Sixth, the parody of the
waltz in the Seventh — his most wide-ranging scherzos are those of the Fifth

and Ninth Symphonies. They are Mahler's most apocalyptic ländlers. Starting with only a few instruments they grow to enormous proportions. In the Fifth Symphony the scherzo is the centerpiece of the entire symphony, being Part II of a tripartite symphonic design. Notable here, as in the scherzo of the Ninth, is the use of three different time scales, perhaps to represent past, present and future. The movement is a gigantic dance of life, panoramic in conception and operating on multiple levels of consciousness. This scherzo, which has 819 bars and lasts approximately seventeen minutes — longer than any of the other movements —, begins in a moderate tempo but slows down at measure 136 to a reminiscent waltz which is suddenly cut off without transition by the original ländler (meas. 174); this dance turns "wild" (meas. 201) and undergoes a startling key change at measure 218 that heightens the music's temperature and leads to the scherzo's first climax. After numerous echoing flourishes and waltz fragments — musical remnants of the crisis — a spectral pizzicato waltz ensues, that gradually becomes more luminous and in an increasingly wild transition leads back to the first ländler. This time it sounds richer, and the mood is more hectic. At measure 574, the direction "press forward" *(drängend)* catapults the music into a wild melee that continues with two brief let-ups to the movement's climax (at meas. 696), where the ländler bursts all bonds and bounds — harmonic, rhythmic, metric and emotional — and reaches for the cosmos (especially at meas. 704). It takes a long while and many fragments in far-off keys — "horns echoing and re-echoing as if across mountain distances"[31] — to subside, but as soon as it does, a fast and wild coda picks it up again and hurls it to a tumultuous conclusion.

It is Mahler's largest scherzo and probably the largest ever written. It elevates the scherzo to a human comedy and transforms an Alpine peasant dance into an epic round and at times a *danse macabre*. The harmonic freedom, flexibility of tempo, instrumental sophistication and extreme emotional range free Mahler's ländler from all traces of rusticity or regionalism and make it a metaphor for the fullness of life. It is a monumentalized ländler, capturing the essence of ländler-hood, which means that it is far removed from the original dance. Unlike Schubert and Bruckner, Mahler could never have danced a ländler.

His ländlers are sublimations of the real thing, but also a comment on it by a keen observer who could not accept its rusticity at face value. Mahler's ländlers symbolize a culture in crisis, as an outsider might perceive it with special sensitivity.

The scherzo of the Ninth Symphony is entitled "At the pace of a leisurely ländler" but has three distinct tempos: the basic ländler (Tempo I — "Somewhat clumsy and very robust"), a faster, brusquer section (Tempo II — Poco più mosso subito) and a slow, wistfully romantic dance (Tempo III — "Ländler, quite slow") which Adorno calls a "a quasi trans-Austrian, supratemporal ländler theme."[32] Thus the movement is built on multiple levels of time and space, long before the age of stereophony. (The tempo changes, combined with the dimension of the piece, make it very difficult to conduct, the problem being how to find one's way back to Tempo I.) The temporal dispositions make this ländler timeless: looking backward and forward, sometimes without transition, this dance, too, becomes an encompassing metaphor for the earthly life. Scherzos usually represent reality, the here-and-now, the texture of life, in contrast with the more philosophical or ideological movements of the symphony; in Mahler, by reason of their large time scale and synchronicity, the scherzos expand this reality to an all-embracing existential drama, in which the different tempos and tonalities indicate different phases of life.

By comparison with the ländler in the Fifth Symphony, this one is less vital and more resigned. It opens quietly and more like a ländler, with the main theme marked "heavy" and the second violins carrying the tune marked "like country fiddles," but the sophisticated treatment is evident in the stress on the second beat, in the trills and grace notes, in the countermelody in bassoons and violas, and in the bold, hard-to-play horn flourishes. This movement is, in fact, the most subtle, moving and insinuating scherzo that Mahler wrote. Though it, too, has its parody of village band music (meas. 147-208, 423-486), which speeds up and vulgarizes the music of Tempo II, it is not mainly grim or ironic. It is melancholy, retrospective, sorrowful music.[33] The climax which abruptly ends the parodistic band music (meas. 515-522) is not shattering as in the previous scherzos, but leads back to the original ländler, now diminished and bereft-sounding. The shift from C major to C minor at measure 576 and especially at measure 578 with its muted low brass is more shattering than any eruption could be, for it presages the end of the ländler. The remaining bars bring the dance hesitantly to its end, as a few instruments play disembodied fragments of the original ländler. After this no more ländlers are possible, a conclusion that is not invalidated by the two scherzos in the Tenth Symphony.[34]

In the scherzos of the Fifth and Ninth Symphonies Mahler has written the apotheosis of the ländler while simultaneously presiding over its end. A comparison with Ravel's *La Valse*, intended as an epitaph for the Viennese waltz and originally entitled "Vienna,"[35] shows important differences between the two composers and between impressionism and expressionism as well. In contrast to Mahler, Ravel was not Austrian and he wrote the piece after World War I with the benefit of hindsight. Moreover, Ravel wrote a virtuosic "choreographic poem," a genre work in a lush, bravura style, whereas Mahler wrote a multi-layered symphonic movement in a more differentiated orchestral idiom and, being more deeply involved, dug deeper. His apocalyptic dances are echoed in the grim ländler fragments of Alban Berg's "Reigen" (Rounds) from his Three Pieces for Orchestra (opus 6), in his opera *Wozzeck* and in the far-off, infinitely poignant Carinthian ländler in his Violin Concerto. Deeply indebted to Mahler are Shostakovich's scherzos, but these are not ländlers and they have a strongly national tone that is absent in Mahler.

Like his unmartial marches, Mahler's dances show his alienation from the folk spirit. His deep affection for the ländler and the waltz is evident, but he always stylizes them into large-scale, indeed cataclysmic statements about a dying civilization which he loved but to which he could never quite belong. Leaving all traces of folklore far behind, these dances are the expression of a remarkably agitated and unassimilated imagination.

3. Folksongs

In 1885, when Mahler was conducting at the opera in Kassel, he wrote orchestral arrangements or incidental music for an extended poem entitled "Das Volkslied" ("The Folksong") by Salomon von Mosenthal.[36] The work was performed in Kassel on 20 April and 29 May 1885.[37] Though Mahler's music for this work has not survived, his participation in this project is of some interest. Mosenthal's poem, in eight tableaus framed by a prologue and an epilogue, is — typically for a Central European Jewish writer — not a national work, as the title might suggest, but a tribute to music and song as an international art expressive of the spirit of many different peoples. The first tableau depicts the grieving Jews after their dispersion; this is followed by scenes in medieval France, late medieval Germany, Naples, Austria, nineteenth-century Germany, the Rhine and the Alps, each with a representative folksong. There follows a tribute to other nations' folksongs, and the work concludes with a paean to folksongs: "May the folksongs of all peoples soar heavenward/Borne by the tongues of all children." The concluding scene shows "The Folksong" as it is borne upward by the children of all nations.[38]

Even with the preponderance of German tableaus, this work was made considerably more Germanic for the Kassel performances — the Jewish song, which must have been too much for the producer, was replaced with a German song, and the work strikes a more patriotic note in its revised form[39] — but at least a semblance of internationalism remains. This non-national or supra-national attitude, so uncharacteristic of folksongs, which tend to promote the opposite, typifies Mahler's outlook. Though he often chose what seem to be folkloristic texts, most of them turn out to be quite sophisticated or at least existential rather than regional, or he changed them in that direction. When he did set less sophisticated texts, such as "Rheinlegendchen" ("Rhine Legend") or "Verlor'ne Müh" ("Wasted Effort") (in dialect) or "Wer hat dies Liedlein erdacht?" ("Who thought up this little song?"), the resulting songs are among his weaker ones. Almost invariably he turned quasi-folksongs into personal or human dramas by eliminating the folk element.

    An example is the early song-cycle *Lieder eines fahrenden Gesellen (Songs of a Wayfarer)* (1884). The title was used a few years earlier (1878) by a minor German poet, Rudolf Baumbach, to name a collection of his poems that quickly became a best-seller.[40] So popular was this book that two years later the author wrote a sequel, *Neue Lieder eines fahrenden Gesellen*. By 1907, 51,000 copies of Baumbach's *Lieder eines fahrenden Gesellen* were in print — an astonishingly large number for a volume of poems. Many of these poems are drinking songs; as the opening poem makes clear, the author is writing about a happy-go-lucky travelling student or apprentice mainly interested in wine, women and song.[41] A greater contrast with Mahler's own texts for his song-cycle is hard to imagine: whereas Baumbach's poems resemble fraternity songs and are, moreover, tinged with nationalism and anti-Catholicism, Mahler's lyrics, though stylistically derivative and in one case almost directly borrowed,[42] express a deep personal involvement. They tell of the wanderer's jilted love, his search for forgetfulness in nature and his thoughts of sleep and death as escape from his sorrow. (The two parts of the final song end like a funeral march.) A mere reading of the words shows an expressive power and depth that are simply beyond Baumbach's reach.[43] The third song in particular has an emotional intensity, in words and music, that goes beyond what is usually found in folk music. The first stanza reads:

Ich hab' ein glühend Messer,	I have a fiery knife
ein Messer in meiner Brust,	a knife in my breast,
o weh! O weh!	o woe! O woe!
Das schneid't so tief	That cuts so deep
in jede Freud' und jede Lust,	into all joy and all desire,
so tief! So tief!	so deep! So deep!
Es schneid't so weh und tief!	It cuts so sharp and deep!

    The idiom may be folkloristic — the words are simple, short and direct, the thoughts uncomplicated, the form balladesque — but the emotions and especially the stormy music with its eruptive climax[44] followed by the music's disintegration are characteristically and penetratingly individual. Mahler was only twenty-four when he wrote the cycle, which was inspired by a personal experience; as he grew older, the texts he chose were less subjective, and the music, while always retaining his sharply personal stamp, tended away from the folkloristic toward what is universally human.

A striking example is the posthorn episode in the third movement of the Third Symphony. It is an extended melody for a small brass instrument (usually played by a trumpet player), which is repeated twice in a slightly different form and brings the movement and the symphony practically to a halt. Remarkable about this music is its exposed character — the posthorn melody is accompanied by few other instruments and is not connected thematically with any other music in this symphony. Functioning as the trio of the Scherzo, it has the character of some of Schubert's and Bruckner's trios, which are much more relaxed, more songful and more reflective than their bustling scherzos. (Examples occur in Schubert's A minor piano sonata D. 845 and in Bruckner's Seventh Symphony.) But this trio has in addition a significant feature: its melody suggests six different German folksongs and one Spanish dance.[45] That is to say, the posthorn melody contains, in its course, phrases or turns that recall some phrases in these folksongs. Furthermore, the posthorn melody shows a marked resemblance to a section in Liszt's piano piece *Rhapsodie Espagnole* and to Glinka's orchestral rhapsody *Jota Aragonesa*, both of which use the same Spanish dance tune. It turns out that Mahler conducted Liszt's piece in Busoni's arrangement for piano and orchestra on 22 October 1894 in Hamburg, with Busoni as soloist.[46] When Busoni later wondered how this melody found its way into Mahler's symphony, he must have forgotten that he and Mahler had performed the Liszt piece together.[47]

The fact that this performance took place leaves no doubt whatever that Mahler is alluding to the Liszt piece or improvising on it or free-associating to it. The date of the performance means that Mahler heard the Liszt piece only about eight or nine months before he composed the scherzo of the Third Symphony;[48] it must have taken hold of him in some way, just as "Frère Jacques" and "Funiculì, funiculà" did.[49] But whereas Richard Strauss quotes "Funiculì" literally in his tone poem *Aus Italien (From Italy)* and uses it realistically to represent an Italian scene, Mahler transmutes Liszt's Spanish theme into a haunting chant, a kind of valedictory to folk music. Not a trace of Spanish flavor remains in this music, which has become an emblematic song from a lost romantic realm. The tempo is considerably slower than in Liszt and Glinka; the pace is "free" (p. 154)[50] with many changes and shifts; the rhythm is broken by numerous tied notes and distentions, particularly in the reprise; the harmony shows chromaticism in the accompanying violins (p. 155 top and p. 173) and a sudden shift to the minor key (p. 155); the orchestration has a delicate accompaniment of muted violins and a counterpointed horn chant, a combination of clarinets, triangle, two harps and violas in the brief interlude passage (p. 155), and divided violins are played close to the bridge with harp support as the strings take over the posthorn melody (p. 173). Exact repetitions are avoided. Moreover, the posthorn is intoned very softly "as from a great distance" and finally fades away (see p. 158 and p. 174). It is thus set off from the symphonic context, both by being at a distance (off stage) and by being introduced by a trumpet signal that announces an entirely new music. Finally, the posthorn itself is not a traditional orchestral instrument, but was used "initially only as a signal instrument for the arrival and departure of mail coaches . . . and later as an actual musical instrument to consciously promote folksongs."[51]

As a folksong instrument the posthorn plays a melody that is reminiscent of a folk tune but does not quote a particular one. Tibbe suggests that it is neither Mahler's song nor anyone else's, yet it sounds familiar.[52] By alluding to six different folksongs without settling on one specific song, the melody is representative of the folksong idiom, the "folksong as such"[53] — 'folksong' as an idea rather than an individual example — universal and abstract rather than particular and specific. In its extreme nostalgia and sophistication, this melody is the creation of a composer who knew and loved folk music but would never have sung a folksong himself. It is not folk music but a distillation of it. And recalling as it does a Spanish jota and in its subsidiary phrase a Bohemian hulán,[54] this episode is a richly allusive, multi-layered passage that brings together Spanish, Czech and German folk music in such a way that the national elements are completely eliminated. And by placing this episode in the midst of a gigantic symphonic cosmos, Mahler completes the process of monumentalizing and memorializing folk music.

Mahler's various and sometimes conflicting explanations of this scherzo point to a contrast between nature and man, between the animal world and the world of the spirit, with the posthorn music evoking the latter realm.[55] Undoubtedly there are two musical realms here: worldly and otherworldly, realistic and idealistic, present and past, ironic and transfigured. And undoubtedly there is an intrusion of something spiritual into the real world. Perhaps the outburst at the end of the episode is the clash between the irreal and the real that must occur when a dream comes to an end and the reality principle returns with full force. The extraordinary major-minor ending of the scherzo with its offbeat C minor brass chords flings the listener back into the tumult of life.

But a specific interpretation seems inadequate to this music. Just as Mahler magnifies a folksong, a ländler or a march into a universal statement, so he takes this scherzo beyond its traditional scope into a multi-dimensional music, thereby transcending his own title ("What the animals in the forest tell me") and the song "Ablösung im Sommer" ("Replacement in Summer") on which the movement is based. On this heightened level the posthorn interlude sounds like a memory of a better world, a world of innocence, perhaps of lost childhood, a lost paradise. Since it contains so many different folk music allusions, this music evokes a memory recollected in tranquility, a folksong world of simplicity and harmony that Mahler could never be a part of, a golden age that is gone forever if it ever existed. This music offers a glimpse of beauty and serenity in a scherzo that represents the bustling present, the here-and-now, life as it is lived on earth. Even a parody of rustic merry-making is included (meas. 432-454). But what strikes me as most significant is that Mahler strips this music of its regional connotations and raises it to a music of the spheres. The posthorn episode is one of Mahler's most inspired moments.

He used a similar approach in his songs by deepening many of the texts he set. He did this by omitting mundane lines or positive endings or simply by rewriting them to that end. In the early song, "Ich ging mit Lust durch einen grünen Wald ("I walked joyfully through a green wood"), Mahler omitted the last two stanzas of the original poem, entitled "Waldvögelein" ("Forest Bird"), which tell explicitly that the girl's lover had, after a drinking bout, been unfaithful to her and nearly forgotten her.[56] Mahler replaced these lines with one stanza of his own which tells of the lovers' union but warns the girl of her lover's infidelity without going into specifics. This change makes the song more sophisticated, emotionally more complex, more ambivalent, more artful.

In "Zu Strassburg auf der Schanz" ("On Strassburg's Ramparts") Mahler omitted the last two stanzas, the first of which contains the deserter's plea that he be shot at once "so that my blood spurts out," while the last stanza contains his prayer to God to keep his soul.[57] The omissions eliminate the physical aspects of the execution and the faith in a caring God, thus making the song both less naturalistic and more tragic. The music hauntingly intensifies this mood.

In "Wer hat dies Liedlein erdacht?" ("Who thought up this little song?") about an attractive young country girl, the second stanza makes wealth, abstemiousness and thrift the conditions for a suitor. Mahler eliminated this stanza and substituted a longer one which speaks poetically about the girl's beauty and her ability to heal the sick and revive the dead.[58] Whether these lines are his own or are borrowed from another poem, they change the rather simple-minded text to a more lyrical, richer poem that is also less naive. Again the music matches this shift in content by moving into far-off tonalities and richer sonorities (meas. 46-47) that belie the folksong origin of the text. The result is a song that is too sophisticated for its text, as often happens when Mahler sets a light-hearted poem. Besides, the textual change makes the last stanza — that three geese brought the song with them — too lightweight by comparison.

The most far-reaching changes occur in "Wo die schönen Trompeten blasen" ("Where the shining trumpets blow"), one of Mahler's finest songs. Mahler's text is based on two separate poems from *Des Knaben Wunderhorn*, "Bildchen" ("Little Portrait") and "Unbeschreibliche Freude" ("Indescribable Joy"), which share a number of lines.[59] In "Bildchen" a girl is pining away for her beloved when she hears him knock at her door. She doesn't want to admit him until after her parents have gone to bed, but he insists. She lets him in and weeps, but he promises to marry her within a year. First he has to go to war on green meadows; "where the shining trumpets blow there is my home of green meadow." He'll have a picture painted of her which he'll carry with him so that he won't forget her. — This poem could take place in the girl's imagination; Deryck Cooke interprets it as an account of a visit by the dead soldier's ghost,[60] but I take it to be the girl's fantasy or dream in which the soldier's death is foreshadowed.

"Unbeschreibliche Freude" deals with the same basic situation but does not end tragically. After promising to marry the girl, the boy who is not a soldier adds that their love is so great that even if all the fields were made of paper and all the students were writing on it, they still would not be able to describe it. Not surprisingly, Mahler omitted the last stanza about the fields of paper and he also omitted the stanza in "Bildchen" in which the girl refuses to admit the boy until her parents have gone to sleep. He purified the poems of all dross and telescoped them into a tragic ballad. Emphasizing the tragic element, he eliminated the final stanza of "Bildchen" about the girl's picture and ended his version with the two lines that foretell the soldier's death: "Where the shining trumpets blow, there is my home, my home of green grass." ("Allwo dort die schönen Trompeten blasen, da ist mein Haus, mein Haus von grünem Rasen.") The music ends quietly and starkly, the trumpets playing in the minor key as a sign that these are not military flourishes but taps. As elsewhere, his change in title shows his tendency to universalize what is specific and to make it tragic.[61]

Mahler's music for these songs is invariably highly sophisticated, which produces a somewhat uneasy mixture of popular texts, often themselves quite sophisticated, and ultra-refined, knowing music, particularly in the orchestral songs. (An example is "Der Schildwache Nachtlied" ["The Sentinel's Night Song"] with its unresolved ending.) Similarities between numerous songs by Mahler and corresponding folk tunes to these texts show that Mahler was familiar with many folksongs and that he changed them drastically in each case from simple folk tunes to harmonically, technically, rhythmically, musically subtle songs.[62] The orchestral settings — rare for songs — increase the disparity between folk music and art music.

Folk music, whether it be songs, dances or marches, lends itself to being stylized. That is to say, its directness or familiarity invites composers to change it in such a way as to conform to a particular conception or style. Stylization usually involves the imposition of an artistic design on material that is spontaneous or unreflected; often this is done by exaggerating its inherent features and omitting details. For example, in his first two Rasumovsky quartets Beethoven introduces Russian folksongs and fits them into the formal structure and distilled musical context of a string quartet; in the last movement of his Fourth Symphony Tchaikovsky incorporates a different Russian folksong into his symphonic design. The effect is fourfold: 1. it gives folk music a place in art music; 2. it gives the listener a new perspective on folk music; 3. it defines the composer's relationship to folk music; 4. it makes a comment on folk music. In the Tchaikovsky example, the inflation of a simple folk tune to a stentorian pronouncement in the brass or a yearning plaint in the strings makes a telling statement about the composer's love of and alienation from folk music. Since this song is part of the carnival music, its interruption by the fate motif creates a split between the composer and the folk. This ambivalent attitude developed in the nineteenth century, as the artist became more and more sophisticated and socially more disaffiliated. In Mahler's case this disaffiliation combined with his modernism to produce a particularly extreme example of personal and artistic alienation. No other composer comes to mind in whom the conflict between folk music and art music is more intense.

Mahler did not make arrangements of folksongs, as Beethoven, Brahms, Vaughan Williams and Britten have done, nor did he compose in the spirit of folk music or use its inflections, as Janáček and Bartók did, nor did he write folksong symphonies, as Roy Harris did. As a recent critic points out, folk music served Mahler as a constituent element in musical structure and form.[63] The waltz, ländler, march, folksong absorb, or serve to shape, a large form; as they lose their folkloristic origin they become compositional types. But the fact of this origin makes his music more vivid even as the folk element becomes abstracted.[64] It is this abstraction or distance that defines Mahler's relation to the folk idiom: he stands aside or apart, seeing folk music wistfully as an affectionate bystander or abstractly as an expressionistic artist — in either case being barred by his personal and social situation from participating in it. It is this perspective that gives his music its extraordinarily haunting quality; it is the music of an exile, an extraterritorial.

4. Expressionism

Mahler's defamiliarization of folk music, his spiritualization of marches, dances and folksongs, shows an affinity with the tendency to abstraction found in expressionism. He shares with the expressionists a need to universalize what is inherently specific or regional. Edvard Munch's famous picture "The Cry" shows a human figure breaking out into a primal scream that fills the entire picture. Not only the figure — unidentified as to sex or age — but the seacoast and blood-red sky are drawn into this scream by Munch's strongly emotional style. This picture shows not a specific fear, but an existential anxiety that is heightened by the unconcern of two passersby. The titles of Munch's paintings — The Cry, The Kiss, The Dance of Life — point up the emphasis on what is representative rather than on what is individual. A similar tendency is the practice of not giving personal names to characters in expressionist plays, but of identifying them merely by such titles as The Man or The Woman, The Son or The Daughter. This emphasizes what is human at the expense of what is personal or national.

The denationalization of marches, dances and folksongs is carried to an extreme by Schoenberg, Berg and Webern. Their development of atonality eliminates all differences between the notes of the scale, thereby abolishing the basis for all national music. Generic forms of music are subjected to a disintegrating process that barely leaves their basic rhythm intact. The March in Berg's Three Pieces for Orchestra (opus 6) is a cataclysmic work which sounds the death knell of the march as we know it. Typically entitled 'March,' it avoids any references to specific events, even though it was completed on 23 August 1914, just after the outbreak of World War I. Clearly descended from Mahler's Sixth Symphony from which it quotes, it shares his apocalyptic mood and his practice of "investing forms with spiritual significance."[65] An analogous example is Webern's treatment of the passacaglia in his opus 1. As in Mahler, this defamiliarization is coupled with a deep affection for these musical forms.

The approach to folksongs in expressionist music also follows Mahler's example. In the second movement of Schoenberg's Second String Quartet, he introduces the popular song "O du lieber Augustin, alles ist hin." Suddenly appearing amid much tortured romanticism and embroidered with a countermelodic canon, this ditty makes a much more startling effect than the folksongs in Mahler's symphonies because of the much greater disjunction between the song and the surrounding music. Schoenberg's statement that "all is gone" ("alles ist hin") is *not* ironical" but has "a real emotional significance"[66] — meaning perhaps that folksong romanticism is gone forever — and shows a correspondingly greater disparity between folk music and Schoenberg's marginality as a person and composer. His atonal variations on the popular German folksong "Ännchen von Tharau," in the third movement of the Suite opus 29, defamiliarize this song beyond all recognition. Presumably he liked this song, but his treatment of it is one of the most extreme distortions of folk music ever composed. So wide is the distance between folksong simplicity and musical complexity that the effect is grotesque rather than ironic. More vivid are similar passages in Berg's opera *Wozzeck* because the dramatic situation clarifies the musical intention. Most moving is the chorus of apprentices and soldiers in Act II who break into Wozzeck's agony with a harmonically and rhythmically distorted version of a romantic German hunting song.[67] The extreme dissociation between Wozzeck's music and the hunting chorus is an example of tragic irony, for Wozzeck, one of the world's hunted, is being taunted by the hunters. Musically, Berg goes beyond Mahler to suggest the end of all romantic hunting songs and fanfares ever written. The distortions of marches and dances in this opera strongly recall Mahler; the soldier Wozzeck reminds us of the tragic military figures in Mahler's songs. To say that the mood is anti-military is too obvious; a deep compassion for society's victims informs this music.[68]

The combination of several musics — the synchronicity of different musical levels — recalls Mahler's stereophonic experiments in *Das klagende Lied* and the Second and Third Symphonies as well as his practice of bringing together several different musical idioms simultaneously or without transition. Apart from the modernity of combining two or more disparate styles, this practice is closely related to the suspension of time, space and causality in expressionism. It is in this respect that Kafka, whose style is not expressionist, shows an affinity with this movement. His stories are not defined as to time and place, and his plots do not follow a logical progression. They require an imaginative leap between the multiplicity of precise detail and the dark background against which this detail is projected. Similarly, Mahler uses a vivid orchestration which is, like Kafka's writing, precise but surreal and serves an increasingly dark metaphysics. Mahler's symphonies are spiritual journeys, comparable to expressionist pilgrimage plays like Strindberg's *Till Damaskus (To Damascus)* and Kaiser's *Die Bürger von Calais (The Citizens of Calais)*, and to Kokoschka's cityscapes in which cities are projected into the cosmos.

Mahler shares with the expressionists a markedly anti-realist stance. They are subjective artists who do not seek to imitate reality but internalize their experience or spiritualize it by placing it in an abstract context. In the first movement of Mahler's First Symphony he directs the clarinets to "imitate the call of a cuckoo,"[69] but they play a fourth whereas a real cuckoo uses a third.

In true expressionist practice his nature sounds are not imitations but transformations of nature. Mahler's symphonies are landscapes of the soul.

A comparison with Richard Strauss makes this immediately clear. When Strauss uses cowbells in the *Alpine Symphony* he paints a realistic scene of cows grazing on a mountain meadow, whereas Mahler's cowbells in the Sixth and Seventh Symphonies, lacking such a context, are symbolic, transfigured sounds that are literally not of this world. Strauss' cowbells are specific and localized; Mahler's are disembodied and suspended in cosmic space. Whereas Strauss describes a day in the Alps, Mahler gives an expressionist synthesis of the Alpine spirit.

Since realism in literature and art is equivalent to a firm tonal basis in music, Mahler's gradual move to polytonality makes his music less realistic and more abstract. Put in another way, the disjunction between his vivid orchestration and his growing departures from tonality increase the tension between the palpable surface of the music and the spiritualization of the content. Mahler anticipated the disparity between the intense colors and the abstract vision of expressionist painters. The expressive intensity of his music and its unusual sound derive to a considerable degree from his scoring, which emphasizes the outermost range of the instruments. "If I want to produce a soft, subdued sound, I don't give it to an instrument which produces it easily, but rather to one which can get it only with effort and under pressure — often by forcing itself and exceeding its natural range. I often make the basses and bassoon squeak on the highest notes, while my flute huffs and puffs down below."[70] This extreme expressive range, which gives his music its unmistakable sound, is akin to the similarly heightened style of expressionist art, literature and music. Mahler also preceded the expressionists in combining disparate stylistic levels without any transition, as in the clash between the martial first theme and parodistic second theme in the last movement of the Seventh Symphony (meas. 51).

Mahler's visionary music anticipated the sharp division between inner and outer reality that is typical of expressionist art. Like Mahler, many expressionists were culturally marginal figures with the outsider's critical view of reality. Their exposed social position reveals itself in the lack of popular or regional accents in their work. As cosmopolitans without strong roots, they addressed humanity in a new language. The difference between Mahler and the expressionist composers, both of whom found a natural base in supranational Vienna, is that Mahler's voice is a solitary one, while the expressionists formed communities, issued pronouncements and even took part in social action. Though Mahler was too individualistic to have done this, he was artistically speaking an activist. Violating traditional standards of beauty, harmony, balance and restraint, he wrote music of such naked emotional force and arrestingly vivid sound that its expressive weight overburdens the traditional form and harmony he used. One might say that it is unassimilated music, in the sense that it is not in the mainstream and lacks any trace of virtuosity or showmanship. Breaking through all previous expressive limits, it has something extreme, larger-than-life, something "traumatic,"[71] which gives it its uniquely affective tone. Mahler's music is the lament of the homeless, of those who stand between nations and cultures.

NOTES FOR CHAPTER V: TRANSNATIONAL MUSIC

[1] Stefen Zweig, *Die Welt von gestern*. Erinnerungen eines Europäers (Stockholm: Bermann-Fischer Verlag, 1946), p. 41.

[2] Adolf D. Klarmann, "Grillparzer und die Moderne," *Die Neue Rundschau*, vol. 67 (1956), p. 137 and p. 145.

[3] An example is the poem "Wahrhaftig" in Heine's early collection *Buch der Lieder*.

[4] Constant Lambert, *Music Ho!* (London: Faber and Faber, 1937), pp. 113-114.

[5] The most apt regional identification of Mahler that I have found is "älplerisch" (in H. F. Redlich's essay on Mahler in *Die Musik in Geschichte und Gegenwart*, ed. Friedrich Blume [Kassel: Bärenreiter-Verlag], vol. 8 (1960), p. 1496). This word means 'quasi-Alpine' or 'in an Alpine manner or style,' which expresses very well Mahler's elusive mixture of unearthliness and a Central European accent.

[6] Even Brahms and Bruckner wrote some patriotic music: Brahms's *Triumphlied*, op. 55, written in 1870-71 to commemorate the Franco-Prussian War and dedicated to the newly proclaimed German Emperor, and Bruckner's *Helgoland* (1893).

[7] Alma Mahler, *Gustav Mahler: Memories and Letters*, ed. Donald Mitchell (Seattle: University of Washington Press, 1975), p. 92.

[8] A comparison between Liszt's *Faust* Symphony and Mahler's Eighth Symphony, the second part of which is also based on Goethe's *Faust*, shows that Liszt's first movement is an orchestral characterization of the protagonist Faust, whereas this Teutonic hero never appears in Mahler's symphony. Of interest in this connection is Mahler's reported statement that this work was dedicated "To the German Nation." (See Guido Adler, *Gustav Mahler* [Vienna-Leipzig: Universal-Edition, 1916], p. 92. — De La Grange states that "this symphony is a gift to the Nation"; see his liner notes for the recording of the Eighth Symphony on Epic Records SC-6004 by the Rotterdam Philharmonic Orchestra under Eduard Flipse.) Since no sources are given and no corroborating evidence is available, it may be that Mahler expressed this thought orally to Adler or some one else but then had second thoughts about it, for the symphony carries no such dedication. However, there is written evidence that Mahler intended to dedicate this symphony to his wife and even had the dedicatory page prepared. (See Alma Mahler, *Gustav Mahler: Memories and Letters*, ed. Donald Mitchell, pp. 178-179 and 334-335), yet the printed score does not contain this dedication either. Whether Mahler or Alma had a change of heart or whether the dedication was, after all, intended to be personal rather than official, is a matter of speculation. Certainly the two dedications are in conflict and may have been impulsive gestures of the moment, which on cold reflection proved unwise. To my knowledge, Mahler never dedicated any of his works. But with regard to the planned dedication "To the German Nation," there is deep irony in the contrast between this wholly uncharacteristic gesture and this totally unnational symphony.

[9] The references are to the orchestral score of "Waldmärchen" (Melville, N. Y.: Belwin-Mills Publishing Corporation, 1973).

[10] See the orchestral score of *Das klagende Lied* (Vienna: Universal Edition, 1978), vol. XII of the Critical Edition of Mahler's works as edited by the International Gustav Mahler Society in Vienna.

[11] Deryck Cooke, "Delius: A Centenary Evaluation," in *Vindications: Essays on Romantic Music* (Cambridge-New York: Cambridge University Press, 1982), pp. 117-118. A better word than 'race' would be 'country' or 'culture.'

1. Marches

[12] Henry-Louis de La Grange, *Mahler* I (Garden City, N. Y.: Doubleday, 1973), p. 18.

[13] *Riemann Musik-Lexikon: Sachteil*, 12th ed., ed. Hans Heinrich Eggebrecht (Mainz: B. Schott's Söhne, 1967), p. 546.

[14] All references are to the score of the Third Symphony in the Critical Edition of Mahler's works, edited by the International Gustav Mahler Society (Vienna: Universal Edition, 1974).

[15] See Theodor W. Adorno, *Mahler: Eine musikalische Physiognomik* (Frankfurt/Main: Suhrkamp Verlag, 1960), p. 109.

[16] Henry-Louis de La Grange, *Mahler* I, p. 375. — Mahler's untypically militaristic statement that "the victorious columns of troops that instantly overthrow the enemy rabble are just like the Prussian armies" is not borne out by the unmilitary sound of his music, which was ahead of his thought.

[17] Theodor W. Adorno, *Mahler*, pp. 180-181. Adding that Mahler was incapable of writing a happy end, Adorno argues persuasively that Mahler's only successful final movements are those that avoid a victorious ending.

[18] After hearing the Second Symphony many years after Mahler's death, Alma found his "constant telephoning with God" a bit trying. See Alma Mahler-Werfel, *Mein Leben* (Frankfurt/Main: S. Fischer Verlag, 1965), pp. 185-186.

[19] See p. 175 of the score of the Second Symphony in the Critical Edition of Mahler's works, edited by the International Gustav Mahler Society (Vienna: Universal Edition, 1970).

[20] Deryck Cooke, *Gustav Mahler: An Introduction to his Music* (Cambridge-New York: Cambridge University Press, 1980), p. 84.

[21] Alma Mahler, *Gustav Mahler: Memories and Letters,* ed. Donald Mitchell (Seattle: University of Washington Press, 1975), p. 70 and p. 100.

[22] All references are to the score of the Sixth Symphony in the Critical Edition of Mahler's works, edited by the International Gustav Mahler Society (Lindau: C. F. Kahnt, 1963).

[23] See Theodor W. Adorno, *Mahler*, pp. 131-136, and Erwin Ratz, "Zum Formproblem: Das Finale der VI. Symphonie," in *Gustav Mahler* (Tübingen: Rainer Wunderlich Verlag, 1966), pp. 90-122.

[24] All references are to the score of the Seventh Symphony in the Critical Edition of Mahler's works, edited by the International Gustav Mahler Society (Berlin-Wiesbaden: Bote und Bock, 1960).

[25] Alma Mahler, *Gustav Mahler: Memories and Letters,* ed. Donald Mitchell, p. 135.

[26] The final song in *Das Lied von der Erde*, "Der Abschied" ("The Farewell"), though it begins as a funeral march, closes in free rhythm in the major key, having gone beyond the end of a friendship or of life to reach a realm where there are no more marches.

[27] One explanation for Mahler's penchant for off-beat accents and syncopations may lie in his irregular gait. His daughter reports that he often "shifted gear," and Klemperer remembers that he "seemed not to be able to walk properly." The interview with Anna Mahler is included in Columbia Masterworks Set M3X-31437 which contains Mahler's Fourth and Fifth Symphonies, performed by Leonard Bernstein and the New York Philharmonic. Klemperer's statement appears in *Gustav Mahler* (Tübingen: Rainer Wunderlich Verlag, 1966), p. 61.

[28] They are "Zu Strassburg auf der Schanz," "Nicht Wiedersehen!," "Der Schildwache Nachtlied," "Lied des Verfolgten im Turm," "Wo die schönen Trompeten blasen," "Revelge" and "Der Tamboursg'sell."

[29] Referring to the disparity between text and music, a recent writer cites the march in the fourth song from *Das Lied von der Erde*: ". . . when the contralto soloist sings of maidens plucking lotus blossoms in the sunlight, a squadron of winds and percussion suddenly bursts on the scene in a furious cavalry quickstep, provoked by nothing more martial than a reference in the text to 'handsome lads on spirited horses.' But the musical effect is utterly electrifying." Frederic V. Grunfeld, *Prophets without Honor* (New York: McGraw-Hill, 1980), p. 44.

[30] A literary parallel to Mahler's interpretation of the march is Joseph Roth's novel *Radetzkymarsch* (1932), which uses Johann Strauss's well-known march as a backdrop for events that are tragic and grotesque. A famous imperial march becomes a metaphor for the declining empire. Roth, who came from Eastern Galicia — literally from the margins of the empire — had a similarly dark world view, but he was of course writing *after* World War I.

2. Dances

[31] Deryck Cooke, *Gustav Mahler: An Introduction to his Music*, p. 82. — The musical references are to the score of the Fifth Symphony in the Critical Edition of Mahler's works, edited by the International Gustav Mahler Society (Frankfurt/Main-London-New York: C. F. Peters, 1964).

[32] ". . . einem quasi überösterreichischen, zeitlupenhaften Ländlerthema. . . ." See Theodor W. Adorno, *Mahler*, p. 209. — The musical references are to the score of the Ninth Symphony in the Critical Edition of Mahler's works, edited by the International Gustav Mahler Society (Vienna: Universal Edition, 1969).

[33] I emphatically disagree with Cooke's judgment that this ländler is "divested of all charm, life and significance." See Deryck Cooke, *Gustav Mahler: An Introduction to his Music*, p. 117.

[34] Schnitzler's famous play *Reigen (La Ronde)* (1900) shows a similar disjunction between the innocence of the title and the enormity of the content. Despite the differences in medium, tone and style, Schnitzler also uses the title to suggest a dance into the abyss, as becomes clear in the final scene if not before.

[35] Arbie Orenstein, *Ravel: Man and Musician* (New York-London: Columbia University Press, 1975), p. 72.

3. Folksongs

[36] Mosenthal was a minor author, mainly of plays, who was born in Kassel and settled in Vienna. He was an assimilated Jew, best known for his play *Deborah* (1850), which deals with anti-Semitic prejudice in a small Austrian town, and for his librettos to Otto Nicolai's opera *The Merry Wives of Windsor* and Karl Goldmark's opera *The Queen of Sheba*. For more detailed information about Mosenthal, see Charlene A. Lea, *Emancipation, Assimilation and Stereotype: The Image of the Jew in German and Austrian Drama, 1800-1850* (Bonn: Bouvier, 1978), pp. 61-69.

[37] Henry-Louis de La Grange, *Mahler* I, p. 126.

[38] S. H. Mosenthal, "Das Volkslied." Ein Gedicht mit Liedern und Bildern. In: S. H. Mosenthal, *Gesammelte Werke* (Stuttgart-Leipzig: Eduard Hallberger, 1878), vol. 6, pp. 328-341.

[39] Henry-Louis de La Grange, *Mahler* I, p. 705.

[40] See Edward F. Kravitt, "The Trend towards the Folklike, Nationalism, and their Expression by Mahler and his Contemporaries in the Lied," *Chord and Discord*, vol. 2, no. 10 (1963), p. 53,

and Jens Malte Fischer, "Das klagende Lied von der Erde. Zu Gustav Mahlers Liedern und ihren Texten," *Zeitschrift für Literaturwissenschaft und Linguistik* 9 (1979), Heft 34, pp. 59-60.

[41] Rudolf Baumbach, *Lieder eines fahrenden Gesellen* (Stuttgart: Cotta, 1907).

[42] Compare the first poem of Mahler's cycle with the poem "Wenn mein Schatz Hochzeit macht" in the folksong collection *Des Knaben Wunderhorn*, collected by Achim von Arnim and Clemens Brentano, ed. Willi A. Koch (Munich: Winkler-Verlag, 1957), pp. 704-705.

[43] A similar comparison could be made between the literary quality of Joseph Victor von Scheffel's narrative poem *Der Trompeter von Säckingen* and the musical quality of what remains of Mahler's incidental music for it, namely the *Blumine* movement from the first version of his First Symphony. Of interest is Mahler's connection with this inferior and provincial literature and his characteristic elevation of it.

[44] See measure 68 in the score of *Lieder eines fahrenden Gesellen*, edited by the International Gustav Mahler Society (Vienna-Frankfurt/Main-London: Josef Weinberger, 1982).

[45] They are: Freut euch des Lebens
                 Es zogen drei Burschen wohl über den Rhein
                 Ich ging durch einen grasgrünen Wald
                 Wie lieblich schallt durch Busch und Wald
                 Man schafft so gern sich Sorg und Müh
                 Es kann mich nichts Schöneres erfreuen
                 Jota aragonesa

[46] Henry-Louis de La Grange, *Mahler* I, p. 315. Only Samuel Lipman mentions this fact, in his essay "The Mahler Everyone Loves," *Commentary*, vol. 64, no. 5 (November 1977), p. 59. Lipman questions Mahler's musical integrity because he used the Liszt theme, but the resulting music is so different that Mahler has created an entirely new piece. Besides, Liszt too had borrowed the theme.

[47] Ferruccio Busoni, "Wert der Bearbeitung," in Ferruccio Busoni, *Von der Einheit der Musik* (Berlin: Max Hesse, 1922), p. 152.

[48] The scherzo was written in June and July of 1895; see Henry-Louis de La Grange, *Mahler* I, p. 804.

[49] Ibid., p. 540.

[50] Page references are to the score of the Third Symphony, edited by the International Gustav Mahler Society (Vienna: Universal Edition, 1974).

[51] Curt Sachs, *Handbuch der Instrumentenkunde*, second ed. (Leipzig: Breitkopf und Härtel, 1930), p. 255; quoted by Hans Heinrich Eggebrecht, *Die Musik Gustav Mahlers* (Munich-Zurich: R. Piper Verlag, 1982), p. 182. — Karbusicky believes that since Mahler could only have traveled by mail coach between Prague and Iglau in 1871, the posthorn melody may be a reminiscence of what he heard on that trip. See Vladimir Karbusicky, *Gustav Mahler und seine Umwelt* (Darmstadt: Wissenschaftliche Buchgesellschaft, 1978), pp. 49-50.

[52] Monika Tibbe, *Über die Verwendung von Liedern und Liedelementen in instrumentalen Symphoniesätzen Gustav Mahlers* (Munich: Musikverlag Emil Katzbichler, 1971), p. 86.

[53] Hans Heinrich Eggebrecht, *Die Musik Gustav Mahlers*, p. 195.

[54] Vladimir Karbusicky, *Gustav Mahler und seine Umwelt*, pp. 45-49. — De La Grange mentions two other childhood reminiscences as possible sources; see Henry-Louis de La Grange, *Mahler* I, p. 371 and p. 897.

[55] Henry-Louis de La Grange, *Mahler* I, pp. 805-806.

[56] The complete text of the poem is in *Des Knaben Wunderhorn*, collected by Achim von Arnim and Clemens Brentano, ed. Willi A. Koch (Munich: Winkler-Verlag, 1957), p. 677. Mahler's setting

may be found in Gustav Mahler, *Lieder und Gesänge for High Voice* (Melville, N. Y.: Belwin-Mills Publishing Corporation, n.d.) (Kalmus Vocal Series No. 6840), pp. 20-23.

[57] The complete text of the poem is in *Des Knaben Wunderhorn*, pp. 98-99; Mahler's setting is in Gustav Mahler, *Lieder und Gesänge for High Voice*, pp. 30-33.

[58] The original text is in *Des Knaben Wunderhorn*, p. 144; Mahler's setting is in Gustav Mahler, *Des Knaben Wunderhorn*, vol. I (Vienna-London: Universal Edition, n.d.) (Philharmonia Score No. 219), pp. 63-73.

[59] Both poems are in *Des Knaben Wunderhorn*: "Bildchen" on pp. 676-677, "Unbeschreibliche Freude" on p. 696.

[60] Deryck Cooke, *Gustav Mahler: An Introduction to his Music*, pp. 42-43.

[61] Folksongs are often tragic, but it seems to me that by comparison with American folksongs German ones are more introverted and possibly more sentimental, both textually and musically. This has something to do with the fact that German has a wider emotional range than English and with the strongly romantic strain in German culture.

[62] Examples of such correspondences are between Mahler's song "Ich ging mit Lust durch einen grünen Wald" and "Der leichtfertige Liebhaber" in *Deutscher Liederhort*, collected and annotated by Ludwig Erk and Franz M. Böhme, reprint of Leipzig edition of 1893-1894 (Hildesheim: Georg Olms, and Wiesbaden: Breitkopf und Härtel, 1963), vol. II, p. 390; between Mahler's song "Zu Strassburg auf der Schanz" and "Der Schweizer" (Erk-Böhme, vol. III, pp. 261-262); between Mahler's song "Nicht Wiedersehen!" and "Herzlieb im Grabe" (Erk-Böhme, vol. I, pp. 606-607); between Mahler's song "Trost im Unglück" and "Husarenliebe" (Erk-Böhme, vol. III, pp. 281-282). See also Henry-Louis de La Grange, *Mahler* I, pp. 762-779.

[63] Mathias Hansen, "Zur Funktion von Volksmusikelementen in Kompositionen Gustav Mahlers," *Beiträge zur Musikwissenschaft*, vol. 23 (1981), no. 1, p. 33.

[64] Ibid.

4. Expressionism

[65] Charles Rosen, *Arnold Schoenberg* (New York: Viking Press, 1975), p. 14. The quotation is not literal.

[66] Dika Newlin, *Bruckner-Mahler-Schoenberg* (London: Marion Boyars, 1979), p. 235.

[67] "Ein Jäger aus der Pfalz" is the title of the song. See measures 560-577, 581-589 and 636-639 in the score of *Wozzeck*, edited by H. E. Apostel (Vienna: Universal Edition, 1955). — Twice Berg quotes a theme from the march in Mahler's Third Symphony, each time satirizing the posturing, strutting drum major who destroys Wozzeck. See measures 349-354 in Act I and measures 392-395 in Act II.

[68] See Theodor W. Adorno, *Mahler*, p. 216.

[69] Measure 30 in the score edited by the International Gustav Mahler Society (Vienna: Universal Edition, 1967).

[70] Natalie Bauer-Lechner, *Recollections of Gustav Mahler*, tr. Dika Newlin, ed. Peter Franklin (Cambridge-New York: Cambridge University Press, 1980), p. 160.

[71] Theodor W. Adorno, *Mahler*, p. 70.

CONCLUSION

When Mahler died in Vienna on 18 May 1911, he had not only lived a hectically productive life, but his path had taken him from a tiny Bohemian village to many of the cities of Eastern and Western Europe and even to the New World. He had met most of the composers and performers of his time and many other prominent persons. But despite his many artistic and social contacts he was not a gregarious man; he was, in fact, quite self-absorbed and was basically a "loner," as his relationship to his wife reveals. It is amazing that this introspective man, to whom his compositions were more important than anything else, attended successfully to the manifold duties, artistic and managerial, of an opera director, while challenging the musical establishment with his anti-traditional policies. His imperial appointment did not stop him from resisting musical requests even from the Emperor when it was a matter of maintaining the artistic integrity of the Vienna Opera. But his outsider's status clearly made his uncompromising stand on artistic matters much more difficult to maintain and undoubtedly made more enemies for him. He lived the hyphenated existence of the assimilated Jew who, even with Mahler's gifts, is not fully accepted by Gentiles. And he was marginal, too, in that he lived and created at the extreme ends of the emotional scale.

Being Czech by birth but German by education, Mahler was neither Czech nor German, which intensified his marginality but gave him a uniquely transnational outlook. After some early cultural and national sympathies for Germany, inspired by a group of young intellectuals he met during his student days, Mahler became a truly international figure who was at home nowhere except perhaps in the supranational ambience of Vienna. Though his main creative impulses came from the Austro-German symphonic tradition, he retained an affection for his Czech background and for Czech music, which occasionally shows up in his own music and which places him somewhat outside of German music. And because he was Jewish he was perhaps more critical of tradition — any tradition — than a non-Jew. To this constellation must be added his liberal use of musical irony and his emergence as a composer at a time when the harmonic language of music was crumbling. This combination of personal, social, historical and musical factors explains his singular lack of national affiliation as a man and artist.

Mahler's most original contribution as a composer, in my view, is his denationalizing transformation of marches, dances and folksongs. He achieved this by freeing them from their traditional harmonic and rhythmic context and infusing them with irony by juxtaposing them against a totally different music. The effect of this treatment is to defamiliarize popular forms of music to such an extent that all local, regional and national elements are eliminated. In Mahler's hands marches, dances and folksongs are transmuted into universal statements while retaining a distant link to folk music, which makes them extraordinarily haunting. They are the expression of someone who loves folk music yet cannot partake of it himself. While this view of folk music looks back to a lost innocence, at the same time it looks forward to the spiritualization of reality and the leveling out of national differences found in expressionism. In his ironic treatment of folk music Mahler was both innovative and prophetic.

Mahler's reception in Germany and Austria has been problematic precisely, I think, because his music is unnational and filled with irony. German and Austrian associations have been filtered through a critical mind. Moreover, during the 1930s and 1940s it was banned in that area, which considerably delayed its acceptance there. The national trauma of those years continues to linger in matters relating to Jewish issues. Outside of the German-speaking area, especially in the United States, Mahler's reception in recent years has been phenomenal. This may be a sign of our turbulent times, to which his music addresses itself eloquently, or it may simply be that non-German audiences, not being privy to his Central European allusions, can concentrate on the more purely musical aspects. His appeal may also be that of the stranger who speaks a well-known language but in a fascinatingly different, uniquely expressive idiom. Mahler was a mediator between cultures, who communicates a rich German-Jewish-Slavic heritage and who exemplifies the tragically brief German-Jewish symbiosis at its most intense.

BIBLIOGRAPHY

This bibliography includes all works cited in the footnotes as well as all those that have been consulted, with the exception of general reference works.

Adler, Guido. *Gustav Mahler.* Vienna-Leipzig: Universal-Edition, 1916.

.... "Gustav Mahler." *Biographisches Jahrbuch und deutscher Nekrolog*, 16 (1911). Ed. Anton Bettelheim. Berlin: G. Reimer, 1914, pp. 1-41.

.... "Gustav Mahlers Persönlichkeit." in *Das Mahler-Fest, Amsterdam, 1920.* Ed. C. Rudolf Mengelberg. Vienna-Leipzig: Universal-Edition, 1920, pp. 17-20.

.... *Wollen und Wirken: Aus dem Leben eines Musikhistorikers.* Vienna-Leipzig: Universal-Edition, 1935.

Adorno, Theodor W. "Alban Berg." In *Klangfiguren: Musikalische Schriften I.* Frankfurt/Main-Berlin: Suhrkamp, 1959, pp. 121-137.

.... *Mahler: Eine musikalische Physiognomik.* Frankfurt/Main: Suhrkamp, 1960.

.... "Mahler." In *Quasi una fantasia: Musikalische Schriften II.* Frankfurt/Main: Suhrkamp, 1963, pp. 115-154.

.... "Philosophie und Lehrer." In *Eingriffe: Neun kritische Modelle.* Frankfurt/Main: Suhrkamp, 1963, pp. 29-53.

.... *Versuch über Wagner.* Frankfurt/Main-Berlin: Suhrkamp, 1952.

.... "Wien." In *Quasi una fantasia: Musikalische Schriften II.* Frankfurt/Main: Suhrkamp, 1963, pp. 274-305.

.... "Zu einer imaginären Auswahl von Liedern Gustav Mahlers." In *Impromptus.* Frankfurt/Main: Suhrkamp, 1968, pp. 30-38.

Allgemeines Deutsches Kommersbuch. Ed. Hermann and Moritz Schauenburg. Musical editors Friedrich Silcher and Friedrich

Erk. 156th ed. Lahr/Schwarzwald: Moritz Schauenburg, 1966.

Apel, Willi. *Harvard Dictionary of Music.* 2nd ed. Cambridge, Mass.: Harvard University Press, 1969.

Arendt, Hannah. *Antisemitism.* New York: Harcourt, Brace and World, 1968.

Bahr-Mildenburg, Anna. *Erinnerungen.* Vienna-Berlin: Wiener Literarische Anstalt, 1921.

Barford, Philip. *Mahler Symphonies and Songs.* BBC Music Guides, 12. Seattle: University of Washington, 1971.

Barker, A. W. "Gustav Mahler and German Literature." In *Focus on Vienna 1900: Change and Continuity in Literature, Music, Art and Intellectual History.* Ed. Erika Nielsen. Munich: Fink, 1982, pp. 131-139.

Barssova, Inna. "Mahler und Dostojewski." In *Beiträge '79-81: Gustav Mahler Kolloquium 1979.* "Beiträge" der Österreichischen Gesellschaft für Musik, No. 7. Ed. Rudolf Klein. Kassel: Bärenreiter, 1981, pp. 65-75.

Batka, Richard. "Das Jüdische bei Gustav Mahler." *Der Kunstwart*, 23 (1910), pp. 97-98.

Bauer-Lechner, Natalie. *Erinnerungen an Gustav Mahler.* Leipzig-Vienna-Zurich: E. P. Tal, 1923.

.... *Recollections of Gustav Mahler.* Trans. Dika Newlin. Ed. Peter Franklin. New York: Cambridge University Press, 1980.

.... *Fragmente: Gelerntes und Gelebtes.* Vienna: R. Lechner, 1907.

Baumbach, Rudolf. *Lieder eines fahrenden Gesellen.* Stuttgart: Cotta, 1907.

Bein, Alex. *Die Judenfrage: Biographie eines Weltproblems.* 2 vols. Stuttgart: Deutsche Verlags-Anstalt, 1980.

Bekker, Paul. *Gustav Mahlers Sinfonien.* Berlin: Schuster und Loeffler, 1921.

.... *Die Sinfonie von Beethoven bis Mahler.* Berlin: Schuster und Loeffler, 1918.

Berl, Heinrich. *Das Judentum in der Musik.* Stuttgart-Berlin-Leipzig: Deutsche Verlagsanstalt, 1926.

Bernstein, Leonard. "Mahler: His Time Has Come." *High Fidelity*, 17, No. 9 (1967), 51-54.

.... *The Unanswered Question: Six Talks at Harvard.* Cambridge, Mass.: Harvard University Press, 1976.

Bethge, Hans. *Die chinesische Flöte: Nachdichtungen chinesischer Lyrik.* Wiesbaden: Insel-Verlag, 1956.

Blaukopf, Kurt. *Gustav Mahler oder Der Zeitgenosse der Zukunft.* Vienna: Molden, 1969.

Blessinger, Karl. *Judentum und Musik: Ein Beitrag zur Kultur- und Rassenpolitik.* Berlin: Hahnefeld, 1944.

Bloch, Ernest. Letter to Alma Mahler, 2 January 1948. (Unpublished) Mahler-Werfel Collection. University of Pennsylvania Library, Philadelphia, Pa.

Boulez, Pierre. "Gustav Mahler up-to-date?" In *Gustav Mahler in Vienna,* ed. Sigrid Wiesmann, tr. Anne Shelley. New York: Rizzoli International Publications, 1976, pp. 11-28.

Braunthal, Julius. *Victor und Friedrich Adler: Zwei Generationen Arbeiterbewegung.* Wiener Neustadt: Verlag der Wiener Volksbuchhandlung, 1965.

Brecht, Bertolt. "Kurze Beschreibung einer neuen Technik der Schauspielkunst, die einen Verfremdungseffekt hervorbringt." In Vol. 15 of *Gesammelte Werke in 20 Bänden.* Frankfurt/Main: Suhrkamp, 1967, pp. 341-357.

.... "Über experimentelles Theater." In Vol. 15 of *Gesammelte Werke in 20 Bänden.* Frankfurt/Main: Suhrkamp, 1967, pp. 285-305.

Brod, Max. *Gustav Mahler: Beispiel einer deutsch-jüdischen Symbiose.* Vom Gestern zum Morgen, 13. Frankfurt/Main: Ner-Tamid-Verlag, 1961.

.... "Gustav Mahler (Zu seinem 100. Geburtstag)." *Eckart,* 29 (1960), 205-208.

.... "Gustav Mahlers jüdische Melodien." *Anbruch* 2 (1920), 378-379.

.... "Jüdische Volksmelodien." *Der Jude,* 1 (1916-1917), 344-345.

.... *Der Prager Kreis.* Stuttgart: Kohlhammer, 1966.

Brownlow, Frank. "*Childe Harold* and the *Années de Pèlerinage.*" Unpublished Paper. English Department, Mount Holyoke College, South Hadley, Mass.

Busoni, Ferruccio. "Wert der Bearbeitung." In *Von der Einheit der Musik.* Berlin: Max Hesse, 1922.

Cardus, Neville. *Gustav Mahler: His Mind and his Music.* Vol. I. London: Victor Gollancz, 1965.

Castle, Eduard. *Geschichte der deutschen Literatur in Österreich-Ungarn im Zeitalter Franz Josephs I.* 2 vols. Vienna: Verlag von Carl Fromme, n.d.

Christy, Nicholas P., Beverly M. Christy and Barry G. Wood. "Gustav Mahler and his Illnesses." *Transactions of the American Clinical and Climatological Association,* 82 (1970), 200-217.

Cooke, Deryck. "The Facts concerning Mahler's Tenth Symphony," *Chord and Discord,* 2, No. 10 (1963), 3-27.

.... *Gustav Mahler: An Introduction to his Music.* New York: Cambridge University Press, 1980.

.... *Vindications: Essays on Romantic Music.* New York: Cambridge University Press, 1982.

Cowell, Henry, and Sidney Cowell. *Charles Ives and his Music.* New York: Oxford University Press, 1955.

Craig, Gordon A. *The Germans.* New York: New American Library, 1983.

Cuddihy, John Murray. *The Ordeal of Civility: Freud, Marx, Lévi-Strauss and the Jewish Struggle with Modernity.* New York: Basic Books, 1974.

Danuser, Hermann. "Konstruktion des Romans bei Gustav Mahler." In *Musikalische Prosa.* Studien zur Musikgeschichte des 19. Jahrhunderts, No. 46. Regensburg: Bosse, 1975, pp. 87-117.

Dehmel, Ida. Letter to Alma Mahler, 27 January 1925. (Unpublished) Mahler-Werfel Collection. University of Pennsylvania Library, Philadelphia, Pa.

Decsey, Ernst. *Musik war sein Leben: Lebenserinnerungen.* Ed. Harald R. Hampel. Vienna: Deutsch, 1962.

.... "'Die Welt geht uns etwas an . . .': Stunden mit Mahler." *Neues Österreich,* 6 November 1960, pp. 15-16.

Deutscher, Isaac. *The Non-Jewish Jew and Other Essays.* Ed. Tamara Deutscher. London-New York-Toronto: Oxford University Press, 1968.

A Dictionary of the Social Sciences. Ed. Julius Gould and William L. Kolb. New York: Free Press of Glencoe, 1964.

Döhl, Friedhelm. "Gustav Mahler, eine notwendige Revision: Zur 100. Wiederkehr seines Geburtstages." *Neue Zeitschrift für Musik,* 121 (1960), 234-237.

Eckstein, Friedrich. *"Alte unnennbare Tage!": Erinnerungen aus siebzig Lehr- und Wanderjahren.* Vienna: Reichner, 1936.

Eggebrecht, Hans Heinrich. *Die Musik Gustav Mahlers.* Munich: Piper, 1982.

Eichenauer, Richard. *Musik und Rasse.* Munich: J. F. Lehmanns, 1932.

Ekman, Karl. *Jean Sibelius: His Life and Personality.* London: A. Wilmer, 1936.

Ellert, Frederick C. "Franz Werfel's Great Dilemma." *The Bridge: A Yearbook of Judaeo-Christian Studies.* Vol. 4. Ed. John M. Oesterreicher. New York: Pantheon Books, 1962, pp. 197-224.

Elon, Amos. *Herzl.* New York: Holt, Rinehart and Winston, 1975.

Encyclopedia Judaica. Jerusalem: Keter Publishing House; New York: Macmillan, 1971. 16 vols.

Engelmann, Bernt. *Deutschland ohne Juden: Eine Bilanz.* Munich: Schneekluth, 1970.

Erk, Ludwig, and Franz M. Böhme. *Deutscher Liederhort.* 3 vols. Leipzig, 1893-1894; rpt. Hildesheim: Olms; Wiesbaden: Breitkopf und Härtel, 1963.

Filler, Susan Melanie. "Editorial Problems in Symphonies of Gustav Mahler: A Study of the Sources of the Third and Tenth Symphonies." Diss. Northwestern 1977.

Fischer, Jens Malte. "Das klagende Lied von der Erde: Zu Gustav Mahlers Liedern und ihren Texten." *Zeitschrift für Literaturwissenschaft und Linguistik,* 9, No. 34 (1979), 55-69.

Fischer, Theodor. "Aus Gustav Mahlers Jugendzeit." *Deutsche Heimat.* Sudetendeutsche Monatsschrift für Literatur, Kunst, Heimat- und Volkskunde, 7 (1931), 264-268.

Floros, Constantin. *Gustav Mahler.* Vol. I: *Die geistige Welt Gustav Mahlers in systematischer Darstellung.* Vol. II: *Mahler und die Symphonik des 19. Jahrhunderts in neuer Deutung.* Wiesbaden: Breitkopf und Härtel, 1977.

Foerster, Josef Bohuslav. *Der Pilger: Erinnerungen eines Musikers.* Trans. from the Czech by Pavel Eisner. Prague: Artia, 1955.

Freyenfels, Jodok. "Mahler und der 'fesche Pepi': Eine Konfrontation der Elemente." *Neue Zeitschrift für Musik,* 132 (1971), 178-183.

Gartenberg, Egon. *Mahler: The Man and his Music.* New York: Schirmer Books, 1978.

Gay, Peter. *Freud, Jews and Other Germans: Masters and Victims in Modernist Culture.* New York: Oxford University Press, 1978.

Gollerich, August. *Anton Bruckner.* Ed. Max Auer. Vol. IV. Regensburg: Bosse, 1936.

Gradenwitz, Peter. "Mahler and Schoenberg." *Leo Baeck Institute Year Book* V (1960), pp. 262-284.

Gross, Harvey. "Gustav Mahler: Fad, or Fullness of Time?" *The American Scholar,* 42 (1973), 484-488.

Grunfeld, Frederic V. *Prophets without Honour: A Background to Freud, Kafka, Einstein and their World.* New York: McGraw-Hill, 1980.

Hansen, Mathias. "Zur Funktion von Volksmusikelementen in Kompositionen Gustav Mahlers." *Beiträge zur Musikwissenschaft,* 23 (1981), 31-35.

Hefling, Stephen E. "The Road not Taken: Mahler's *Rübezahl.*" *The Yale University Library Gazette,* 57 (1983), 145-170.

Heine, Heinrich. "Gedanken und Einfälle." In Vol. 7 of *Sämtliche Werke.* Ed. Ernst Elster. Leipzig-Vienna: Bibliographisches Institut, 1893, pp. 400-452.

Heine, Heinrich. "Über Polen." In Vol. 7 of *Sämtliche Werke.* Ed. Ernst Elster. Leipzig-Vienna: Bibliographisches Institut, 1893, pp. 188-217.

Heller, Erich. *Thomas Mann: The Ironic German.* Cleveland and New York: Meridian Books, 1961.

Heyworth, Peter. *Otto Klemperer, His Life and Times.* Vol. I: 1885-1933 (Cambridge and New York: Cambridge University Press, 1983).

Hohlbaum, Robert. *Der Zauberstab: Roman des Wiener Musiklebens.* Graz-Göttingen: Leopold Stocker, n.d. [1954].

Holländer, Hans. "Unbekannte Jugendbriefe Gustav Mahlers." *Die Musik,* 20 (1928), 807-813.

Ives, Charles. *Memos.* Ed. John Kirkpatrick. New York: Norton, 1972.

Janik, Allan, and Stephen Toulmin. *Wittgenstein's Vienna.* New York: Simon and Schuster, 1973.

Jews and Germans from 1860 to 1933: The Problematic Symbiosis. Ed. David Bronsen. Reihe Siegen: Beiträge zur Literatur- und Sprachwissenschaft, 9. Heidelberg: Winter, 1979.

The Jews: Their Role in Civilization. Ed. Louis Finkelstein. Vol. 3 of *The Jews.* Ed. Louis Finkelstein. 4th ed. New York: Schocken Books, 1971.

Jewish Encyclopedia. New York-London: Funk and Wagnalls, 1912. Vol. XII.

Johnston, William M. *The Austrian Mind: An Intellectual and Social History 1848-1938.* Berkeley: University of California Press, 1972.

Jones, Ernest. *The Life and Work of Sigmund Freud.* Vol. II: *Years of Maturity, 1901-1919.* New York: Basic Books, 1955.

Jugend in Wien: Literatur um 1900. Eine Ausstellung des Deutschen Literaturarchivs im Schiller-Nationalmuseum Marbach a.N.

Ed. Ludwig Greve and Werner Volke. Sonderaus-
stellungen des Schiller-Nationalmuseums, Katalog
No. 24. Munich: Kösel, 1974.

Kafka-Handbuch. Ed. Hartmut Binder. Vol. I. Stuttgart: Kröner, 1979.

Kahler, Erich. *The Jews among the Nations.* New York: Ungar, 1967.

.... "The Jews and the Germans." In *Studies of the Leo Baeck Institute.* Ed. Max Kreutzberger. New York: Ungar,
1967, pp. 19-43.

Kann, Robert A. *The Habsburg Empire.* New York: Praeger, 1957.

.... *The Multi-National Empire: Nationalism and National Reform
in the Habsburg Monarchy 1848-1918.* Vol. II. New
York: Octagon Books, 1964.

Karbusicky, Vladimir. *Gustav Mahler und seine Umwelt.* Impulse der For-
schung, 28. Darmstadt: Wissenschaftliche Buch-
gesellschaft, 1978.

Karpath, Ludwig. *Begegnung mit dem Genius.* 2nd ed. Vienna-Leipzig: Fiba-
Verlag, 1934.

Kennedy, Michael. *Mahler.* The Master Musicians Series. London: Dent, 1974.

Kestenberg-Gladstein, Ruth. "The Jews between Czechs and Germans in the
Historic Lands, 1848-1918." In *The Jews of Czecho-
slovakia: Historical Studies and Surveys.* Vol. I. Phila-
delphia: The Jewish Publication Society of America;
New York: Society for the History of Czechoslovak
Jews, 1968, pp. 21-71.

Kienzl, Wilhelm. *Meine Lebenswanderung: Erlebtes und Erlauschtes.* Stuttgart:
J. Engelhorns Nachfolger, 1926.

Klarmann, Adolf D. "Grillparzer und die Moderne." *Die Neue Rundschau,*
67 (1956), 137-152.

Klemperer, Otto. *Meine Erinnerungen an Gustav Mahler.* Zurich: Atlantis, 1960.

Klopstock, Friedrich Gottlieb. "Die Auferstehung." In *Sämtliche Werke.* Vol.
7. Leipzig: Göschen, 1823, pp. 118-119.

Klose, Friedrich. *Meine Lehrjahre bei Bruckner: Erinnerungen und Betrachtungen.*
Regensburg: Bosse, 1927.

Klusen, Ernst. "Gustav Mahler und das Volkslied seiner Heimat." *Journal of
the International Folk Music Council,* 15 (1963), 29-37.

Des Knaben Wunderhorn: Alte deutsche Lieder. Collected by Achim von Arnim
and Clemens Brentano. Ed. Willi A. Koch. Munich:
Winkler, 1957.

Kohn, Hans. "Before 1918 in the Historic Lands." In *The Jews of Czechoslovakia: Historical Studies and Surveys.* Vol. I. Phila-

delphia: The Jewish Publication Society of America;
New York: Society for the History of Czechoslovak
Jews, 1968, pp. 12-20.

Komma, Karl Michael. *Das böhmische Musikantentum.* Kassel: Hinnenthal,
1960.

Kralik, Heinrich. *Gustav Mahler.* Ed. Friedrich Heller. Österreichische Kom-
ponisten des 20. Jahrhunderts, No. 14. Vienna: Lafite
and Österreichischer Bundesverlag, 1968.

Kralik, Richard. "Gesichter und Gestalten: Victor Adler und Pernerstorfer."
I.N. 106.071, fol. 1^r-6^r, MS. Manuscript Collection.
Wiener Stadtbibliothek, Vienna.

.........................*Tage und Werke: Lebenserinnerungen.* Vienna: Vogelsang, 1922.

Kravitt, Edward F. "The Trend toward the Folklike, Nationalism, and their
Expression by Mahler and his Contemporaries in the
Lied." *Chord and Discord,* 2, No. 10 (1963), 40-56.

La Grange, Henry-Louis de. Liner notes for a recording of Mahler's Eighth
Symphony by soloists, combined Rotterdam Choirs
and the Rotterdam Philharmonic Orchestra, cond.
Eduard Flipse. Epic, SC-6004, 1954.

.... *Mahler.* Vol. I. Garden City, N. Y.: Doubleday,
1973.

Lambert, Constant. *Music Ho!: A Study of Music in Decline.* 2nd ed. London:
Faber and Faber, 1937.

Lea, Charlene A. *Emancipation, Assimilation and Stereotype: The Image of the
Jew in German and Austrian Drama, 1800-1850.* Bonn:
Bouvier, 1978.

Lea, Henry A. "Mahler: German Romantic or Jewish Satirist?" In *Jews and
Germans from 1860 to 1933: The Problematic Symbiosis.*
Ed. David Bronsen. Reihe Siegen: Beiträge zur Lite-
ratur- und Sprachwissenschaft, 9. Heidelberg: Winter,
1979, pp. 288-305.

.... "Mahler: Man on the Margin." In *Views and Reviews of Modern
German Literature: Festschrift for Adolf D. Klarmann.*
Ed. Karl S. Weimar. Munich: Delp, 1974, pp. 92-104.

.... "Mahler und der Expressionismus." In *Aspekte des Expressionismus: Periodisierung, Stil, Gedankenwelt.* Ed.
Wolfgang Paulsen. Poesie und Wissenschaft, 8. Heidelberg: Stiehm, 1968, pp. 85-102.

.... "Musical Expressionism in Vienna." In *Passion and Rebellion: The Expressionist Heritage.* Ed. Stephen E. Bronner and Douglas Kellner. South Hadley, Mass.: J. F. Bergin, 1983, pp. 315-331.

Lipman, Samuel. "The Mahler Everyone Loves." *Commentary*, 64, No. 5 (1977), 55-60.

Loschnigg, Franz. "The Cultural Education of Gustav Mahler." Diss. Wisconsin-Madison 1976.

Louis, Rudolf. *Die deutsche Musik der Gegenwart.* Munich-Leipzig: Müller, 1909.

Macartney, C. A. *The Habsburg Empire 1790-1918.* New York: Macmillan, 1969.

Mahler, Alma. *Gustav Mahler: Erinnerungen und Briefe.* Amsterdam: Allert de Lange, 1940.

.... *Gustav Mahler: Memories and Letters.* 3rd ed. Trans. Basil Creighton. Ed. Donald Mitchell. Seattle: University of Washington Press, 1975.

Mahler-Werfel, Alma. *And the Bridge is Love.* In collaboration with E. B. Ashton. New York: Harcourt, Brace, 1958.

.... *Mein Leben.* Frankfurt/Main: Suhrkamp, 1963.

Mahler, Arnošt. "Gustav Mahler und seine Heimat." *Die Musikforschung,* 25 (1972), 437-448.

Gustav Mahler. Tübingen: Rainer Wunderlich, Hermann Leins, 1966.

Gustav Mahler: Briefe 1879-1911. Ed. Alma Maria Mahler. Vienna: Zsolnay, 1925.

Selected Letters of Gustav Mahler. Trans. Eithne Wilkins, Ernst Kaiser and Bill Hopkins. Ed. Knud Martner. New York: Farrar, Straus and Giroux, 1979.

Gustav Mahler: Briefe. Expanded edition by Herta Blaukopf. Bibliothek der Internationalen Gustav Mahler Gesellschaft. Vienna: Zsolnay, 1982.

Gustav Mahler: Unbekannte Briefe. Ed. Herta Blaukopf. Bibliothek der Internationalen Gustav Mahler Gesellschaft. Vienna: Zsolnay, 1983.

"Briefe Gustav Mahlers an Ferruccio Busoni." Ed. Jutta Theurich. *Beiträge zur Musikwissenschaft*, 19 (1977), 212-215.

Gustav Mahler und Richard Strauss: Briefwechsel 1888-1911. Ed. Herta Blaukopf. Bibliothek der Internationalen Gustav Mahler Gesellschaft. Munich: Piper, 1980.

Gustav Mahler: Ein Bild seiner Persönlichkeit in Widmungen. Ed. Paul Stefan. Munich: Piper, 1910.

Gustav Mahler: Im eigenen Wort — Im Worte der Freunde. Ed. Willi Reich. Zurich: Verlag der Arche, 1958.

Gustav Mahler: Sinfonie und Wirklichkeit. Ed. Otto Kolleritsch. Studien zur Wertungsforschung, 9. Graz: Universal Edition and Institut für Wertungsforschung, 1977.

Gustav Mahler in Vienna. Trans. Anne Shelley. Ed. Sigrid Wiesmann. New York: Rizzoli International Publications, 1976.

Mahler: A Documentary Study. Trans. Paul Baker, Susanne Flatauer, P. R. J. Ford, Daisy Loman and Geoffrey Watkins. Ed. Kurt Blaukopf. New York: Oxford University Press, 1976.

Mahler - eine Herausforderung: Ein Symposion. Ed. Peter Ruzicka. Wiesbaden: Breitkopf und Härtel, 1977.

Mann, Thomas. *Briefe 1889-1936.* Ed. Erika Mann. Frankfurt/Main: S. Fischer, 1962.

.... *"Death in Venice" and Seven Other Stories.* Trans. H. T. Lowe-Porter. New York: Vintage Books, 1954.

.... *Doctor Faustus.* Trans. H. T. Lowe-Porter. New York: Knopf, 1970.

.... *Doktor Faustus.* Vol. 6 of Gesammelte Werke in 13 Bänden. Frankfurt/Main: S. Fischer, 1974.

Martner, Knud, and Robert Becqué. "Zwölf unbekannte Briefe Gustav Mahlers an Ludwig Strecker." *Archiv für Musikwissenschaft,* 34 (1977), 287-297.

Marx, Joseph. *Betrachtungen eines romantischen Realisten: Gesammelte Aufsätze, Vorträge und Reden über Musik.* Ed. Oswald Ortner. Vienna: Gerlach und Wiedling, 1947.

Matter, Jean. *Connaissance de Mahler: Documents, analyses et synthèses.* Lausanne: Editions l'Age d'Homme, 1974.

May, Arthur J. *The Habsburg Monarchy 1867-1914.* Cambridge, Mass.: Harvard University Press, 1951.

.... *Vienna in the Age of Franz Josef.* Norman: University of Oklahoma Press, 1966.

McGrath, William J. *Dionysian Art and Populist Politics in Austria.* New Haven: Yale University Press, 1974.

.... "Mahler and Freud." In *Beiträge '79-81: Gustav Mahler Kolloquium 1979.* "Beiträge" der Österreichischen Gesellschaft für Musik, No. 7. Ed. Rudolf Klein. Kassel: Bärenreiter, 1981, pp. 40-51.

Mitchell, Donald. *Gustav Mahler: The Early Years.* Ed. Paul Banks and David Matthews. Berkeley: University of California Press, 1980.

——————— *Gustav Mahler: The Wunderhorn Years.* Boulder: Westview Press, 1976.

——————— *The Language of Modern Music.* London: Faber and Faber, 1966.

Monson, Karen. *Alma Mahler: Muse to Genius.* Boston: Houghton Mifflin, 1983.

Morgan, Robert. P. "Ives and Mahler: Mutual Responses at the End of an Era." *19th Century Music,* 2 (1978), 72-81.

Mosenthal, Salomon von. "Das Volkslied." In Vol. 6 of *Gesammelte Werke.* Stuttgart-Leipzig: Hallberger, 1878, pp. 328-341.

Moser, Hans Joachim. *Das deutsche Lied seit Mozart.* 2nd ed. Tutzing: Hans Schneider, 1968.

——————— *Geschichte der deutschen Musik.* Rev. ed. Vol. III: *From Beethoven to the Present.* 1928; rpt. Hildesheim: Olms, 1968.

——————— *Kleine deutsche Musikgeschichte.* Rev. ed. Stuttgart: Cotta, 1949.

——————— *Die Musik der deutschen Stämme.* Vienna: Wancura, 1957.

——————— *Musikgeschichte in hundert Lebensbildern.* 3rd ed. Stuttgart: Reclam, 1958.

Muecke, D. C. *The Compass of Irony.* London: Methuen, 1969.

——————— *Irony and the Ironic.* London: Methuen, 1982.

The Music Hour. Fourth Book. Ed. Osbourne McConathy, W. Otto Miessner, Edward Bailey Birge and Mabel E. Bray. New York-Boston-Chicago-San Francisco: Silver Burdett Co., 1937.

The New Grove Dictionary of Music and Musicians. Ed. Stanley Sadie. 20 vols. London: Macmillan, 1980.

The New Standard Jewish Encyclopedia. Revised ed. Ed. Cecil Roth and Geoffrey Wigoder. London: W. H. Allen, 1975.

Newlin, Dika. *Bruckner - Mahler - Schoenberg.* London: Marion Boyars, 1979.

——————— "Mahler's Opera." *Opera News,* 18 March 1972, pp. 6-7.

Noe, Günther von. "Das musikalische Zitat." *Neue Zeitschrift für Musik* 124 (1963), 134-137.

Orenstein, Arbie. *Ravel: Man and Musician.* New York: Columbia University Press, 1975.

Pamer, Fritz Egon. "Gustav Mahlers Lieder." *Studien zur Musikwissenschaft,* 16 (1929), 116-138, and 17 (1930), 105-127.

Park, Robert E. *Race and Culture.* Glencoe, Illinois: The Free Press, 1950.

The Penguin Book of Lieder. Ed. and trans. S. S. Prawer. Harmondsworth, England, and New York: Penguin, 1979.

Pfohl, Ferdinand. *Gustav Mahler: Eindrücke und Erinnerungen aus den Hamburger Jahren.* Ed. Knud Martner. Hamburg: Karl Dieter Wagner, 1973.

Pirchan, Emil, Alexander Witeschnik and Otto Fritz. *300 Jahre Wiener Operntheater.* Vienna: Fortuna, 1953.

Politzer, Heinz. *Franz Kafka, der Künstler.* Frankfurt/Main: Fischer, 1965.

Prieberg, Fred K. *Musik im NS-Staat.* Frankfurt/Main: Fischer, 1982.

Pulzer, Peter G. J. *The Rise of Political Anti-Semitism in Germany and Austria.* New York: Wiley, 1964.

Redlich, Hans Ferdinand. Essay on Mahler in *Die Musik in Geschichte und Gegenwart: Allgemeine Enzyklopädie der Musik.* Ed. Friedrich Blume. Vol. 8. Kassel: Bärenreiter, 1960, col. 1489-1500.

.... *Gustav Mahler: Eine Erkenntnis.* Nürnberg: Hans Carl, 1919.

Reich-Ranicki, Marcel. *Über Ruhestörer: Juden in der deutschen Literatur.* Munich: Piper, 1973.

Reik, Theodor. *The Haunting Melody: Psychoanalytic Experiences in Life and Music.* New York: Grove Press, 1960.

Reilly, Edward R. *Gustav Mahler and Guido Adler: Records of a Friendship.* Cambridge and New York: Cambridge University Press, 1982.

.... *Gustav Mahler und Guido Adler. Zur Geschichte einer Freundschaft.* Trans. Herta Singer-Blaukopf. Bibliothek der Internationalen Gustav Mahler Gesellschaft. Vienna: Universal Edition, 1978.

Riemann Musik-Lexikon. 12th ed. *Sachteil.* Ed. Hans Heinrich Eggebrecht. Mainz: Schott's Söhne, 1967.

Ritter, William. "Un symphoniste viennois: M. Gustave Mahler." In *Etudes d'art étranger.* Paris: Société du Mercure de France, 1906, pp. 244-288.

Rölleke, Heinz. "Gustav Mahlers 'Wunderhorn'-Lieder: Textgrundlagen und Textauswahl." *Jahrbuch des Freien Deutschen Hochstifts* (1981), 370-378.

Rosen, Charles. *Arnold Schoenberg.* New York: Viking Press, 1975.

Rosensaft, Menachem Z. "Jews and Antisemites in Austria at the End of the Nineteenth Century." *Leo Baeck Year Book* XXI (1976), 57-86.

Russian Formalist Criticism: Four Essays. Trans. Lee T. Lemon and Marion J. Reis. Lincoln: University of Nebraska Press, 1965.

Sachs, Curt. *Handbuch der Instrumentenkunde.* 2nd ed. Leipzig: Breitkopf und Härtel, 1930.

Sammons, Jeffrey. *Heinrich Heine: A Modern Biography.* Princeton: Princeton University Press, 1979.

Sartre, Jean-Paul. *Anti-Semite and Jew.* Trans. George J. Becker. New York: Schocken, 1965.

Schacherl, Lillian. *Mähren: Land der friedlichen Widersprüche.* Munich: Prestel-Verlag, 1968.

Schaefer, Hans Joachim. *Gustav Mahler in Kassel.* Kassel: Bärenreiter, 1982.

Schlegel, Friedrich. *Kritische Schriften.* Ed. Wolfdietrich Rasch. Munich: Hanser, 1964.

Schnitzler, Arthur. *Jugend in Wien.* Ed. Therese Nickl and Heinrich Schnitzler. Vienna: Molden, 1968.

.... *Tagebuch 1909-1912.* Vienna: Verlag der Österreichischen Akademie der Wissenschaften, 1981.

Scholem, Gershom. "Jews and Germans." In *On Jews and Judaism in Crisis: Selected Essays.* Ed. Werner J. Dannhauser. New York: Schocken, 1976, pp. 71-92.

Schorske, Carl E. *Fin-de-Siècle Vienna: Politics and Culture.* New York: Random House, 1981.

Schreiber, Wolfgang. *Gustav Mahler in Selbstzeugnissen und Bilddokumenten.* Rowohlts Monographien, 181. Reinbek bei Hamburg: Rowohlt, 1971.

Schumann, Karl. *Das kleine Gustav Mahler-Buch.* Reinbek bei Hamburg: Rowohlt, 1982.

Shanet, Howard. *Philharmonic: A History of New York's Orchestra.* Garden City: Doubleday, 1975.

Simmel, Georg. "Exkurs über den Fremden." In *Soziologie: Untersuchungen über die Formen der Vergesellschaftung.* 3rd ed. Munich-Leipzig: Duncker und Humblot, 1923, pp. 509-512.

Small, Christopher. *Music, Society, Education: A Radical Examination of the Prophetic Function of Music in Western, Eastern and African Cultures with its Impact on Society and its Use in Education.* London: Calder, 1977.

Specht, Richard. *Gustav Mahler.* Stuttgart-Berlin: Deutsche Verlags-Anstalt, 1925.

Stefan, Paul. *Das Grab in Wien: Eine Chronik 1903-1911.* Berlin: E. Reiss, 1913.

.... *Gustav Mahler: Eine Studie über Persönlichkeit und Werk.* 4th ed. Munich: Piper, 1912.

.... "Gustav Mahler in der Literatur." *Moderne Welt,* 3, No. 7 (1921-1922), 8-9.

Stölzl, Christoph. *Kafkas böses Böhmen: Zur Sozialgeschichte eines Prager Juden.* Munich: edition text + kritik, 1975.

Stonequist, Everett V. *The Marginal Man.* New York: Scribner, 1937.

Storck, Karl. *Die Musik der Gegenwart.* Stuttgart: Muth, 1919.

Storjohann, Helmut. "Gustav Mahlers Verhältnis zur Volksmusik." *Musica* (Kassel), 14 (1960), 357-359.

Stössinger, Felix. "Hermann Broch." In *Deutsche Literatur im 20. Jahrhundert.* Ed. Otto Mann and Wolfgang Rothe. 5th ed. Vol. II. Bern-Munich: Francke, 1967, pp. 202-218.

Thiel, Eberhard. *Sachwörterbuch der Musik.* Kröners Taschenausgabe, 210. Stuttgart: Kröner, 1962.

Thomson, Philip. *The Grotesque.* The Critical Idiom, 24. London: Methuen, 1972.

Tibbe, Monika. *Lieder und Liedelemente in instrumentalen Symphoniesätzen Gustav Mahlers.* Berliner musikwissenschaftliche Arbeiten, 1. Munich: Musikverlag Emil Katzbichler, 1971.

Urbach, Reinhard. *Schnitzler-Kommentar zu den erzählenden und dramatischen Schriften.* Munich: Winkler, 1974.

Vaget, Hans Rudolf. "Film and Literature. The Case of *Death in Venice:* Luchino Visconti and Thomas Mann." *German Quarterly,* 53 (1980), 159-175.

Veblen, Thorstein. "The Intellectual Pre-Eminence of Jews in Modern Europe." In *The Portable Veblen.* Ed. Max Lerner. New York: Viking, 1948, pp. 467-479.

Vogel, Jaroslav. *Leoš Janáček.* Rev. and ed. Karel Janovický. New York: Norton, 1981.

Briefwechsel zwischen Cosima Wagner und Fürst Ernst zu Hohenlohe-Langenburg. Stuttgart: Cotta, 1937.

Cosima Wagner's Diaries. Trans. Geoffrey Skelton. Ed. Martin Gregor-Dellin and Dietrich Mack. Vol. II: 1878-1883. New York: Harcourt, Brace and Jovanovich, 1978.

Wagner, Cosima. *Das zweite Leben: Briefe und Aufzeichnungen 1883-1930.* Ed. Dietrich Mack. Munich: Piper, 1980.

Wagner, Richard. "Aufklärungen über 'Das Judentum in der Musik.'" In *Sämtliche Schriften und Dichtungen.* 5th ed. Vol. 8. Leipzig: Breitkopf und Härtel/C. F. W. Siegel [R. Linnemann], 1911, pp. 238-260.

Wagner, Richard. "Erkenne dich selbst." In *Sämtliche Schriften und Dichtungen.* 5th ed. Vol. 10. Leipzig: Breitkopf und Härtel/C. F. W. Siegel [R. Linnemann], 1911, pp. 263-274.

.... "Das Judentum in der Musik." In *Sämtliche Schriften und Dichtungen.* 5th ed. Vol. 5. Leipzig: Breitkopf und Härtel/C. F. W. Siegel [R. Linnemann], 1911, pp. 66-85.

.... "Judaism in Music." In *Stories and Essays.* Ed. Charles Osborne. London: Peter Owen, 1973, pp. 23-39.

Richard Wagner: Wie antisemitisch darf ein Künstler sein? Ed. Heinz-Klaus Metzger and Rainer Riehn. Musik-Konzepte, 5. Munich: edition text + kritik, 1978.

Walter, Bruno. *Gustav Mahler.* Vienna: Herbert Reichner, 1936.

.... *Thema und Variationen: Erinnerungen und Gedanken.* Stockholm: Bermann-Fischer, 1947.

Wapnewski, Peter. "Der Zeitgenosse unserer Zukunft: Gustav-Mahler-Festival in achtzehn Städten Nordrhein-Westfalens — eine Eröffnungsrede." *Die Zeit,* No. 43, 26 October 1979, Feuilleton, p. 19.

Werner, Eric. "The Jewish Contribution to Music." In *The Jews: Their Role in Civilization.* Ed. Louis Finkelstein. 4th ed. Vol. 3 of *The Jews.* Ed. Louis Finkelstein. New York: Schocken, 1971, pp. 116-153.

Wessling, Berndt W. *Gustav Mahler: Ein prophetisches Leben.* Hamburg: Hoffmann und Campe, 1974.

Whaples, Miriam K. "Mahler and Schubert's A minor Sonata D. 784." *Music and Letters,* 65 (1984), 255-263.

Wiskemann, Elizabeth. *Czechs and Germans: A Study of the Struggle in the Historic Provinces of Bohemia and Moravia.* 2nd ed. London: Macmillan; New York: St. Martin's Press, 1967.

Wolf, Ernest. "A Case of Slightly Mistaken Identity: Gustav Mahler and Gustav Aschenbach." *Twentieth Century Literature,* 19 (1973), 40-52.

Wooldridge, David. *From the Steeples and Mountains: A Study of Charles Ives.* New York: Knopf, 1974.

Wulf, Joseph. *Musik im Dritten Reich.* Eine Dokumentation. Gütersloh: S. Mohn, 1963.

Zuckerkandl, Bertha. *Österreich Intim: Erinnerungen 1892-1942.* Ed. Reinhard Federmann. Frankfurt/Main-Berlin-Vienna: Propyläen/Ullstein, 1970.

Zweig, Stefan. *Die Welt von gestern: Erinnerungen eines Europäers.* Stockholm: Bermann-Fischer, 1946.

Mahler's Works Mentioned in this Study

A. The following compositions have thus far appeared in the Complete Critical Edition of Mahler's works:

Vol. XII: *Das klagende Lied (The Song of Lament).* For soprano, contralto, tenor, mixed chorus and large orchestra. Text by Mahler, based on a story found in Grimm and Ludwig Bechstein. Vienna, 1978.

Vol. IX: *Das Lied von der Erde (The Song of the Earth).* For tenor and contralto (or baritone) and orchestra. Texts from *Die chinesische Flöte (The Chinese Flute)* by Hans Bethge. Vienna, 1964.

Vol. XIV, Part 1: *Lieder eines fahrenden Gesellen (Songs of a Wayfarer).* For solo voice and orchestra. Texts by Mahler. Vienna, 1982.

Vol. I: Symphony No. 1 for large orchestra. Vienna, 1967.

Vol. II: Symphony No. 2 for soprano, contralto, mixed chorus and large orchestra. Texts from *Des Knaben Wunderhorn (The Youth's Magic Horn)* and Friedrich Gottlieb Klopstock's poem "Auferstehung" ("Resurrection"). Vienna, 1970.

Vol. III: Symphony No. 3 for contralto, boys' choir, women's choir and large orchestra. Texts by Nietzsche and from *Des Knaben Wunderhorn.* Vienna, 1974.

Vol. IV: Symphony No. 4 for soprano and large orchestra. Text from *Des Knaben Wunderhorn.* Vienna, 1963.

Vol. V: Symphony No. 5 for large orchestra. Vienna, 1964.

Vol. VI: Symphony No. 6 for large orchestra. Vienna, 1963.

Vol. VII: Symphony No. 7 for large orchestra. Vienna, 1960.

Vol. VIII: Symphony No. 8 for eight solo voices, boys' choir, two mixed choirs and large orchestra. Texts: The Latin hymn "Veni Creator Spiritus" and the final scene of Goethe's *Faust.* Vienna, 1977.

Vol. X: Symphony No. 9 for large orchestra. Vienna, 1969.

Vol. XIa: Adagio from Symphony No. 10 for large orchestra. Vienna, 1964.

B.   The following cited works have appeared in the following editions:

Blumine (Chapter of Flowers): Symphonic Movement from Symphony No. 1. Bryn Mawr, Pennsylvania: Theodore Presser Co., 1968.

Des Knaben Wunderhorn (The Youth's Magic Horn), a collection of German folksongs edited by Achim von Arnim and Clemens Brentano:

Ablösung im Sommer (Replacement in Summer). For solo voice and piano. In Gustav Mahler, *Lieder und Gesänge.* Melville, New York: Belwin-Mills Publishing Corporation, n.d. Kalmus Vocal Series No. 6840.

Des Antonius von Padua Fischpredigt (Anthony of Padua's Sermon to the Fishes). For solo voice and orchestra. In Gustav Mahler, *Des Knaben Wunderhorn,* II. Vienna and London: Universal Edition, n.d. Philharmonia Score No. 220.

Ich ging mit Lust durch einen grünen Wald (I Walked Joyfully through a Green Wood). For solo voice and piano. Melville, New York: Belwin-Mills Corporation, n.d. Kalmus Vocal Series No. 6840.

Lied des Verfolgten im Turm (Song of the Prisoner in the Tower). For solo voice and orchestra. In Gustav Mahler, *Des Knaben Wunderhorn,* II. Vienna and London: Universal Edition, n.d. Philharmonia Score No. 220.

Nicht Wiedersehen! (Never to Meet Again). For solo voice and piano. In Gustav Mahler, *Lieder und Gesänge.* Melville, New York: Belwin-Mills Publishing Corporation, n.d. Kalmus Vocal Series No. 6840.

Revelge (Reveille). For solo voice and orchestra. In Gustav Mahler, *Sieben letzte Lieder.* Vienna: Wiener Philharmonischer Verlag, 1926. Philharmonia Score No. 253.

Rheinlegendchen (Little Rhine Legend). For solo voice and orchestra. In Gustav Mahler, *Des Knaben Wunderhorn,* II. Vienna and London: Universal Edition, n.d. Philharmonia Score No. 220.

Der Schildwache Nachtlied (Sentinel's Night Song). For solo voice and orchestra. In Gustav Mahler, *Des Knaben Wunderhorn,* I. Vienna and London: Universal Edition, n.d. Philharmonia Score No. 219.

Der Tamboursg'sell (The Drummer Boy). For solo voice and orchestra. In Gustav Mahler, *Sieben letzte Lieder.* Vienna: Wiener Philharmonischer Verlag, 1926. Philharmonia Score No. 253.

Trost im Unglück (Consolation in Misfortune). For solo voice and orchestra. In Gustav Mahler, *Des Knaben Wunderhorn,* I. Vienna and London: Universal Edition, n.d. Philharmonia Score No. 219.

Verlor'ne Müh' (Wasted Effort). In Gustav Mahler, *Des Knaben Wunderhorn,* I. For solo voice and orchestra. Vienna and London: Universal Edition, n.d. Philharmonia Score No. 219.

Wer hat dies Liedlein erdacht? (Who Made up this Little Song?). For solo voice and orchestra. In Gustav Mahler, *Des Knaben Wunderhorn,* I. Vienna and London: Universal Edition, n.d. Philharmonia Score No. 219.

Wo die schönen Trompeten blasen (Where the Splendid Trumpets Sound). For solo voice and orchestra. In Gustav Mahler, *Des Knaben Wunderhorn,* II. Vienna and London: Universal Edition, n.d. Philharmonia Score No. 220.

Zu Strassburg auf der Schanz (On the Ramparts of Strassburg). For solo voice and piano. In Gustav Mahler, *Lieder und Gesänge.* Melville, New York: Belwin-Mills Publishing Corporation, n.d. Kalmus Vocal Series No. 6840.

Waldmärchen (A Forest Legend). Part I of *Das klagende Lied.* For four solo voices, mixed chorus and large orchestra. Text by Mahler. New York: Belwin-Mills Publishing Corporation, n.d.

INDEX OF NAMES